Prague English Studies and the Transformation of Philologies

edited by
Martin Procházka and Ondřej Pilný

CHARLES UNIVERSITY IN PRAGUE
KAROLINUM PRESS 2012

The publication of this volume was supported from the "Programme for the Development of Research Areas at Charles University, P09, Literature and Art in Intercultural Relations," sub-programme "Transformations of the Cultural History of the Anglophone Countries: Identities, Periods Canons." / Tato kniha byla vydána v rámci Programu rozvoje vědních oblastí na Univerzitě Karlově č. P09, Literatura a umění v mezikulturních souvislostech, podprogram Proměny kulturních dějin anglofonních zemí: identity, periody, kánony.

Cataloguing-in-publication – National Library of the Czech Republic
Prague English Studies and the Transformation of Philologies / Martin Procházka, Ondřej Pilný (eds.). – 1st ed. – Prague : Karolinum Press, 2013
Published by: Charles University in Prague
ISBN 978-80-246-2156-2
80(=111)+908(=1.100=111) * 82.0 * 81-116 * 80 * (437.3)
- anglistics – Czechia – 20th century
- literary studies – Czechia – 20th century
- structural linguistics – Czechia – 20th century
- philology
- collective monographs

400 – Language [11] 80 – Philology [11]

Published by Charles University in Prague
Karolinum Press
Ovocný trh 3, 116 36 Praha 1
Prague 2012

Editor vice-rector Prof. PhDr. Ivan Jakubec, CSc.
Reviewers PhDr. Ladislav Nagy, PhD, PhDr. Petr Chalupský, PhD
Cover Jan Šerých
Typeset by OP
Printed by Karolinum Press
First Edition

ISBN 978-80-246-2156-2

Published on the occasion of the centenary of
Prague English Studies.

*This book is dedicated to Zdeněk Stříbrný,
on the occasion of his 90th birthday.*

CONTENTS

Martin Procházka
Introduction   9

1. LEGACIES:
   VILÉM MATHESIUS AND FOLLOWERS

Martin Procházka
The Value of Language: Rhetoric, Semiology, Philology
   and the Functional Approach   25

Helena Znojemská
Vilém Mathesius as Literary Historian   43

Bohuslav Mánek
Vilém Mathesius as Translator and Theoretician of Translation   64

Pavla Veselá
A Structuralist History of Zdeněk Vančura   83

Zdeněk Beran
Jaroslav Hornát's Critical Method in His Studies of Charles
   Dickens   103

2. CONTEXTS AND OUTCOMES:
   FROM PRAGUE STRUCTURALISM TO RADICAL PHILOLOGY

Robert J.C. Young
Structuralism and the Prague Linguistic Circle Revisited   121

David Vichnar
Functional Linguistics as the "Science of Poetic Forms":
   An ABC of the Prague Linguistic Circle's Poetics   154

Erik Roraback
A Gateway to a Baroque Rhetoric of Jacques Lacan and
   Niklas Luhmann   166

Ondřej Pilný
Jan Grossman, Structuralism, and the Grotesque   184

Louis Armand
Attesting / Before the Fact   198

Contributors   207
Index   211

INTRODUCTION

Martin Procházka

This book commemorates the centenary of Prague English Studies, officially inaugurated in 1912 by the appointment of Vilém Mathesius (1882-1945), the founder of Prague Linguistic Circle (1926) and the first Professor of English Language and Literature at Charles University. The volume is divided into two sections: the first part reassesses the significance of Mathesius's legacy in literary and translation studies and revisits the work of some of his followers, especially Zdeněk Vančura (1903-1974) and Jaroslav Hornát (1926-1990); while the second explores the diverse contexts and implications of Structuralism (as the major influence on Prague English Studies) from political aspects of Russian Formalist theories and the poetics of the Czech avant-garde, via the aesthetic of the grotesque and the rhetorical features of the works of late Structuralists (Jacques Lacan and Niklas Luhmann), to recent theories of text and hypertext.

Theoretically, the individual approaches are fairly diverse: from interpretations of Mathesius's functionalism in epistemological, semiological or aesthetic contexts, to Post-structuralist views of the relationship between symbols and facts (or fictions) in philology. Discussing the methodological problems related to the transformations of philology, our approach distinguishes several stages in the process: the formation of humanistic philology in the fifteenth and sixteenth centuries influenced by Classical rhetoric (especially by Aristotle and Quintilian), the emergence of modern philology from a wider Romantic project of cultural studies and, finally, the repudiation of the "historical method" of modern philology by Structuralist linguistics. This last event is reinterpreted in the wider context of the evolution of philology and with respect to different approaches to (and strategies of) inter-disciplinarity in humanistic and modern philologies and in Structuralism.

Following Paul de Man,[1] the major concern of the methodological agenda of this book can be identified as *the problem of rhetoric*, which is further expanded in the opening chapter to the second part and contextualized with respect to the crucial issues of nineteenth-century philology as modulated by Prague Structuralism. The main aspects of this problem are rhetoric's liminal position between grammar and logic, structure and meaning, and its concerns with truth, performativity and the value of language. Reassessment of these issues appears vital to an understanding of the dynamics of recent transformations of Structuralist methodologies (exemplified by the works of Lacan and Luhman) and of philology (in textual genetics) which are discussed in the concluding section. The other, closely related problem, is that of the methodology of cultural theory and literary history. Although the representatives of Prague English studies succeeded in overcoming the rigidity of the Saussurean synchronic approach, their treatment of dynamic structures is still considerably indebted to traditional notions of value and nineteenth-century views of literature as the representation of national identity and unity. While Mathesius demonstrates that value is founded on the internal dynamism of structure, especially on the "potentiality of language phenomena" (explained as an "oscillation" generating functional relationships and leading to constant changes of theoretical perspectives), his historical approach is characterized by the hypothesis of the "community of language users," whose totalizing and teleological moments point back to Romantic organicism and nineteenth-century biologism and virtually preclude wider application of the functional method. Despite this, individual studies, such as the research of Renaissance Euphuism

---

[1]   See his *Allegories of Reading* (New Haven and London: Yale University Press, 1979); *Blindness and Insight*, 2nd ed. (London and New York: Routledge, 1984); *The Rhetoric of Romanticism* (New York: Columbia University Press, 1984) and especially "Resistance to Theory," *Yale French Studies* 18 (1979): 1-23. A relevant commentary on de Man's project, particularly on its Nietzschean background, is Carlo Ginzburg's *History, Rhetoric and Proof* (Hanover, NH, and London: University Press of New England, 1999).

undertaken in the 1930s and 40s by Zdeněk Vančura, have demonstrated the possibilities of Mathesius's functionalism, especially in histories of genres and other literary forms. The initial chapter of the second part of this book then demonstrates the ways in which the limits of functionalism were transcended by Nikolay Troubetzkoy and Roman Jakobson.

The first part of this volume entitled "Legacies: Vilém Mathesius and Followers" opens with Martin Procházka's analysis of Mathesius's functional approach in several historical and theoretical contexts of Classical rhetoric, Saussurean semiology and Romantic philology. The chapter entitled "The Value of Language: Rhetoric, Semiology, Philology and the Functional Approach" discusses first the epistemological, political and ethical implications of "arbitrariness" in Aristotelian rhetoric and Saussurean semiology and shows the importance of the former approach for the critical orientation of humanistic philology represented by the fifteenth-century Italian humanist Lorenzo Valla. Mathesius's "synchronistic" and functional approach is here contrasted with the project of Romantic philology (represented by Friedrich Schlegel), which generated, among others, the historical study of language, typical of the German school of "Neogrammarians" (*Junggrammatiker*), whose methods were repudiated by Mathesius and other Structuralists.

The concluding part of the chapter shows that Mathesius's approach is based on a different notion of development than the linear growth typical of the schemes of the "Neogrammarians." His system develops by virtue of its internal dynamism described by Mathesius as the "oscillation of speech among individuals inside the communities of language." This oscillation, which is later used in the context of Michel Foucault's theory of discourse as a paradigm by New Historicism, generates a plethora of potentialities whose materializations can either contribute to the system's "dynamic stability" ("norm") or, more importantly, can provide the means for the expression of individual active attitudes to reality. From this perspective, the expressive function of language, or "language instinct," fully realized in leading literary works, appears more significant than the communicative function dominating the social uses of language.

As a consequence, Mathesius's approach (influenced, among others, by Croce's expressive aesthetics) is, on the one hand, desirable, as a possibility of transcending a narrowly functionalist view of language. On the other hand, it involves some risk, since it may lead to the transgression of generally valid language norms and "styles" (Mathesius and other Prague Structuralists use the term "functional styles of language" to include its communicative and expressive functions). Mathesius attempts to control this tension between invention and stability by means of two strategies. Firstly, he avoids the question of "literariness" discussed by Roman Jakobson (1896-1982) and other Russian Formalists, and focuses instead on the linguistic interpretation of literary language thereby subordinating rhetorical to linguistic phenomena. Despite its primarily regulative function, this approach is also productive, providing a different perspective on rhetorical figures as being the results of the interaction of phenomena at different language levels (phonological, morphological, syntactic, thematic) and their different expressive functions. The second strategy that regulates Mathesius's approach is the application of the hypothesis of the "language community" which also dominates the theories of many other representatives of Structuralism. Based on the obsolete Romantic notion of the "organic community" and infused by contemporary biological views of the nation ("national biology"), this concept not only represents a totalizing, ideological aspect of Mathesius's method (introducing modern functionalism into nineteenth-century ideological notions of language and literature as principal signs of the excellence and exceptional character of a specific nation), but also imposes a restriction on the development of literary theoretical aspects in his later work. In Mathesius's opinion, the major purpose of literature is to contribute to the growth of the nation's organic structure. As a result, one of the major potentialities of Mathesius's revolutionary functionalism, namely the transformation of philology into modern literary and cultural theory, has remained undeveloped. This is evident when comparing Mathesius's project with other twentieth-century attempts to transform philology – especially Mikhail Bakhtin's historical poetics.

The following chapter by Helena Znojemská discusses "Vilém Mathesius as Literary Historian." Although Mathesius progressively focused on linguistic problems in his scholarly output, he also produced the monumental, though truncated, *History of English Literature*, and continued to comment on issues of literary criticism in texts of a more popular nature such as "The Origins and Nature of Critical Judgement" and "On the Functions and Tools of Literary Criticism." Despite the fact that the *History of English Literature* has been hailed as a foundational act of Prague English Studies, no systematic attempt has been made at a detailed analysis of the evolution of his thought on aesthetics and literary criticism, nor on their potential affinities with the theories of other members of the Prague Linguistic Circle (René Wellek, 1909-1997; Jan Mukařovský, 1891-1975). Znojemská's chapter remedies this lack and confronts Mathesius's specific methodology and findings with the propositions voiced in the more theoretical statements on the nature of literary criticism, and in his linguistic works. It also searches for possible continuities between Mathesius's propositions on the nature of a literary work of art and the much more refined theoretical positions developed by Wellek and Mukařovský (e.g., the structural unity of the work of art as a basis of its evaluation, or the concept of art as semiotic fact). Particularly important in this second line of enquiry is the concept of "norm" and its links to Mathesius's notions of "dynamic stability" and, as a function of its wider applicability, "dynamic classicism."

In the next chapter on "Vilém Mathesius as Translator and Theoretician of Translation," Bohuslav Mánek discusses Mathesius's principal translations, that of H.G. Wells's collection of essays *An Englishman Looks at the World* and a selection from Chaucer's *The Canterbury Tales*. Mánek also analyses the translations of the extracts from diverse authors interspersed throughout his *History of English Literature*, which was written in Czech; subsequently, he defines Mathesius's position in the development of Czech translation theory and practice and discusses his theoretical approach to translation and its individual techniques (derived from his functional approach). Special attention is given to Mathesius's analysis and criticism of Czech translation practice and of its specific problems, such as the translation of blank verse.

Mathesius's legacy in terms of the work of his pupils and followers among Czech scholars in English and American literature is the topic of the two following chapters, both of which also discuss the impact of the political upheaval resulting from the instalment of the communist totalitarian regime, whose ideology was, by and large, hostile to Structuralism. In the first chapter, entitled "A Structuralist History of Zdeněk Vančura," Pavla Veselá traces "the ruptures and continuities" in the work of this leading Czech Americanist of the mid-twentieth century. Her analysis of Vančura's work starts from with his early studies of Renaissance and Baroque prose and periodization in early modern English and American literature. These writings are discussed in the context of Russian Formalism, Prague Structuralism and Mathesius's functional approach. Vančura's conclusions about literary history, typical of his early work, are confronted with the major tendencies in his later writings which are influenced by the political changes in Czechoslovakia after the victory of communism in 1948.The chapter explains Vančura's efforts to repudiate Structuralism under ideological pressure from the totalitarian regime, but it also demonstrates that it was not unreservedly negative as these historical changes also stimulated Vančura to develop and expand upon his previous positions and to establish a certain, though not unproblematic, continuity of his later approaches with the functional method.

The chapter on "Jaroslav Hornát's Critical Method in His Studies of Charles Dickens" by Zdeněk Beran concludes the first part of the book. As a detailed case study it deals with Hornát's interpretation of Dickens's oeuvre in a series of essays, which accompanied the project of its modern Czech translation for the *Knihovna klasiků* (The Classics Library). As a result, the chapter documents the interrelationship of literary studies with translation practice, an important aspect of the modern transformation of philology and focuses on the Structuralist influences on Hornát's approach to Dickens, especially Jan Mukařovský's theory of "norm" (closely related to Mathesius's functionalism), Felix Vodička's (1909-1974) concept of "concretization," and their notions of narrative structure, chiefly the relationship of "*fabula*" and "*sujet*" discussed first by the Russian Formalists. Although Hornát's method can be said to follow and expand upon Vančura's Structuralist analysis of

Euphuism and its rhetoric (this is evident from Hornát's study *Anglická renesanční próza* – English Renaissance Prose, 1970), in his essays on Dickens's novels Hornát evidently develops the Structuralist approach, deepening it especially in terms of a functional analysis of motifs and the emotional expressivity of Dickens's style.

The second part of the book, "Contexts and Outcomes: From Prague Structuralism to Radical Philology," opens with an extensive chapter "Structuralism and the Prague School Revisited" by Robert J.C. Young. Using the expertise of his highly influential work on Post-colonialism and critical theory, Young demonstrates that Structuralism did not emerge as a mere "literary methodology relating to grammar, phonology and stylistics (as in the work of Vilém Mathesius and Jan Mukařovský)," but also, and perhaps more importantly, "as a broader cultural project in a self-conscious anti-Western strategy, directed against the hierarchical imperialist cultural and racialist assumptions of European thought." As a consequence suggests Young, the Structuralist projects of Nikolai Troubetzkoy (1890-1938) and Roman Jakobson (1896-1982) "can be affiliated [...] to the huge body of anti-colonial thought that was developed round the world during the first half of the twentieth century and which now forms the basis of Postcolonial Studies." Young's stimulating interpretation of the synchronic approach as "anti-ethnocentric general theory to put all cultures, high/low, west/east/ south, on a level playing field" indicates that it possesses an undeveloped potentiality. It can be argued (as Jacques Derrida did as early as 1966, pointing out the "rupture" in Lévi-Strauss's ethnological project[2]) that the failure of Structuralism to fulfil its promise of becoming a general methodology of the "human sciences" led to a steep decline of its influence – even to the extent that few today seem to take it seriously.

If Structuralism is so easy to dismiss now, asks Young, why were so many of the most pre-eminent intellectuals of the era, such as Lévi-Strauss, Lacan, Foucault, Althusser, and Barthes so taken with it? To answer

---

[2] Jacques Derrida, "Structure, Sign and Play in the Discourse of Human Sciences," *Writing and Difference*, trans. Alan Bass (Chicago and London: University of Chicago Press, 1978) 273-92.

this requires the kind of assiduous reconsideration of the origins of Structuralism in the work of Jakobson and Troubetzkoy that Young's chapter contains. Although no more than "outsiders to the Prague Circle," these Russian scholars were responsible for formulating the method and indeed the very name – Structuralism. Arguing that "the conceptual basis of Structuralism was created [...] in part as a form of émigré culture, underpinned by a form of Russian nationalism," Young points out the interdisciplinary basis of their project, which effected the transformation of the approaches of nineteenth-century philology: "Troubetzkoy like many linguists of his time was also an ethnologist and anthropologist, folklorist and dialectologist." Nonetheless, Troubetzkoy's 'philological' orientation was clearly based on a critique of the ethnocentric culture of Europe and constituted "the espousal of a new kind of Russian nationalism, centring its identity in Eurasia," the subsequent idealization of early medieval Slavic history, the so-called "Great Moravia," or even, as T.G. Masaryk conceived it, the notion of Czechoslovakia as a "bridge" between the East and the West. Unsurprisingly, these notions evolved from the Romantic idea of "organic unity" used to cover up subversive aspects of "hybridity," which then came to dominate the work of Mikhail Bakhtin. Unlike Bakhtin's approach, Troubetzkoy's project is characterized by a repudiation of Eurocentrism: a "radical critique of European culture from the point of view of the world outside Europe," which also involves an attack on current Western notions of "progress," as "the forced acquisition, through imperialism, of European modernity by other cultures around the world."

Although Troubetzkoy might have been inspired by the ideology of Pan-Slavism, he transcends its Romantic framework in inclining towards a Structuralist (and even Post-structuralist) perspective, where hierarchical differences among cultures are discarded in favour of the "synchronic" approach: "There is neither higher nor lower. There is only [the] similar and dissimilar." According to Young, this theoretical stance anticipates Lyotard's views that the "value of different cultures [...] marked by [...] the *différend*, their 'qualitative incommensurability' or their untranslatability," reflected also in Benedict Anderson's theory of "imagined communities" and Edward Said's critique of colonialism. From this angle, Troubetzkoy's project appears as a "complete restructuring of the ethnocentric cultural hierarchy that operated at the foundation of western imperial civilization in the disciplinary formation of its knowledges." Roman Jakobson's reflections, which stimulated both Lacan's analysis of the unconscious and Lévi-Strauss's approach to the "savage mind," had developed from the same source.

Analyzing the Structuralist approach to language development, Young shows that "[t]he Prague School doctrines were both [...] technical and ideological: the emphasis on synchrony was deliberately opposed to the historicist Indo-European comparative linguistics of the nineteenth century that had been dominated by German historical scholarship, and which had been committed to implicitly racialist notions of linguistic hierarchy that assumed the superiority of European languages." Against the tree model (*Stammbaumtheorie*) of the "Neogrammarians," Troubetzkoy came up with the theory of the *Sprachbund*, or the convergence of languages on "non-genetic basis" designed to explain "the linguistic cohesion of Eurasia." Significantly, this theory shifted "the language model from a linear to a spatial evolution, from the language tree to the linguistic chain, net or, to move to Deleuzian terms, the rhizome." The importance of the *Sprachbund* results from the facts that it "denies simple nationalist identifications with languages on the European model" and makes "an important distinction between language and culture: cultural zones, such as Eurasia, are formations of the same kind as language zones, but they are not necessarily to be identified with them." In other words, although the zones of language and culture are separate, Troubetzkoy's "diffusionist" approach also emphasizes the "formative role of language on culture so that genetically unrelated languages begin to cohere within a single geographic and cultural historical zone." Young clearly demonstrates the features of Troubetzkoy's model that anticipate Post-structuralist notions of an open, dynamic totality of the sort explored by Derrida and Deleuze. His analysis is expanded by a stimulating comparison of different approaches to hybridity and assimilation in linguistic, ethnic and cultural terms, confronting the works of the eccentric Soviet linguist Nikolai Yakovlevitch Marr (1865-1934), Troubetzkoy and Jakobson.

All this clearly shows an important dimension, added by Troubetzkoy and Jakobson to the project of the Prague School and to Structuralism in general. Thanks to their ambitious revision of many of the principal tenets of nineteenth-century philology, Structuralism became "a cultural and political project whose epistemological reach formed a wide-ranging challenge to the Eurocentric presuppositions of European positivism and the forms of knowledge that had been developed under its aegis."

The following chapter on "Functional Linguistics as the 'Science of Poetic Forms'" by David Vichnar discusses the major features of the poetics of the Prague Linguistic Circle. Vichnar shows how the poetic theory of Prague Structuralism grew out of direct engagement with poetic practice, which in turn was informed by contemporary advances in the field of poetics. This is exemplified by the friendships and close collaborative relationships of Jakobson with a number of Russian and Czech poets, but especially with Vítězslav Nezval. The heritage of Vilém Mathesius is then revisited as a source of inspiration for two of his followers in the fields of poetics and aesthetics: Bohuslav Havránek (1893-1987) and Jan Mukařovský. On the basis of their engagement in a vital public discussion concerning the matter of prescriptive poetics and literary criticism, Vichnar argues that although the part played by Mathesius and his followers in the debates of the 20s and 30s on Czech "Poetism" (*poetismus*) and Surrealism may have been overshadowed by their more illustrious Russian co-member, their importance for, and alliance with, the Czech avant-garde is not to be underestimated.

Specific points in the impact of Structuralism, mentioned at the outset of Robert Young's analysis, are the focus of Erik Roraback's chapter, "A Gateway to a Baroque Rhetoric of Jacques Lacan and Niklas Luhmann." Interpreting major features of the ideological content and rhetoric of selected works by this French psychoanalytic thinker and the German systems theorist, Roraback compares them to the phenomenological Structuralism of the Czech-born Husserlian philosopher, Ladislav Rieger (1890-1958) and of the theories of the Prague Linguistic Circle. In this context, Rieger's ground-breaking essay, "The Semantic Analysis of Philosophical Texts" (which addresses the problem of representation), is used to highlight contentious areas in Luhmann's systems-theory, which otherwise builds upon Husserl in many key respects. The chapter uses aspects of Mathesius's functional approach (developed in the "Theses" of the Prague Linguistic Circle presented at the Prague Congress of Slavists, 1929) to reveal the connections of Prague semantic analysis with the problems of rhetoric in both Lacan and in Luhmann.

The chapter on "Jan Grossman, Structuralism, and the Grotesque" by Ondřej Pilný examines the use of the Structuralist method by Jan Grossman (1925-1993), a pupil of Jan Mukařovský and Václav Černý, and arguably one of the most influential figures of twentieth-century Czech theatre. It focuses on Grossman's essays on Alfred Jarry's *Ubu* plays, Kafka's *The Trial*, and the plays of Václav Havel and uses these texts as the basis of an exegesis of Grossman's staging of Jarry, emphasizing the use of the grotesque in the context of totalitarian Czechoslovakia. Grossman's theoretical and practical development of Structuralist methodology within the context of a restrictive political regime is linked with stimuli from Mathesius's functional approach and contrasted with Mukařovský's 1940s essays on the theatre in which the latter's Structuralism begins to slide towards a totalizing ideology and ultimately advocates agit-prop. Grossman's version of absurdist drama, developed in close collaboration with Václav Havel, is seen to promote the theatre as a space in which the recipient is not to regulate what is produced but is rather to engage in a free conversation with a work of art that ultimately unmasks recondite evil. The use of the grotesque represents a principal ingredient in this version of absurdism; its form stands as an inheritor of the concept of the medieval grotesque outlined by Mikhail Bakhtin, who identified in it a "power to liberate from dogmatism, completeness, and limitation."

The final chapter of the volume, "Attesting / Before the Fact" by Louis Armand, opens with a discussion of "radical philology," a term coined by Geert Lernout, one of the representatives of "textual genetics," in his analysis of Joyce's *Finnegans Wake* notebooks. Any philology, from historical approaches to language to the study of language acquisition, must take into account its "incompletion" (resulting from the incompatibility of intuitive approaches to what exists before signification and the semiotic study of communication). As a result, philology can be only an "approximative method" (or a system of knowledge) bound up with the materiality of signifying. This poses important problems concerning the relation of signs or "symbols" to facts: the impossibility of distinguishing between them. Since a decisive part of philology has consisted in "enumerating sets of facts that correspond with language" in symbolic, rhetorical or poetic terms, the problem of the verifiability of this correspondence arises. This problem entails symbolization and becomes "a theoretical fiction" which refers to the question of responsibility and the relation to the Lacanian Real or the Other. In this way, "radical philology" problematizes the value of language, relating it to the questions of fiction and of the unspeakable. Although these issues were not directly addressed by Prague Structuralists, they were arguably anticipated by them, especially in Mukařovský's analysis of "unintentionality."[3]

The present volume does not pretend to list, explain and define all relevant aspects of the transformation of philology within the development of Prague English Studies and in the broader framework of Prague Structuralism. Inspired by Mathesius's functional approach and also provoked by the powerful theoretical and methodological stimuli presented by Troubetzkoy and Jakobson, this volume attempts to cast light on selected genetic and contextual aspects of the Structuralist transformation of philology. These features are typical both of its local dimensions within the framework of Prague English Studies and of its broader contextual relationships with dominant trends in nineteenth-century philology and twentieth-century linguistics, anthropology and cultural theory. In several ways it also demonstrates the interdependence of the theoretical and practical moments of this process, tracing its links to the rhetoric of theoretical writing, translation projects, avant-garde poetry and stage practice.

We are pleased to acknowledge an important aspect of the genesis of this volume by way of a final remark: apart from commemorating the centenary of Prague English Studies, this book is intended as a tribute to the doyen of Prague Anglicists, Professor Zdeněk Stříbrný, whose ninetieth birthday coincided with the centenary of English Studies.

---

3   Jan Mukařovský, "Intentionality and Unintentionality," *Structure, Sign and Function: Selected Essays by Jan Mukařovský*, ed. and trans. John Burbank and Peter Steiner (New Haven and London: Yale University Press, 1978) 89-128.

Professor Stříbrný's life-long work, dedicated chiefly to the study of Shakespeare, made a vital contribution in its own right to the transformation of philology. This is particularly evident from the anthology *Charles University on Shakespeare* (1966) edited by him and containing contributions by Jan Mukařovský, and by Vilém Mathesius's followers – Zdeněk Vančura and Bohumil Trnka (1895-1984). Stříbrný's interpretations of Shakespeare, especially his study "The Genesis of Double Time in Pre-Shakespearean and Shakespearean Drama" (1969),[4] in turn form an original development of the dynamic and perspectivist features of Mathesius's functionalist thought.

---

[4] See Zdeněk Stříbrný, *The Whirligig of Time*, ed. Lois Potter (Newark: University of Delaware Press, 2007) 79-97. For an analysis of theoretical aspects of Stříbrný's approach see Martin Procházka, "'Techniques' and 'Philosophies' of Time in Shakespeare's Plays and Individual Life," *Litteraria Pragensia* 18.35 (2008): 100-104.

1. LEGACIES: VILÉM MATHESIUS AND FOLLOWERS

THE VALUE OF LANGUAGE: RHETORIC, SEMIOLOGY, PHILOLOGY AND THE FUNCTIONAL APPROACH

Martin Procházka

Language, law and truth have always been closely linked. From the fragments of the pre-Socratic thinkers it is evident that the dichotomy *physis – nomos* (nature – law) was not only connected with the establishment of social inequality and repression of sensuous activity, but also with the control of language and its epistemological power. According to the treatise *On Truth* by Antiphon the Sophist,

> [m]ost of the things which are legally just are [none the less...] inimical to nature. By law it has been laid down for the eyes what they should see and what they should not see; for the ears what they should hear and they should not hear; for the tongue what it should speak, and what it should not speak; [...].[1]

The relation between language and law is problematized in Aristotle: the power of speech[2] is no longer identified with *physis*, nor linked with

---

1 Antiphon the Sophist, "On Truth," quoted in *Sources in Greek Political Thought from Homer to Polybius*, ed. Donald Kagan (New York: The Free Press, 1965) 217-19.

2 Here, speech is not understood in opposition to "language," as in Ferdinand de Saussure's *parole* vs. *la langue* dichotomy ("Language is speech *less speaking*." Ferdinand de Saussure, *Course in General Linguistics*, ed. Charles Bally and Albert Sechehaye in collaboration with Albert Reidlinger, trans.

the application of available methods, but connected with the open-ended nature of "deliberation," judicial or political reasoning which can discover "alternative possibilities":[3]

> The duty of rhetoric is to deal with such matters as we deliberate upon without arts or systems to guide us, in the hearing of persons who cannot take in at a glance a complicated argument, or follow a long chain of reasoning. The subjects of our deliberation are such as seem to present us with alternative possibilities [...].[4]

These "possibilities" are understood as "probabilities," that is, things "contingent" (neither necessarily true nor necessarily false, but true under certain circumstances), or "variable" (varying statistically across a certain domain):

> A Probability is a thing that usually happens; not, however, as some definitions would suggest, anything whatever that usually happens, but only if it belongs to the class of the "contingent" or "variable." It bears the same relation to that in respect of which it is probable as the universal bears to the particular.[5]

Wade Baskin [London: Peter Owen, 1960] 77; emphasis added.) but as "speaking" – a specific *act of speech*, a *performance* of the qualities of the language a system.

3   Aristotle's thought may be said to anticipate modern and contemporary theories of "deliberative democracy" based on morally sound, legitimate and qualified political decisions and not on a mere aggregate of preferences (e.g., in voting by ballot) or on the inequality of political power and wealth or the pressures of interest groups, lobbyists, etc. These theories were anticipated by late eighteenth- and early nineteenth-century thinkers, such as Edmund Burke, Benjamin Franklin, Thomas Jefferson, Alexander Hamilton, John Adams, John Jay, Alexis de Tocqueville and John Stuart Mill. They are influential in contemporary political thought (Jürgen Habermas, John Rawls, James Fishkin, Joshua Cohen, James Fearon or Carne Ross). See, e.g., John Elster (ed.), *Deliberative Democracy* (Cambridge: Cambridge University Press, 1998); James Fishkin, *When the People Speak* (New York and Oxford: Oxford University Press, 2011).

4   Aristotle, *Rhetoric* (I.2.1357a), ed. W.D. Ross, trans. W. Rhys Roberts (New York: Cosimo Books) 9.

5   Aristotle (I.2.1357a) 10.

Evidently, "possibilities" and "probabilities" are closely linked: the former are products of a rhetorical activity called deliberation and the latter are its subjects.

Moreover, Aristotle discusses possibilities and probabilities as specific "signs" (determined by the relation of the particular to the universal). These "signs" are *arbitrary* in the sense of presenting no necessary connection between a proposition and a conclusion made about a certain thing or event. Their arbitrariness is characterized by "deliberation," because they can be "refuted."[6]

The connection of Aristotle's notion of "sign" (*sēmeion*) with the above-mentioned problems of probability and the possibility of a "complete proof" derived from an "infallible sign" (*tekhmērion*),[7] accounts for the complex nature of arbitrariness outlined in *Rhetoric*. According to Aristotle, the main social task of rhetoric is to help making just decisions in "definite cases" and solving problems unforeseen by lawgivers: "whether something has happened or has not happened, will be or will not be, is or is not."[8] Concerned "with modes of persuasion" and aiming to "produce conviction," rhetoric is the art which by working with signs establishes *a vital link between probabilities and truths*: "[t]he true and the approximately true are apprehended by the same faculty."[9] As Aristotle points out, the success of this process cannot be predetermined and is never complete: the function of rhetoric "is not simply to succeed in persuading, but rather to discover the means of coming as near such success as the circumstances in each particular case allow." In this respect, rhetoric is like medicine which does not "make a man quite healthy" but puts people "as far as may be on the road to health."[10] In Aristotle's *Rhetoric*, the arbitrariness of signs matters as a *value* relevant for *the search for truth*, in specific cases which can be decided only by negotiation using the persuasive powers of speech.

A completely different understanding of arbitrariness is typical of one of the key examples of its modern use – de Saussure's conception of

6   Aristotle (I.2.1357b) 10.
7   Aristotle (I.2.1357b) 10.
8   Aristotle (I.1.1354b) 4.
9   Aristotle (I.1.1355a) 5.
10   Aristotle (I.1.1355b) 6.

language as a semiotic system: "language is a convention and the nature of the sign that is agreed upon does not matter."[11] The assumption that signs are arbitrary (conventional) implies that language, as a system depending "solely on a rational principle, is free and can be organized at will."[12] The corrective to the individual reason and will is not the nature of language as a social institution, since "group psychology" does not operate on a "purely logical basis" and "contacts between individuals" may therefore include "anything that deflects reason."[13]

Although de Saussure sees "the action of time combined with the social force" as an important feature of arbitrariness, he does not understand arbitrariness as a condition opening a field of possibilities and enabling deliberation on probabilities, evidence and truth. The *Course of General Linguistics* defines arbitrariness of the sign as a means establishing "[l]anguage" as "a self-contained whole and principle of classification" and giving "unity" to speech. This approach evades the complexity of speech and the interdisciplinary nature of its research:

> Taken as a whole, speech is many-sided and heterogeneous; straddling several areas simultaneously – physical, physiological and psychological – it belongs both to the individual and to the society; we cannot put it to any category of human facts, for we cannot discover its unity.[14]

Evidently, de Saussure's notion of speech focuses on its articulation ("physical" and "physiological" areas) and perception ("psychological") and does not take into account its epistemological function and persuasive power, since these can only be functions of language as a system of signs. Moreover, the *Course* identifies language as a contrived system with "a natural order" and the only possible means of classification, conflating the *physis–nomos* opposition: "As soon as we give language the first place among the facts of speech, we introduce a *natural order* to a *mass* that lends itself to *no other classification* [...] what is natural to mankind,

11   Saussure 10.
12   Saussure 78.
13   Saussure 78.
14   Saussure 9.

is not speech, but the faculty of constructing a language, i.e., a system of distinct signs corresponding to distinct ideas."[15] The arbitrariness of this process becomes evident when the "constructing of language" is paradoxically identified with the acceptance of law, and not with lawgiving, as it might appear.[16] Moreover, the social consensus about signs is a mere "idea" (or fiction) which does not have a "real" existence.[17] According to Saussurean semiology, "the essential quality of the sign," its arbitrariness, "escapes individual or social will."[18] Therefore it can be identified either with *the natural law* or with *randomness*.

All this, however, does not mean that language as a sign system is not a social or collective phenomenon: it is called "something social, [...] collective," "a communal good" or "communal property."[19] Nonetheless, the principal question is whether it should be studied only in this framework of reference, as a mere outcome of communal ownership, or rather approached as something *outside* the community but "related" ("corresponding") to it.[20] The main reason for this shift in perspective is the notion of the arbitrariness of the sign, resulting no longer (as in Aristotle) from the social negotiation of the relationship between the signifier and the signified, but from the assumption of the *randomness* of this relationship: "there is no guarantee that the individual reason

---

15 Saussure 9-10 (emphasis added).
16 Albert Riedlinger, notes to the second and third lectures of the *Course*. "Genfer Vorlesungsmitschriften," Fedinand de Saussure, *Linguistik und Semiologie: Texte, Briefe und Dokumente aus der Nachlaß*, ed. and trans. Johannes Fehr (Frankfurt M.: Suhrkamp, 1997) 500: "Wenn es einen Bereich gibt, in dem die Gesetzgebung als Gesetz erscheint, das man hinnehmen muß und das man nich schafft, da ist es jener der Sprache [>langue<]." All translations from this source are mine.
17 "Den Moment, in dem sich man über die Zeichen einigt, gibt es real nicht, bloß als Vorstellung." Riedlinger 500.
18 "Das, was sich in der Sprache [>langue<] dem individuellen oder sozialen Willen entzieht, ist das wesentliche Eigenschaft des Zeichens [...]." Riedlinger 502.
19 "etwas Soziales, etwas Kollektives," "das Gut einer Gemeinschaft." Riedlinger 503.
20 "Tatsächlich, wenn ein semiologischer System das Gut einer Gemeinschaft wird, ist es vergeblich, dieses außerhalb dessen betrachten zu wollen, was sich für es aus dieser kollektiven Eigenschaft ergibt, und es genügt, um sein Wesen zu erfassen, das zu untersuchen, was es gegenüber der Gemeinschaft ist." Riedlinger 503.

directs the relationship between the sign and the idea in mind."[21] This is because of the unpredictability of the development of the community of language users which affects the evolution of language as a system: "we do not know in advance which forces will interfere with the life of the sign system."[22]

Following this assumption, de Saussure chose the interaction between the sea and the ship as a model of the community – language relationship. Due to the unpredictability of the ocean as a *natural* system, the course of the ship cannot be determined chiefly on the basis of its construction, i.e., the intrinsic qualities of the *human-made* system. The major problems of this model are the naturalistic idea of the community (a highly complex and little known system, like the sea, must obviously appear unpredictable) and a technological idea of language as a constructed communication (transport) device. The representation of community as the sea overinflates the aspects of potentiality and indeterminacy by its emphasis on the disputable *wholeness* of the system. It is questionable whether a community can be modelled like a sea; recent notions of "imagined communities" emphasize their fragmented structure and the importance of technological media and economic forces in their formation.[23] Because of its totalizing perspective, the model does not emphasize the potentialities of language but rather its most general purpose: "the sign system is created for the community and not for an individual, like the ship is made for the sea."[24] The result is a certain duality of Saussurean arbitrariness, which combines randomness of natural processes with the imperative of communal purpose.

As already stated, this approach establishes a fundamentally different relationship between language, law and truth than that articulated in Aristotle's *Rhetoric*. While Aristotle stresses the function of speech in those areas of social life where exact truths cannot be determined,

---

[21] "nichts garantiert, daß eine individuelle Vernunft den Bezug zwischen Zeichen und Vorstellung leitet." Riedlinger 503.

[22] "*A priori* wissen wir nicht, welch Kräfte sich einmischen werden ins Leben des Zeichensystems [...]." Riedlinger 503.

[23] See, e.g., Benedict Anderson, *Imagined Communities*, 2nd ed. (London: Verso, 1991) 36 (on "print-capitalism") and *passim*.

[24] "Das Zeichensystem ist für die Gemeinschaft gemacht und nich für ein Individuum, wie das Schiff fürs Meer geschaffen ist." Riedlinger 503.

Saussurean semiology attempts to overcome this indeterminacy by pointing both to the unpredictability of communal life (comparing it to a complex and little understood natural phenomenon – the sea) and to the dominant communal function of language and its status as a "social product."[25]

The difference between the function of the sign in Aristotelian rhetoric and Saussurean linguistics can also be exemplified by the discussion of *value* which is in an essential relationship to the question of truth. De Saussure compares the signifier – signified relationship to that between wages and labour in political economy. In both disciplines the relationship between the atemporal and temporal principles of classification (axes of *"simultaneities"* and *"successions"*)[26] establishes the notion of value, as conditioned by time, and, simultaneously, independent from time:

> A value – so long as it is somehow rooted in things and in their natural relations, as happens with economics (the value of a plot of ground, for instance, is related to its productivity) – can to some extent be traced in time if we remember that it depends at each moment upon a system of coexisting values. Its link with things gives it, *perforce, a natural basis, and the judgements that we base on such values are never completely arbitrary; their variability is limited. But we have just seen that natural data have no place in linguistics.*[27]

As a result, the values "rooted in things and in their natural relations" (that is, characterized by the Aristotelian relationship between probabilities and truths) must be excluded from the system of language as "never completely arbitrary [...] natural data" that "have no place in linguistics." Evidently, the science of linguistics dealing with *exact values* of language signs can be founded only by means of abstracting from the *social value* of language. This is confirmed by Riedlinger's notes from the third lecture of the *Course*:

---

[25] "soziales Produkt." Riedlinger 503.
[26] Saussure 80.
[27] Saussure 80 (emphasis added).

> This means that the language [>langue<] is a semiological product and the semiological product is a social product. *Yet, what is it in closer perspective?* Any semiological system consists of a number of units (more or less complex units of different orders) and the true nature of these units – what prevents them from being confused with others – consists in their being *values.* This system of units, which is a system of signs, is also a system of values. [...] The value is difficult to define in different orders [...], but at least we are on a defined ground, from the outside at any rate.[28]

In Saussurean terms, *the value of language coincides with the value of sign as the system unit*, within an externally determined territory of linguistics as a semiological discipline. Although this *intrinsic* value is a means of establishing the system, "what prevents [its specific units] to be confused with others," it is also most generally defined as a social product: "the sign will have a value only through the confirmation of the community."[29]

As a consequence, Saussurean theory has to admit a *dual nature of value*, "as if there were two values in the sign (*value in itself* and *that which it has received from the community*)," and at the same time, eliminate this duality by an ideological statement which declares the community (distanced so far as a complex natural system), an indisputable origin of both types of values: "Where is, in any order, a system of values, if not that [originated] through the community?"[30] This ideology neglects the value of language as a means of discussing the relationship of law and truth, which is the prerequisite of deliberative democracy. Giving up

28 "Das heißt, daß die Sprache [>langue<] ein semiologischer Produkt ist und das semiologische Produkt ein soziales Produkt. *Aber was für eines ist es, näher betrachtet?* Irgendein semiologisches System setzt sich zusammen aus der Menge von Einheiten (mehr or weniger komplexer Einheiten verschiedener Ordnungen), und die wahrhafte Natur dieser Einheiten – was verhindert sie mit anderen Einheiten zu verwechseln – besteht darin, daß sie *Werte* sind. Dieses System von Einheiten, welches ein Zeichensystem ist, ist ein System von Werten. [...] Der Wert in der verschiedenen Ordnungen ist sehr schwierig zu definieren [...], aber wir sind immerhin auf einem definierten Terrain, wenigstens äußerlich." Riedlinger 504.

29 "das Zeichen is sich einen Wert haben wird nur durch die Bestätigung der Gemeinschaft." Riedlinger 504.

30 "Wo gibt es, in irgendeiner Ordnung, ein System von Werten, wenn nicht durch die Gemeinschaft." Riedlinger 504.

the exploration of the social function of language, its performative force and rhetorical means, Saussurean linguistics establishes language as an *abstract system of values* which can be 'naturalized' as an empirical object.

It is a well-known fact that this tendency led to the distinction between the "synchronic" and the "diachronic" study of language.[31] The Prague Structuralist approach, represented, for instance, by Vilém Mathesius's (1882-1945) essay "Functional Linguistics" ("Funkční lingvistika," 1929) rephrases this dichotomy as the opposition between the "non-historical, synchronistic" study of language and the "historical method."[32] As a representative of the "historical" study of language, the "Neogrammarian" school (Junggrammatiker) is chosen, which stressed the value of the knowledge of "deeper historical roots of the later stages" of language development.[33] This rather schematized representation of the history of linguistics erases its earlier phases, especially the critical achievement of humanistic philology.

It is generally accepted that the re-discovery of Quintilian's *Institutio Oratoria*, one of the most important treatises on rhetoric in later antiquity, led to the development of humanistic philology heavily based on rhetoric.[34] Carlo Ginzburg has shown how one of the founders of humanistic philology, Lorenzo Valla (ca. 1407-1457), "was totally foreign, and even hostile, to the cult of Cicero" as the chief representative of the Classical rhetoric in the early Renaissance and emphasized the role of Quintilian in preserving and transmitting "Aristotle's intellectual legacy."[35] In contrast to Cicero, who stressed the power of rhetoric to affect and manipulate mass emotions, and in continuity with Aristotle

---

[31] Saussure 81.

[32] Vilém Mathesius, "Functional Linguistics" (Funkční lingvistika, 1929), trans. Libuše Dušková, *Praguiana*, ed. Josef Vachek (Prague: Academia, 1983) 121.

[33] Mathesius, "Functional Linguistics" 122.

[34] See especially Paul Oskar Kristeller, "Humanism and Scholasticism in the ItalianRenaissance," *Byzantion* 17 (1944-45): 346-74; *Studies in Renaissance Thoughtand Letters*, 4 vols. (Rome: Edizioni di storia e letteratura, 1956-1996) 1:553-83; 2:357, 382-83, 420; 4:90, 235. On the importance of Kristeller's work in relation to Post-structuralist approaches to rhetoric influenced by Nietzsche, see Carlo Ginzburg, *History, Rhetoric, and Proof* (Hanover, NH, and London: University Press of New England, 1999) 58.

[35] Ginzburg 63.

and Quintilian, Valla understood rhetoric as the "scrutiny of proofs" dealing with the so-called "inartificial" evidence, such as "prejudices, rumours, tortures, documents [*tabulae*], oaths and witnesses," that is examining the truthfulness of signs/proofs produced by other than rhetorical means.[36] Valla, whose later reputation among early modern editors, paleographers and text critics, especially Jean Mabillon (1632-1707) and Bernard de Montfaucon (1655-1741),[37] had been established by his demonstration that an important document, the so-called *Donation of Constantine*, bestowing a third of the Roman Empire on the Catholic Church, was a medieval forgery, can be seen as a humanist philologist using rhetoric as a method for a critical analysis of a legally and politically relevant text. Despite the traditional features of Valla's approach, especially the rhetorical form of *declamatio*, "based on the alternating demonstration of the opposite arguments,"[38] his stylistic and grammatical analysis of the forged legal document can be said to have anticipated a trend, which, among others, led to Josef Dobrovský's (1753-1829) substantial critique of the authenticity of the so-called "Manuscripts," believed by nineteenth-century Czech nationalists to be a principal historical source documenting the ancient origins of the Czech language, culture, law and government. Evidently, there were also other historical tendencies in philology, incompatible with the "historical method" of the "Neogrammarian" school.

Here it must be pointed out that the historical approach of the "Neogrammarians" can be traced back to the more comprehensive and wide-ranging project of Romantic philologists, namely Sir William Jones

[36] Ginzburg 61. On "inartificial" (*atekhnoi*) proofs see Quintilian, *Institutes of Oratory*, trans. John Selby Watson, ed. Lee Honeycutt (Iowa State University, 2006), online, accessed 28 December 2012: "But though these species of proof are devoid of art in themselves, they yet require, very frequently, to be supported or overthrown with the utmost force of eloquence, and those writers, therefore, appear to me highly deserving of blame who have excluded all this kind of proofs from the rules of art." Similar to Aristotle, Quintilian stresses the importance of rhetoric in interpreting these proofs only seemingly unconnected with "the art of speaking."

[37] See Ginzburg 64, mentioning "Valla's sensitivity to linguistic anachronisms," which stemmed from his attempts to "revive classical Latin as a purified language."

[38] Ginzburg 60.

(1746-1794) and brothers Friedrich (1772-1829) and August Wilhelm von Schlegel (1767-1845). Their main purpose was to make the comparative study of languages a key to understanding the philosophy, mythology and laws of ancient cultures.[39] In his treatise *On the Language and Wisdom of the Indians* (*Über die Sprache und Weisheit der Indier*, 1808), Friedrich Schlegel developed William Jones's comparative grammar and anticipated Jacob Grimm's (1785-1863) law of consonantal shift ("Erste Lautverschiebung"), which later became the example of an "exceptionless sound law" that according to the Neogrammarians established historical linguistics as a natural science.[40] However, he also pioneered the typological and functional comparison of languages based on the structural view of their morphology:

> The decisive aspect that will clarify everything is the internal structure of languages or the comparative grammar, which will lead us to entirely new conclusions concerning the genealogy of languages in a similar way as the comparative anatomy had thrown light on the history of higher nature.[41]

Here, the analogy between comparative linguistics and the study of complex living organisms is crucial, since it establishes the authority of

---

[39] In the case of Schlegel's principal work *On the Language and Wisdom of the Indians*, the study of language is the point of departure to the exploration of the ancient Indian *Laws of Manu* (*Manusmṛti*) and of the philosophical aspects of the Vedic texts as the origins of Indian culture. See Friedrich Schlegel, *Über die Sprache und Weisheit der Indier. Ein Beitrag zur Begründung der Alterthumskunde* (Heidelberg: Mohr und Zimmer, 1808) 96-97 and *passim*.

[40] See Hermann Osthoff und Karl Brugmann, *Morphologische Untersuchungen auf dem Gebiete der indogermanischen Sprachen*, Vol. 1 (Leipzig: S. Hirzel, 1878) xiii: "Aller Lautwandel, soweit er mechanisch vor sich geht, vollzieht sich nach ausnahmslosen Gesetzen, d.h. die Richtung der Lautbewegung ist bei allen Angehörigen einer Sprachgenossenschaft, außer dem Fall, daß Dialektspaltung eintritt, stets dieselbe, und alle Wörter, in denen der Lautbewegung unterworfene Laut unter gleichen Verhältnissen erscheint, werden ohne Ausnahme von der Veränderung ergriffen."

[41] "Jener entscheidende Punkt aber, der hier alles aufhellen wird, ist die innre Structur der Sprachen oder die vergleichende Grammatik, welche uns ganz neue Aufschlüsse über die Genealogie der Sprachen auf ähnliche Weise geben wird, wie die vergleichende Anatomie über die höhere Naturgeschichte Licht verbreitet hat." Schlegel 28. All translations from this source are mine.

language and culture as the product of natural development and its laws, invoked later by the "Neogrammarians" and other nineteenth-century linguists, for instance August Schleicher (1821-1868), who came up with a theory representing languages as perfect natural organisms.[42] Yet at the same time, similar to Saussurean linguistics, language is defined as an autonomous and self-structuring system. Schlegel puts an emphasis on inflexion (specifically on declension and conjugation)[43] which is the evidence of the internal principle of organic form[44] manifesting itself in the clearest and simplest way in Sanskrit. This sacred literary language is chosen by Schlegel as a demonstration of "the structural law" ("das Gesetz der Structur") in its most ancient and creatively, inventively productive ("kunstreicher") form,[45] that is, not as a schematic matrix but,

---

[42] See, e.g., August Schleicher, *Compendium der vergleichenden Grammatik der indogermanischen Sprachen.Kurzer Abriss der indogermanischen Ursprache, des Altindischen, Altiranischen, Altgriechischen, Altitalischen, Altkeltischen, Altslawischen, Litauischen und Altdeutschen*, 2 vols. (Weimar: H. Böhlau, 1861/62). See also Mathesius's criticism of Schleicher's organic theory of language in "On the Potentiality of the Phenomena of Language" (O potenciálnosti jevů jazykových, 1911), trans. Josef Vachek, *Praguiana* 36: "The influence of natural history and exact sciences, most drastically manifested by Schleicher's conception of language as a biological organism, has led, in the Neogrammarian school, to an aprioristic belief in the absolute regularity of sound-laws and thus acted in the same direction." This criticism completely misses the links of Schleicher's theory with the earlier organicism of Romantic philologists and philosophers.

[43] Cf. Schlegel 35: "Das Wesentliche ist die Gleichheit des Prinzips, alle Verhältnisse und Nebenbestimmungen der Bedeutung nicht durch angehängte Partikeln oder Hülfsverba, sondern durch Flexion, d.h. durch innre Modification der Wurzel zu erkennen zu geben."

[44] Schlegel 41-42 uses the Kantian and Romantic dichotomy of the organic and the mechanic principles of structure: "[...] und man muß zugeben, dass die Structur der Sprache durchaus *organisch* gebildet, durch Flexionen oder inner Veränderungen und Umbiegungen des Wurzellauts in aller seinen Bedeutungen ramificirt, nicht *bloß mechanisch* durch angehängte Worte und Partikeln zusammengesetzt sei, wo den die Wurzel eigentlich unverändert und unfruchtbar bleibt." Emphasis added.

[45] Cf. Schlegel 38: "Hauptsächlich aber besteht der Unterschied doch darin, dass die indische Grammatik in derselben Art, wie die griechische und römische, noch regelmäßiger, demselben Gesetz der Structur, wenn ich so sagen darf, noch treuer und eben dadurch zugleich einfacher und kunstreicher ist als diese."

as a functional relationship.[46] This "structural law" establishes the intrinsic value of language in several traditional as well as innovative ways: as the "infallible sign"[47] of its antiquity, as the productive system which develops by means of "internal changes"[48] and does not need any external support[49] and finally as the outcome of the "scientific, that is, thoroughly historical"[50] (one might say 'consistently structural and functional'), approach to language. As a consequence, the value of language, consisting no longer in its referentiality and social function but in its intrinsic productivity, is confirmed by the "scientific" method of its study. This approach reduces philology to the application of the structural model of language which eliminates any use of rhetoric. As Paul de Man wrote of literary theory, rhetoric becomes "a wild card in the game of serious theoretical disciplines."[51]

Viewed in the manifold context of Classical rhetoric, Saussurean semiology, humanistic philology, Romantic organicism and nineteenth-century notions of language laws, Vilém Mathesius's fundamental study

---

[46] Mathesius, "Functional Linguistics" 123: "the new linguistics [...] proceeds from function to form." Although Schlegel's treatise deals with archaic or 'classical' languages and therefore it cannot be concerned "with the standpoint of the speaker or writer," it does not merely "inquire" about the "meaning" of "ready-made language structures," but "starts from the needs of expression." These "needs" are not individual but *cultural* and are identified also by Mathesius: "a language that would meet the highest demands of cultural life" must also fulfil the requirements of "unimpaired stability," based on "the consensus of good authors." (137-38) Even Mathesius ultimately invokes traditional philological criteria.

[47] "das untrügliches Kennzeichen." Schlegel 41.

[48] "inner[e] Veränderungen." Schlegel 41.

[49] This "support" is necessary for the languages which use "hieroglyphic" script, "painting or picturing" its characters "according to outer natural objects." Schlegel 41-42: "keine hieroglyphische [Schrift] nach äußern Naturgegen-standen malende oder bildernde."

[50] Cf. Schlegel 41: "wenn man die Sprache und ihre Entstehung wissenschaftlich d.h. durchaus historisch betrachten will." In his book, Schlegel uses "historisch" to describe the dynamics of language structure and not primarily to refer to historical development and its specific events. For a similar use of "history" see Jacques Derrida, "Structure, Sign and Play in the Discourse of Human Sciences," *Writing and Difference*, trans. Alan Bass (Chicago and London: University of Chicago Press, 1978) 273-97.

[51] Paul de Man, "The Resistance to Theory," *Yale French Studies* 18 (1979): 8.

"On the Potentiality of the Phenomena of Language" ("O potenciálnosti jevů jazykových," 1911) invites reinterpretation focusing on the notions of value and the transformation of humanistic and "modern" philologies. The "static" (or "synchronistic")[52] method characteristic of Mathesius's approach is based on the concept of value, which is both similar to and different from that typical of the Saussurean semiology. Its similarity to de Saussure is evident mainly from the section dedicated to "semantic analysis." This section comments on Charles Bally's *Traité de stylistique française* (On the Stylistics of French, 1909) and outlines a dual approach to the "oscillation of meaning" as a "semantic potentiality of language." Here, the alternative points of departure are either "a given lexical unit," or "a given idea,"[53] and the value is either identified with a unit of a language system (a signifier in Saussurean terms), or with an idea expressed "by means of language"[54] (a signified). However, in contrast to the fixed and hierarchical relationship between the signifier and the signified determined (and separated) by the Saussurean notion of arbitrariness, Mathesius's approach efficiently combines the focus on the units of the language system with that on the semantic relations between "ideas" and their verbal "expressions," using the notions of "oscillation" and "potentiality." This, among others, transforms the very notion of value and its relation to truth. Whereas de Saussure puts an emphasis on the distinctive function of linguistic value ("the true nature of these units – what prevents them from being confused with others – consists in their being *values*"[55]), for Mathesius the key value of language as a system is the variability of meaning and a flexibility of expressive means, and, consequently, also the plurality and perspectivist nature of truth:

> If, then, we take as our starting point a given lexical unit, the semantic potentiality of language is manifested as actual oscillation of meaning. If, on the other hand, we take as our starting point a given idea and try to find its expression by means of language, the potentiality of language will be manifested as a plurality of expressions, i.e., a possibility of expressing one and the same idea in a variety of ways.[56]

---

52 Mathesius, "On the Potentiality" 3.
53 Mathesius, "On the Potentiality" 29-30.
54 Mathesius, "On the Potentiality" 30.
55 Riedlinger 504 (full quotation see above).
56 Mathesius, "On the Potentiality" 30.

Because of an emphasis on the communicative and expressive potentialities of language manifesting themselves in the activities of individual speakers, Mathesius's pluralism is opposed to Nietzschean relativism, which denies language's grasp of reality and confuses truth with the expression of "a sum of human relations which have been poetically and rhetorically intensified, transferred and embellished, and which, after a long usage, seem to a people to be fixed, canonical and binding."[57]

Although the "potentiality" of language phenomena manifests itself within the system of language, its major aspects, above all its inductive character, point away from Saussurean synchrony and bring linguistics closer to the above discussed rhetorical and philological approaches to the relationship of language, law and truth. As Mathesius puts it: "linguistics examines the speech of the individuals so as to determine the language materials used in the language community."[58] Moreover, Mathesius's concept of potentiality establishes links between linguistics and rhetoric based on the common rules of the use of language material: "specimens of actual speech possessing analogous character or analogous aims display some common features in different speakers of the language."[59] This does not mean that seemingly 'specific' approaches of rhetoric or stylistics have to be supplanted by the 'general' perspective of linguistics, but implies that the very potentiality of language may be viewed from different angles: the "oscillation" characteristic of the use of "language materials" by "individuals" is once seen from the perspective of the whole community and at another time in relation to "concrete literary works."[60] What matters most is the *possibility of the change of perspective*, that is, of the modification of the system based on its practical uses, and not the firm separation of linguistic and rhetorical viewpoints as evident from the Saussurean semiology. This flexibility is the most important prerequisite for the transformation of traditional philological approaches.

---

[57] Friedrich Nietzsche, "On Truth and Lies in Nonmoral Sense," *Philosophy and Truth: Selections from Nietzsche's Notebooks from the Early 1870's*, ed. and trans. Daniel Breazeale (Atlantic Highlands, NJ: Humanity Books, 1979) 83-84.
[58] Mathesius, "On the Potentiality" 30.
[59] Mathesius, "On the Potentiality" 32.
[60] Mathesius, "On the Potentiality" 31.

Despite Mathesius's emphasis on "static" ("synchronistic") aspects of linguistic analysis, his linking of "potentiality" with "oscillation" is vital for the understanding of the dynamic nature of language and its temporality, characteristic also of other cultural phenomena. Instead of the linear growth typical of the schemes of the *Stammbaumtheorie* and connected with the cyclic time of organic forms, Mathesius's system develops by internal dynamism described as the "oscillation of speech among individuals inside the communities of language."[61] This oscillation (used, later, in a different framework, as a paradigm by New Historicism[62]) generates an inexhaustible number of potentialities whose materializations can either contribute to the system's stability by generating the "norm"[63] or, more significantly, provide means for the expression of an active individual attitude to reality. From this perspective, the expressive function of language, or the "language instinct,"[64] fully realized in major literary works, is more important than the communicative function which dominates the social uses of language.

---

[61] Mathesius, "On the Potentiality" 3.

[62] See, e.g., Stephen Greenblatt, "Towards a Poetics of Culture," *The New Historicism*, ed. H. Aram Veeser (London and New York: Routledge, 1989) 8: "effective oscillation between the establishment of distinct discursive domains and the collapse of those domains into one another."

[63] In Mathesius's approach, the problem of "norm" is indicated by the frequent use of the term "limits" which has a decisive meaning for his understanding of "potentiality" as an oscillation within certain boundaries: "It is said here that for each element of speech there exist the limits within which it can be identified. Such limits differ not only in different languages but even in one and the same language for its different elements." The norm can then be understood as a *correlation of different kinds of limits*: "The sound, again, is indefinite physiologically, i.e., its articulation can oscillate in certain limits; but the very large oscillation of articulation is said to be reflected in a relatively small oscillation of the sound." Mathesius, "On the Potentiality" 39, 37. This relational understanding of "norm" surpasses its later definitions, e.g., in the works of Jan Mukařovský (1891-1975) and Felix Vodička (1909-1974).

[64] Mathesius, "Functional Linguistics" 138. Cf. also Vilém Mathesius, "O jazykové správnosti. Několik časových poznámek" (On the Correctness of Language: Several Timely Remarks, 1911-12), *Jazyk, kultura a slovesnost* (Language, Culture and Literature), ed. Josef Vachek (Prague: Odeon, 1982) 62: "The expressive efficiency of language is the very root of its validity [...]." My translation.

This approach (influenced, among others, by Benedetto Croce's aesthetics[65]) is, on the one hand, desirable, since it allows the transcendence of the narrowly functionalist view of language focused on communication, but, on the other hand, potentially dangerous, as it may lead toward the transgression of generally valid language norms and "styles." Mathesius attempts to control this tension by at least two strategies.

First, he avoids the question of *literariness* (discussed by the Russian Formalists and Jakobson) and concentrates on the linguistic interpretation of literary style, subordinating rhetorical to linguistic phenomena (e.g., discussing symbols as specific functions of the process of naming).[66] Despite its primarily regulative function, this approach is also productive, since it provides a different perspective on rhetorical figures as results of the interaction of phenomena at different language levels (phonological, morphological, syntactic, thematic) and their different expressive functions.

The second strategy regulating Mathesius's approach is the application of the hypothesis of the "language community" which also dominates the theories of de Saussure and the representatives of Prague Structuralism. Based on the obsolete Romantic notion of organic community infused by contemporary biological views of the nation ("national biology"[67]), this concept not only represents a totalizing, ideological aspect of Mathesius's approach that restores his modern functionalism to nineteenth-century teleological notions, but also an actual restriction of the development of literary theoretical aspects in his later work. In Mathesius's opinion, the "foremost task" of literature is to contribute to the growth of the nation's organic structure.[68]

---

65 Mathesius, "On the Potentiality" 39.
66 Vilém Mathesius, "Řeč a sloh" (Speech and Style, 1942), *Jazyk, kultura a slovesnost* 100-101. Mathesius tries to cope even with a catachretic metaphor of the Czech Modernist poet Jiří Wolker (1900-1924): "brandish the sword of his heart."
67 Vilém Mathesius, "O úkolech a výzbroji literární kritiky" (On the Tasks and Weaponry of Literary Criticism, 1942-43), *Jazyk, kultura a slovesnost* 212. My translation.
68 Mathesius, "O úkolech a výzbroji literární kritiky" 212-13: "A healthy nation is an organic whole, whose cultural and social structure rises uninterruptedly

As a result, one of the major potentialities of Mathesius's revolutionary functionalism, namely the transformation of philology into a modern literary and cultural theory, has not been realized. This is evident from the comparison of his approach with that of his younger contemporary, Mikhail Bakhtin (1895-1975). Building on the rich legacy of Classical, humanistic and modern philology, as well as on the heritage of Kantian philosophy, Romantic organicism, modern biology and Einsteinean physics, Bakhtin formulated a stimulating theory of literary genres, based on the interdisciplinary notion of the "chronotope."[69] Whereas this theory deals mainly with representational aspects of language structures, it is complemented by the theory of "heteroglossia" or the stylistic polyphony of literary language (dealing with "the problem of internal differentiation and stratification of language"[70]) which bears some resemblance to Mathesius's functionalism, combining the communicative and expressive perspectives on language: "The novel senses itself on the border between the completed, dominant literary language and the extraliterary languages. [...] all these processes of shift and renewal of the national language that are reflected *by* the novel do not bear an abstract linguistic character in the novel, they are inseparable from [...] processes of the renewal of society."[71] Bakhtin's work thus may be said to display, and partially also to fulfil, the unrealized potentialities of Mathesius's approach.

from broad foundations to a narrower summit, without significant gaps between its individual levels. Only in this way a just social rise of gifted individuals and an incessant organic renewal of powers are safeguarded. To contribute to such a structure of the national body is the foremost task of literature [...]." My translation.

[69] Mikhail M. Bakhtin, "Forms of Time and the Chronotope in the Novel," *Dialogic Imagination*, ed. Caryl Emerson (Austin: University of Texas Press, 1981) 84-258.

[70] Mikhail Bakhtin, "From the Prehistory of Novelistic Discourse," *Dialogic Imagination* 67.

[71] Bakhtin, "From the Prehistory of Novelistic Discourse" 68.

VILÉM MATHESIUS
AS LITERARY HISTORIAN

Helena Znojemská

The initiatory role of Vilém Mathesius in the foundation of the Prague Linguistic Circle and the linguistic aspect of Prague Structuralism are well recognized and documented. Linguistic problems were to dominate his scholarly output in later years when his eyesight was failing. Moreover, most of his students who pursued scholarly careers, too, focused on language; therefore it is no wonder that it was this part of his work that received the greatest share of attention. Yet Mathesius was active and productive in other spheres as well: the first professor of English Language and Literature at Charles University, he published a number of articles on literary subjects besides the monumental *History of English Literature*, truncated as it was. In a more popularizing vein he continued to comment on various aspects of Czech cultural life. All this is well known but insufficiently mapped.

The interaction of his linguistic and literary thinking has received only a most general commentary[1] and no attempt has been made to trace in any detail the development of his views on literary history and criticism, nor their potential affinities with the theories of other members of the Prague school. His 'activist' texts then remain isolated from either aspect of his more scholarly production. The present article aims to redress these omissions. It will trace two basic lines of

---

[1] Cf. Libuše Dušková, Jan Čermák, "Dílo" (The Work), Vilém Mathesius, *Paměti a jiné rukopisy* (Memoirs and Other Manuscripts) (Prague: Karolinum, 2009) 24-30.

Mathesius's thinking which run across both the disciplinary and the 'generic' boundaries: the theoretical line, which starts with the objective of establishing "scientific" principles for linguistics and literary history and continues with their application (and which anticipates some of the concepts systematically explored by later Prague School theory), and the line of 'cultural activism' which is determined by emphasis on specific values and which tends to replace and subvert the perspective constituted by the theoretical line.

Reminiscing about his university studies and early academic career, Vilém Mathesius charts the impulses which informed the development of his scholarly interests and positions. Looking back from the distance of some thirty years he finds little inspiration in his official schooling. He presents his intellectual exploits as a lonely venture, guided largely by, as he admits, "haphazard" reading in areas which attracted his interest and by prompts arising from informal friendly and professional relationships and encounters.[2] While his brief assistantship to the visiting Norse linguist Olaf Broch merits a separate paragraph in Mathesius's memoirs as a model of a productive interaction between an established scholar and a younger colleague (a type of relationship which he missed in his professors),[3] he presents as perhaps the most formative influence his friendship with Jaroslav Peklo, a former schoolfellow and biologist. He felt attracted by what he perceived as the superior scientific character of his friend's work, an aspect which he appears to have acutely lacked in his own discipline as it was then pursued at the university. *Scientific analysis* of both language and literature repeatedly appears in Mathesius's memoirs as his early goal: this entails the formulation of a problem specific to the field, solid and explicitly stated theoretical foundations,

---

[2]   Vilém Mathesius, *Paměti* 212-16.

[3]   Mathesius mentions this cooperation as a source of valuable scholarly experience and insight into the problems in phonetics, which was to become one of his fields of interest in linguistics. Apparently, what he valued most was the opportunity to participate in research 'in the making' rather than being presented with the finalized result which, as he saw it, obscured the theoretical foundations and methodological problems of the discipline. Mathesius, *Paměti* 208, 211, 216.

and the application of precise and consistent methodology.[4] His ambitions direct him towards general linguistics and theory of literature.[5]

This scientific aspiration motivates the criticism of the positivist H.A. Taine and his interpretation of Shakespeare's work in Mathesius's 1906 doctoral thesis, his first major scholarly publication.[6] Mathesius here does not find fault with Taine's emphasis on causality, nor does he question the validity of integrating the literary work in a larger social and historical context.[7] His text, tellingly subtitled "Contributions towards the History of Attempts at a Scientific Approach to Literary History,"[8] directs its critical commentary at Taine's failure to correctly establish the "literary-historical facts" and to conduct an analysis of a literary work based on characteristics proper to it: a step which must precede its positioning in relation to possible external influences and determinants. In Mathesius's view, Taine simply failed to formulate the field-specific problem of literary history. Without expressly controverting the principles of positivism, Mathesius therefore challenges Taine's claims to have adopted a strictly scientific approach.[9] Whatever his real stance might

4   Mathesius, *Paměti* 209, 215, 233.
5   In literary analysis he identifies his focus with the systematic description developed by Mukařovský. While we miss even a hint of such acknowledgment or statement of affiliation from the other side, Mathesius himself seems to have seen his approach, and perhaps also some specific concepts, as anticipating the much more refined theory developed by Mukařovský. Mathesius, *Paměti* 233.
6   The first three chapters of the thesis were published in 1907 and 1908, while the fourth remained in manuscript.
7   "As any manner of scientific enquiry, literary history, too, must divide its goal in two: to establish the objectively valid facts and then to place them in a causal relationship with other, better known and delimited facts." Even though the statement is very general and therefore provides little guidance as to what those "other facts" are, the ensuing explanation at least makes it clear that they belong outside literary history proper. Vilém Mathesius, "Tainova kritika Shakespeara" (Taine's Shakespearean Criticism), *Jazyk, kultura a slovesnost* (Language, Culture and Literature), ed. Josef Vachek (Prague: Odeon 1982) 278; cf. also 269. All translations, unless otherwise stated, are mine.
8   "Příspěvky k dějinám pokusů o zvědečtění literární historie," See Mathesius, "Tainova kritika" 252.
9   *Pace* Jindřich Toman, who claims that Mathesius objects to the enquiry into causes and results in general. Cf. Jindřich Toman, *Příběh jednoho moderního projektu: Pražský lingvistický kroužek, 1926-1948*, trans. Vladimír Petkevič

have been at the time (and it tends to be presented as much more visionary in the memoirs[10]), the text is not formulated as a radical critique of established scientific paradigm, but rather as a refinement – an adjustment of focus which should ensure the validity of the analysis and its results.

Mathesius progressively focused on linguistic problems in his scholarly output. However, as his choice of topic for his doctoral dissertation clearly shows, he was initially concerned with the possibilities of systematic scientific description of both language and literature. It appears that the two projects were intimately linked (not in terms of pursuing the same approach in two separate disciplines, but in developing from a specific shared theoretical foundation) in that they formed two aspects of a single undertaking: the concept of expressivity.

While the communicative function defines language as a system of signs, it is the distinctive tendencies in the realization of the expressive function which constitute the unique character of a particular "national" language.[11] Within that scheme literature represents a sovereign domain of the expressive function. In this capacity it can provide guidance in issues of correct usage, defined precisely by the respect for, and conformity with, the individual character of the language. The idea of literature as an indicator of the functional capacity of a given language is introduced as early as 1912 in an article entitled "On Correctness in Language" in polemic with the purists,[12] but it reappears several times in Mathesius's later writings in similar configurations.

Literary work, as the site of a "struggle for expression" which grapples with obstacles absent in automated everyday speech, also provides a rare insight into the mechanisms active in the internal process which precedes any concrete utterance. Mathesius is thus able to break this

(Prague: Karolinum 2011) 99. Originally published as *The Magic of a Common Language: Jakobson, Mathesius, Trubetzkoy, and the Prague Linguistic Circle* (Cambridge, MA: MIT Press 1995).

10   Mathesius, *Paměti* 235.

11   "[...] if we compare several languages of a different structure. In a distinct manner each of them expresses something which the other disregards and which is therefore in fact not necessary for the clarity of communication." Vilém Mathesius, "O jazykové správnosti" (On Correctness in Language), *Jazyk, kultura a slovesnost* 61.

12   Mathesius, "O jazykové správnosti" 60-64.

process down into components which form the basis of his systematic functional description of language: a naming and a relational activity, constituting functional onomatology and syntax respectively.[13] Expression therefore appears to be the foundational concept of Mathesius's theory of language;[14] simultaneously, it gives literature (or verbal art) a privileged though still fundamentally ancillary role in linguistic research.

However, both the chronology of Mathesius's writings and the fact that literature, as documented above, is that sphere of language use which justifies the foregrounding of the expressive function in his early texts on linguistics, suggest that he first developed this notion as part of his proposed scientific approach to literary history. "Expressive potency" ("výrazová mohutnost") indeed plays a central role in the methodology of literary criticism which he elaborated partly in polemic with Taine's reading of Shakespeare and partly in dialogue with other existing descriptive models.[15] Attempting to define the deficiencies of Taine's method, Mathesius states as the first objective of literary history the establishing of "literary-historical facts," i.e., identifying those features of a literary work of art which form the basis of its aesthetic appeal. This he sees as determined by two decisive criteria: the integration of individual elements into a unified whole and the above-mentioned expressive potency.[16]

The first criterion poses few problems: Mathesius here openly embraces the objective orientation (in terms of M.H. Abrams's typology of critical theories[17]) as the groundwork of literary criticism, assigning it priority before any subsequent interrogation into the relations of the literary work to external factors. As implied by Toman, this shift parallels

---

13 Vilém Mathesius, "Functional Linguistics," Josef Vachek (ed. and trans.), *Praguiana: Some Basic and Less Known Aspects of the Prague Linguistic School: An Anthology of Prague School Papers*, 1st ed. (Prague: Academia 1983) 131-32.
14 This seems especially true of Mathesius's early linguistic thought; in the 1930s and 1940s he tends to assign greater importance to the communicative function, though the expressive potential retains pride of place as argument in texts concerned with the cultivation of standard Czech.
15 Mathesius, "Tainova kritika" 278-84.
16 Mathesius, "Tainova kritika" 283.
17 M.H. Abrams, *The Mirror and the Lamp: Romantic Theory and the Critical Tradition* (New York: Oxford University Press 1971) 6-29.

Mathesius's emphasis on the synchronic approach in linguistics;[18] it has to be noted, however, that he did not entirely condemn the validity of diachronic study but relegated it to a secondary position – similar to his restating of priorities in the study of literature.[19] Again, there is a remarkable degree of consistency in the foundations of Mathesius's linguistic and his literary studies. Of equal importance is the procedure of evaluating individual aspects of a literary work of art in terms of their relation to the whole, which finds its expression in the emphasis on an adequate analysis of its construction or "architectonics."[20]

Unfortunately, this early text is Mathesius's only discourse on method in literary criticism and it would be extremely tenuous to posit any direct line of influence from its rather tentatively formulated propositions to later Structuralist theories of literature developed by Mukařovský or Wellek. However, Mathesius's arguments may be seen to anticipate some of Mukařovský's basic tenets, admittedly in a rather diffuse form: thus the subordination of individual elements of the literary work to their interaction in a unified whole suggests the concept of structure, though as yet without the stressing of its dynamic nature and the interplay and balancing of discordant as well as harmonizing tendencies. Such a one-sided understanding of structure may still be seen in Wellek's 1933 reading of *The Pearl*, which represents a reassessment of the relationship of the personal and allegorical levels in the poem in defence of its artistic unity.[21]

---

18 Toman, *Příběh jednoho moderního projektu* 98-106.
19 Toman (*Příběh jednoho moderního projektu*, 106) quotes Mathesius's 1945 letter to Bohuslav Havránek where Mathesius presents his lifelong forceful advocacy of the synchronic method as a strategy for restoring balance to linguistic study, previously dominated entirely by diachrony. Even earlier, however, Mathesius occasionally refers to the necessity of investigating also the state of language in other historical periods, especially with regard to the refining of linguistic characterology; cf. Mathesius, "O jazykové správnosti" 63.
20 The latter term is frequently used especially in Vilém Mathesius, *Dějiny literatury anglické v hlavních jejích proudech a představitelích. Část první: doba anglosaská* (The History of English Literature in Its Chief Tendencies and Representatives. Part I: The Anglo-Saxon Period) (Prague: self-published, 1910) 23 *passim*. Henceforth abbreviated as *Dějiny I*.
21 René Wellek, "*The Pearl*. An Interpretation of the Middle-English Poem," *Příspěvky k dějinám řeči a literatury anglické od členů anglického semináře Karlovy university v Praze / Studies in English by Members of the English*

The objective orientation is in itself a fundamental principle in Mukařovský's literary theory, since the aesthetic function directs attention at the reality which constitutes the aesthetic sign – i.e., the literary work.[22]

The criterion of "expressive potency" represents a much more problematic, complex concept which explicitly combines a number of apparently rather disparate perspectives. The first connects expressivity with the ability to arouse "human interest": a term which Mathesius borrows from M.H. Liddell and which seems to introduce an unexpected extra-literary (or extra-aesthetic) element to Mathesius's theory. The second concerns purely formal aspects, chiefly focusing on poetic qualities of language such as rhythm and melody.[23] A further complication arises from the identification of expressivity with evocative power which calls up specific ideas and emotions in the recipient.[24] What can be made of this configuration? Mathesius's explanation, couched as it is in a series of specifying remarks interspersed through the text, is hopelessly confusing – and perhaps confused.

What seems to be clear is that expressive potency, while posited as a manifestation of the author's artistic capacity, is nowhere defined in terms of Abrams's expressive theory: it has nothing to do with the projection of the author's ideas and emotions. This becomes the more surprising in comparison with Mathesius's later characterization of the expressive function in language as manifest in an "utterance for the sake of expression itself without any regard for the listener."[25] On the contrary, the orientation on the recipient represents an important coordinate of the concept of expressive potency in his literary theory: apart from evoking a specific emotional and intellectual response, it possesses a more

Seminar of the Charles University, Prague, Vol. 4 (Prague: Faculty of Arts, Charles University, 1933) 5-28.

22 Cf. Jan Mukařovský, "Význam estetiky" (The Significance of Aesthetics), *Studie I* (Essays I), eds. Miroslav Červenka and Milan Jankovič, 2nd ed. (Brno: Host, 2007) 65.

23 Mathesius, "Tainova kritika" 284.

24 Mathesius, "Tainova kritika" 283.

25 "[...] vyjadřování pro výraz sám beze všeho ohledu na posluchače," Mathesius, "Functional Linguistics" 37. A late text associates the realization of expressive function with the expression of the *inner state* of the speaker without regard to, or even in defiance of a potential listener. Vilém Mathesius, "Řeč a sloh" (Speech and Style), *Jazyk, kultura a slovesnost* 93.

general potential to activate the "creative participation of the [recipient's] imagination."[26] There is no doubt that such a conception represents a deliberate reaction to Taine's foregrounding of the spontaneous character of Shakespeare's genius: the artist's skill consists precisely in maintaining communication with the recipient through the purposeful and controlled composition of his work.

It might appear that the objective of arousing "human interest" is merely a restatement of this pragmatic aspect of Mathesius's theory. A closer look at the qualities which he associates with this category, namely the vitality, concreteness and complexity featured in the plot, characters, etc., as well as in the language,[27] suggests instead an inclusion of a mimetic and an objective approach. The latter is of course the only relevant framework for the formal analysis of the language of the literary work. The criterion of expressive potency thus represents a conglomerate of qualities and functions seen as responsible for the aesthetic appeal of a literary work of art.

Such an assessment would apparently question Mathesius's success in his foremost ambition, the establishment of the principles of scientific analysis of literature – more specifically, an elaboration of consistent methodology. However, it would be rash to see this as simply a failure of his critical thinking; rather, Mathesius here grapples with the complexity of the matter, attempting a systematic description while trying to avoid a one-sided, reductive approach: two aims resulting in an uneasy and not entirely convincing compromise. Despite the rather casual manner in which Mathesius interconnects all the above-mentioned aspects in a single concept, it would seem that in so doing he at least dimly sensed the relevance of aspects which Mukařovský was later to integrate in a methodical mapping of the relationship between the author and the recipient and the interplay of the aesthetic and extra-aesthetic values in a work of art.

Mukařovský postulated an essential identity between the position of the author and that of the recipient in relation to the work of art in its capacity of a semiotic fact, a sign: to ensure its communicative function, the author must gauge its appeal to the recipient and thus to assume

---

[26] "[Stálé] ponoukání spolutvořící fantazie divákovy, posluchačovy nebo čtenářovy." Mathesius, "Tainova kritika" 289.

[27] Mathesius, "Tainova kritika" 284, 289.

his/her stance.[28] By adopting the semiological perspective in his theory of literature and by systematizing his terminology, Mukařovský validated Mathesius's intuitive and seemingly paradoxical link between the artist's expressive potency and the impact on the recipient. The notion of "human interest" and the values associated with it similarly appear to bear a certain affinity with Mukařovský's explanation of the operation of the work of art as a sign: it relates to the experience of the recipient as a complex of values forming a certain attitude to reality. This is activated by the semantic energy borne by both the thematic and formal aspects of the work which, due precisely to the relation to the recipient's attitude to reality, assume extra-aesthetic values.[29] Again, Mathesius's colourful but rather vaguely defined terms and propositions find here a counterpart in a complex and concise theory. While this does not make Mathesius a precursor of Structuralist literary theory (after all, the above-listed congruences represent only points of minor convergence between Mukařovský's functional approach and Mathesius's essentially much more traditional perspective), it might explain his conviction that in literary criticism – just as in linguistics – he was able to intuit the path later pursued by his younger colleagues in the Prague Linguistic Circle, which he saw as his very own project.[30]

As the foregoing survey makes clear, Mathesius did elaborate a detailed procedure for *literary criticism* in his polemic with Taine. However, with regard to the fact that he proposed to establish the principles of scientific *literary history*, it is rather surprising that he hardly ever transcends the horizon of an individual work of art to define any concept of the historical development in literature. At most, applying the criteria of the gradually

---

[28] Jan Mukařovský, "Osobnost v umění" (Personality in Art), *Studie I* 286-87. It is interesting to note that this article opens with a polemic with alternative models of the relation between the work of art and artistic individuality, among them Taine's determinist approach.

[29] Jan Mukařovský, "Estetická funkce, norma a hodnota jako sociální fakty" (*Aesthetic Function, Norm and Value as Social Facts*), *Studie I* 133-48.

[30] He refers to his having formed "[his] own group of young researchers with scholarly goals similar to [his]." It is unlikely that the statement could refer to any separate group in English Studies; in any case, many of Mathesius's English Studies disciples were also members of the Circle (Trnka, Vachek, Wellek). Mathesius, *Paměti* 235, 237.

evolving formal qualities of language (the expressive potency aspect) and the dexterity and complexity of construction, he observes a development within a single *oeuvre*. Otherwise Mathesius refers vaguely to the tracing of causal links between literary-historical and "other" (historical? social? cultural?) facts as the goal of literary history. He also notes the existence of multiple and varied relations between literature and "other phenomena of life," which may represent an obstacle in isolating valid criteria of literary value.[31] Such extremely non-committal statements are only consonant with the undeclared yet apparent aim of his text – not to completely redefine the discipline but to partially refocus it towards a more extensive attention to the literary work of art in itself.

Whether his thoughts on the subject of literary *history* (rather than literary criticism) matured only gradually or whether they were strategically withheld in his first confrontation with the matter, Mathesius had to formulate his position when he produced the first volume of his history of English literature, surveying the literary production of the Anglo-Saxon period.[32] Unlike the second volume devoted to Middle English literature, the book begins with an introduction defending Mathesius's decision to start his historical overview with the pre-Conquest period, often dismissed, as he argues, on the basis of an ethnic perspective of literature: since a unified English nation emerged from the mixing of various ethnic strands only much later, the texts produced by a people that represents merely one component in the final mixture cannot properly be counted as part of the national literature.[33] Such a conception, he claims, is built on premises external to literary history proper.[34] Instead he posits the criterion of linguistic continuity as the fundamental argument for treating Anglo-Saxon literary monuments as an integral element in the development of English literature. It, however, remains just that; the proposed continuity of literary development has to be substantiated by a detailed and sensitive analysis of individual texts ("literary facts"), supported by an

---

31 Mathesius, "Tainova kritika" 278.
32 Mathesius, *Dějiny I*.
33 Mathesius, *Dějiny I* 1.
34 We may sense here an implicit allusion to Tainean approach to literature as primarily a reflection of national character.

enquiry into the social and cultural context of the period.[35] This statement, as well as the whole project carried out in the first volume, is clearly programmatic: Mathesius here outlines his concept of literary history, specifically as regards the idea of development in literature and its relation to external factors. Literature is to be studied as a phenomenon which evolves internally though not in isolation from the historical (social, cultural) situation. The latter might be said to set the horizons and to supply stimuli for internal reconfigurations in literature, but it does not directly predicate the literary development on any causal principle. While a certain resonance does therefore exist between the two sets of phenomena, the mapping of the historical context remains ancillary in the study of literature.

To a large extent, then, the first volume of Mathesius's history builds on the foundations laid in his criticism of Taine: the procedure used here represents an application of the principles of literary analysis which he articulated in the earlier text, and the introduction supplies the then missing formulation of method in literary history that the book adopts. Central position in the overall argument is given to a series of detailed descriptions of specific texts. The plot or the situation is briefly summarized and the text then characterized in terms of broadly conceived formal aspects, including generic features (e.g., epic / epic song), narrative strategies (narrative / monologue / dialogue; characterization), dominant compositional techniques (variation, contrast), stylistic traits, diction and verse form. Emphasis is placed especially on the integration of these particular facets into a unified, "architectonically pointed" whole.[36] The next level of analysis proceeds to note affinities and correspondences observable in such formal aspects first among individual texts and then groups of texts (e.g., epic and lyric), defining initially genres and subsequently tendencies generally characteristic of the literature at a given stage. In this way, a gradually evolving sequence

---

[35] Mathesius, *Dějiny I* 2.

[36] Mathesius, *Dějiny I* 23 *passim*. The criterion of "expressive potency," unlike that of the unity of structure, is nowhere mentioned explicitly. It is, however, tacitly employed in the detailed commentary on the style and language of individual works. It may be noted that in practical application, Mathesius significantly simplified the concept, focusing exclusively on its formal aspect.

is traced; specific features of the development are explained internally, as a cultivation or transformation of traits present in a rudimentary form in a more archaic phase, or as a response to an external stimulus.

So, for example, the predominance of "static" elements in the composition of *Beowulf* is seen as a progressive step in the development from an epic song (reconstructed as a type on the basis of comparison with texts from other Germanic literatures) towards an ideal type of epic; this is an innovation insofar as it transfers the principle from one aspect of the structure to another. Where it is retained in its original capacity of an attribute of diction or characterization, it represents a regressive residue from the more 'primitive' genre. At the same time, Mathesius observes, the evolution towards epic is unparalleled in related Germanic literatures and therefore unlikely to proceed entirely from internal resources. The external stimulus in this case can be seen in the general acceleration of the cultural development, prompted by the sheltered insular environment saturated by remnants of Latin culture and facilitated by better material conditions provided by advanced agricultural technology.[37] Thus a complex historical situation is presented as an impulse which activates the existing potential for evolution in the literature of the period. The context of the general historical, social and cultural situation is regularly mapped in a separate chapter preceding the systematic description of a proposed phase of literary development. The relevant facts are subsequently highlighted in the analysis of individual texts and a brief reference to major historical events also concludes most of the larger sections. The recurrent pattern appears to reflect the relative weight ascribed to the respective phenomena: while history sets the frame, literature is the core.

Mathesius does not shun value judgments in his analysis; it is symptomatic that artistic deficiency, especially as regards achieving a unity of structure, is regularly detected in works that stand, in his view, at the nexus of two epochs, at a point where the existing literary tradition responds to an external impulse, where, as he puts it, it is confronted with new tasks as is the case with the religious epic or the first Chronicle

---

[37] Mathesius, *Dějiny I* 24-39. The range of disciplines and spheres of activity that Mathesius integrates into a complex portrayal of the period is truly stunning and quite uncommon for the time.

poems. Such an evaluation stems from the essentially teleological perspective of the volume. The proposed continuity of development from "Anglo-Saxon" to "English" literature leads him to promote specific tendencies which he sees emerging in such situations: from epic to romance or chronicle. As in the case of *Beowulf,* Mathesius appears to operate with an ideal generic type which – although not explicitly and fully defined – serves as a basis for the evaluation of the "transitional" texts. A chronicle, even a metrical one, should make its form and diction subservient to the lucid presentation of historical narrative and not allow itself to be too concerned with display of the traditional diction of the epic and steeped in the poetic past. It is this which makes *The Battle of Brunanburh* a less valuable work than the later Chronicle poems – where the strict alliterative verse form and the heavy variation disintegrate, replaced by simple statements rendered in lines of increasingly uniform rhythm. An emergent genre and an emergent verse form thus develop in parallel.[38]

The principle of correlating the impact of non-literary factors with an internal potential for development in the literature itself finally informs also Mathesius's evaluation of individual authors. Here the external input includes, apart from the historical context, also the author's personality which influences the manner in which s/he assumes a position prepared by the evolving literary tradition. Thus the agency of Alfred of Wessex was largely responsible for the establishment of Old English literary prose, his personal concerns laying the foundations for the cultivation of specific genres and subjects by subsequent writers; yet his intervention was only made possible by the existence of a rudimentary prosaic tradition in the South of England.[39] On the contrary, the stage which literary prose had reached by the second half of the tenth century produced an author whose importance lies merely in stylistic refinement and dexterity in the structuring of narrative – not an Alfred but an Ælfric.[40]

What Mathesius postulated as a "scientific" approach to literary history is thus embodied in his first independent treatment of the subject.

[38] Mathesius, *Dějiny I* 134-38.
[39] Mathesius, *Dějiny I* 121-29.
[40] Mathesius, *Dějiny I* 148-51.

The theoretical assumptions are reflected both in the analytical procedure and the overall structure of the book. As if in defiance of a number of remarks that he makes concerning the cataclysmic effects of specific historical events (e.g., the first and the second series of Viking raids[41]) on the continuity of development in literature, the general evolutionary tendencies which Mathesius traces within the entire Anglo-Saxon era remain remarkably stable. This again confirms that he operated on the assumption – perhaps intuited rather than fully conceptualized – that literature evolves primarily through its own internal dynamics, an assumption that resonated with his aim of integrating the Anglo-Saxon period firmly in the history of English literature.

Searching for a term that would characterize the status which Mathesius ascribed to the development of literature in relation to external factors such as the social situation or the historical or cultural context, one might find a suitable match in the concept of *immanence* which Mukařovský explained in a foreword to his 1936 text, *Estetická funkce, norma a hodnota jako sociální fakty*.[42] Replacing the Formalist notion of the autonomy of art, it allows for correlation between the respective phenomena which cannot be reduced to mechanistic causality.[43] Another tentative point of contact with later Structuralist theory may be seen in Mathesius's representation of the role of individual authors. In the identification of authorial "types" (initiatory, elaborative) that emerge at specific points in the evolving sequence he seems to anticipate Mukařovský's views of individual agency in relation to literary tradition. For Mukařovský, the existing state of literature permits at any moment multiple lines of subsequent development; it generates potential "positions" which an individual can assume, while the way this potential is realized depends in turn on the personality of that individual.[44]

[41] Cf. Mathesius, *Dějiny I* 112, 152.
[42] Mukařovský, "Estetická funkce" (The Aesthetic Function), *Studie I* 81-82.
[43] Cf. also Jan Mukařovský, "Strukturalismus v estetice a ve vědě o literatuře" (*Structuralism in Aesthetics and Literary Criticism*), *Studie I* 16.
[44] Jan Mukařovský, "Básník a dílo" (*The Poet and the Work*), *Studie I* 293-97. Cf. also "Problémy individua v umění" (The Individual in Art: Some Issues) or "Strukturalismus v estetice" (Structuralism in Aesthetics), *Studie I* 332 and 16 respectively. The latter text, dating to 1940-41, is probably the first to treat this issue. Here the emphasis is decidedly on the internal determination of

Unlike the partial and relatively marginal congruences in their approach to the literary work of art, the above-mentioned positions apparently shared (at least to some extent) by both scholars represent a core element in their respective concepts of literary history. As in the case of the matter of literary analysis, Mathesius only states what he perceives as the fundamental principles of literary history and leaves the details unexplained, while Mukařovský takes care to interweave all aspects of his theory and relate them to the core postulates. Moreover, Mathesius advances his views as part of a historical survey of a specific literary tradition, whereas Mukařovský's aim in the relevant texts is predominantly theoretical. As a result, their respective positions appear much more distant than they are in reality. Mukařovský himself remained silent on the matter of Mathesius's texts on literature, acknowledging only the inspiration which functional linguistics provided for establishing a Structuralist model of literary/aesthetic theory.[45] Nevertheless, Toman notes that Dmytro Chyzhevsky, who cooperated with the Prague Linguistic Circle, regarded Mathesius as a precursor of literary Formalism,[46] a fact that would support both Mathesius's own remarks on the affinities of his early views with Structuralist theory of literature and the validity of the correspondences, however limited, traced in the present article.

All the same, it is little wonder that Mukařovský does not appear to perceive Mathesius's works on literary history and criticism as in any way relevant to his own project. While Taine was selected as a suitable target by both, by the time Mukařovský was developing his Structuralist theory Mathesius's polemic must have appeared too compromising and insufficiently rigorous to appeal to him, if indeed he was aware of it at all. The *History of English Literature* was a specialized volume which might prove formative for a scholar in English Studies but would almost inevitably be overlooked by a student of Czech and Romance Studies. By the time the two scholars met in the Prague Linguistic Circle,

potential "author-types," while the slightly later texts assume a more balanced perspective which acknowledges the element of fortuitousness introduced by the agency of a specific individual.

45 Jan Mukařovský, "O strukturalismu" (On Structuralism), *Studie I* 26.
46 Toman, *Příběh jednoho moderního projektu* 99.

Mathesius's thinking about literature, to judge from his publications, has undergone a profound transformation.[47]

What was going to stand at the centre of attention in this alternative line of Mathesius's thought is suggested in the last sentence of the first volume of the *History*, a sentence which apparently negates all that he had previously argued:

> Centuries had passed before the darkening haze lifted and an indigenous literature worthy of the name appeared again: it was, however, a literature saturated by a new spirit, written in a new language and savoured by a new nation.[48]

While it seems singularly inapposite as a final word to the first volume, it provides a perfect transition to the second one, symptomatically subtitled "Zápas o národnost" – "The Struggle for Nationhood."[49] The title proves deliberately ambiguous: the book traces the development of

[47] It is true that Mathesius's specialized studies in Czech literature represent detailed formal analyses of specific texts, often relying on statistical methods, and that it might therefore be argued that he maintained a consistent approach throughout his career. However, the articles in question date to the 1940s; it is thus likely that he returned to his early methods precisely on the impulse provided by Mukařovský's literary theory in general and his analysis of the poetic language and Czech verse forms in particular. This is also the period in which Mathesius was writing his memoirs, so his conviction that he worked on essentially the same principles as his younger colleagues in the Circle could have been motivated more by his critical practice at the time than by a detached perspective of the earlier years. Cf. Vilém Mathesius, "Větné základy epického slohu v *Zeyerově Kronice o sv. Brandanu*" (Sentential Foundations of the Epic Style in Zeyer's *Chronicle of St Brandan*), *Jazyk, kultura a slovesnost* 215-24; "Poznámky o překládání cizího blankversu a o českém verši jambickém vůbec" (Notes on Translating Foreign Blankverse and on Czech Iambic Verse in General), *Jazyk, kultura a slovesnost* 227-41.

[48] "Staletí uplynula, než mračný ten závoj se roztrhl a objevila se zase domácí literatura hodná toho jména: byla to však literatura proniklá už novým duchem, psaná novým jazykem a chutnaná novým národem." Mathesius, *Dějiny I* 167.

[49] Vilém Mathesius, *Dějiny literatury anglické v hlavních jejích proudech a představitelích. Část druhá: zápas o národnost* (The History of English Literature in Its Chief Tendencies and Representatives. Part II: The Struggle for Nationhood) (Prague: self-published 1915). Henceforth abbreviated as *Dějiny II*.

English literature in the double sense of the gradual reinstatement of English as a literary language after a period dominated by Latin and French and of the emergence of literature which displays qualities seen as specifically "English," consonant with what Mathesius sees as the English "national character."

The tendency of Mathesius's thinking to assign special position to the national aspect was not limited to this volume. Mathesius's privileging of the expressive function of language in his earliest article concerned with the problems of correct language usage is directly connected to the project of linguistic characterology which he saw as one of the goals of the "new" linguistics. The otherwise consistent emphasis on the synchronic study of language was partially suppressed there, as in this case it might tend to an indiscriminate inclusion of features which typically appear in the language of a specific period but which are not "deeply rooted in the distinctive psychical characteristics" of the language community. Diachronic study was necessary to chart the development of the "general psychical disposition" of the given nation which determined the evolving but still consistent character of the language.[50]

At the close of his career, in a 1942 article on the objectives and tools of literary criticism, Mathesius reiterated his early statements regarding the central role of formal analysis (explicitly naming, again, the structuring of the work and the expressive power as its focal points).This time, however, he added another criterion of evaluation – the function of the work in "national biology." It is true that he presented this aspect as especially vital for what could be seen as historically disadvantaged national communities – undoubtedly reacting to the current situation of the Czech culture – yet he identified this practical function as an inherent aspect of any work of art. An equally important role of literary criticism was also the institution of a national literary tradition through the interpretation of earlier texts.[51]

This is precisely the process which may be observed in the second volume of the *History*. However, the definition of what constitutes a truly English literary tradition is reached by somewhat oblique pathways.

[50] Mathesius, "O jazykové správnosti" 63.
[51] Vilém Mathesius, "O úkolech a výzbroji literární kritiky" (The Objectives and Tools of Literary Criticism), *Jazyk, kultura a slovesnost* 210-14.

The formal analysis of individual works is reduced in scope and depth in comparison with the first part;[52] conversely, the sections devoted to the survey of the historical context are substantially expanded and more closely interwoven with the literary parts. Judging from the role which the ordering of chapters had in highlighting the underlying logic of the basic argument of the first volume (i.e., the postulate of the immanence of literary tradition), it would appear that here it is the historical and social development which provides the main evolutionary line. In fact, the way medieval English history is presented parallels the contrast between the apparent disruptive impact of historical events in the Anglo-Saxon era on the literature of the time and the factual continuity of its development: this time Mathesius occasionally comments on the discrepancy between the outward aspect of an event or period and its potential from the perspective of the future course of events. Thus, for example, the international character of the Angevin empire of Henry II is juxtaposed with the eventual "nation-building" consequences of his reign.[53] Similarly to the first part of the *History*, the perspective assumed in the second volume, too, is by nature teleological – only the weight of the two aspects, the socio-historical and the literary, is reversed.

Mathesius's vision of English history appears to be largely inspired by the Whig interpretation as current in the English historiography of the second half of the nineteenth century.[54] Even though he is not much concerned with its favourite theme of the slow but inexorable progress towards modern parliamentary democracy and constitutional monarchy, nor does he subscribe to its underlying Anglo-Saxonism,[55] he does endorse

---

52 In all due fairness, this may admittedly be at least partly due to the extent of the available material which must be covered.

53 Mathesius, *Dějiny II* 42.

54 The concept is familiar; cf., for example, Krishan Kumar, *The Making of English National Identity* (Cambridge: Cambridge University Press, 2003) 202-207. Some of the historians that Mathesius quotes belong among the chief representatives of this historiographical doctrine: e.g., E.A. Freeman, William Stubbs or Alice Green, the wife of J.R. Green.

55 He does, however, see as significant the interaction of the dominant Germanic element in the *ethnic* makeup of the English people (the Anglo-Saxon base being "reinvigorated" by the Danish and Norman infusion) with Romance cultural influences. Vilém Mathesius, "O vzniku a vývoji kulturní tradice anglické" (The Origin and Development of the English Cultural Tradition), *Naše doba* 34.7, 34.8 (1926, 1926): 389-90.

its other fundamental components: the emphasis on the importance of the bourgeois element, the middle class (what he will later call the "typical concentration along a medial line"[56]), and perhaps even more typically, the concept of English history as characterized by steady continuous evolution, a preference for the middle way and a distrust of all extremes.

It is clear that Mathesius found this latter feature especially congenial. The contrast between the moderation of the English and what he saw as the unhealthy radicalism of Czech culture which proceeded in so many breaks with the past (or, alternatively, was deformed in its development by a preoccupation with past achievements) forms a staple of his 'activist' texts.[57] Similar motives are evident even in some of his linguistic works, especially those targeted at purism: the objective of "flexible stability" in language concerns precisely the gradual transformation of the existing norm of standard language through a sensitively timed incorporation of tendencies in which the norm is transgressed.[58]

In the sphere of literature Mathesius saw these English national characteristics manifested in a consistent tendency towards realism, which he correspondingly installs as a measure of the relative value of specific literary works in the second volume of the *History*. Writers and texts demonstrating a respect for and insight into the reality of their time are presented as founders and important representatives of the English literary tradition: the livelier English lyric, detailed and factual descriptions replacing usual topoi in *Sir Gawain and the Green Knight*,[59] Chaucer's

---

56 Mathesius, "O vzniku a vývoji kulturní tradice anglické" 390.
57 Cf. for example Vilém Mathesius, "Tradice jako princip dynamický" (Tradition as a Dynamic Principle), *Lumír* 55.1 (1928): 19-21; "O úkolech a výzbroji literární kritiky" 214; "Čistá práce" (Neat Work), *Jazyk, kultura a slovesnost* 366-67, etc.
58 Vilém Mathesius, "O potřebě stability ve spisovném jazyce" (On the Need for Stability in Standard Language), *Jazyk, kultura a slovesnost* 66-68.
59 "The romance of *Sir Gawain and the Green Knight* completed the transformation of a foreign genre into an indigenous one by emphasizing and developing elements agreeing with the traditional tendencies of English literary sensibility and by replacing those which were alien to it." ("Dovršil tedy román o panu Gawainovi a Zeleném rytíři přetvoření cizího útvaru v domácí zdůrazněním a rozvitím těch jeho prvků, které byly v souhlase s tradičními

Canterbury Tales, to name but a few of the many examples. In this last case the propensity for "realism," the acuteness of observation and liveliness in characterization, are presented as Chaucer's true talents and his works are analyzed with constant respect to the degree in which it is realized. Such a perspective entirely ignores the equally important "literariness" of Chaucer's texts, the games that he plays with both the reader and the tradition. Nowhere is this more prominent than in Mathesius's evaluation of the characterization of the Pardoner and the Wife of Bath in the respective prologues, where he deplores the lack of realism in the psychology of the figure (the Pardoner) or in the engagement with literary culture (the Wife of Bath and her quotations). Despite such perceived lapses, however, Chaucer represents for Mathesius the completion of the English medieval literary tradition especially in the successful "domestication" of foreign forms and influences.[60]

As the subtitle itself suggested, the second volume of Mathesius's *History* was conceived as charting the English literary tradition in the making. The greater part of the volume was devoted to literary influences and tendencies that had to be either overcome or absorbed and transformed; only the last section of the book follows the triumphant establishment of truly English literature. Inevitably, then, the correlation of national character and national literature in representative authorial types was limited to a handful of illustrative cases. Besides, as a specialist text the book had to dilute its basic argument to cover the required facts: names, titles, dates, even if not directly relevant to the case it was making. Mathesius found the perfect format for his interpretative model in the more popular and condensed article on the English cultural tradition.[61] It is symptomatic that here he locates the beginnings of the "organic growth" of English culture only in the thirteenth century; what precedes it is in a sense merely a preparatory stage. The historical and the literary are systematically interlinked: the former focusing on the already mentioned twin features of middle-class cultural supremacy and the somewhat paradoxically named "conservative

tendencemi anglického cítění literárního a záměnou oněch, jež mu byly vzdáleny."). Mathesius, *Dějiny II* 185.
60   Mathesius, *Dějiny II* 200-231.
61   Mathesius, "O vzniku a vývoji kulturní tradice anglické."

reformism," the latter underscoring, again, the predominance of realistic vision. Nevertheless, similarly to the productive tension intrinsic to an adherence to tradition combined with the reformatory impulse visible in English history, the realistic literary mainstream is kept from stagnation through (what Mukařovský would surely term *dialectical*) confrontation with a submerged current of idealism. Although the literary tradition is thus based on a more nuanced combination of contrary tendencies, there still remains a hierarchy of representative types: the predominantly idealizing authors, whether the Platonic Spenser or the Romantic Shelley, are presented as brilliant aberrations, while Shakespeare, supreme in the poetic rendering of reality, is truly representative of the character of English literature.[62]

Mathesius's perspective of English literature in this later stage of his scholarly career thus shows both a return to and a challenge of the Tainean concept: the former as regards the general approach, the latter in terms of specific conclusions. Like Taine he finally reads literature as a manifestation of national character; the difference lies in what he perceives as its governing feature – not, as Taine would see it, the imaginative spontaneity consonant with the "romantic" English nature,[63] but almost its very opposite: something that comes close to Mathesius's ideal of "dynamic classicism."[64] In both cases, the perspective of the literary historian is to a large extent shaped by his (unreflected?) personal preferences. Mathesius's most monumental literary-historical work thus appears as the nexus where the theoretical and the activist line of his thinking meet; what was conceived as a continuous project ultimately reveals a deep rupture.

---

[62] Mathesius, "O vzniku a vývoji kulturní tradice anglické" 392-93.
[63] Cf. František Sedláček, "Tainova kritika anglického romantismu" (H.A. Taine's Criticism of the English Romantic Movement), *Příspěvky k dějinám řeči a literatury anglické od členů anglického semináře Karlovy university v Praze / Studies in English by Members of the English Seminar of the Charles University, Prague, Vol. 1* (Prague: Faculty of Arts, Charles University, 1924) 65-79.
[64] Cf. Mathesius, "Čistá práce" 363.

VILÉM MATHESIUS AS TRANSLATOR AND THEORETICIAN OF TRANSLATION

Bohuslav Mánek

Vilém Mathesius's oeuvre encompasses several areas, including general and English linguistics, language teaching, literary history and criticism with the related fields of translation studies and the practice of translation, and cultural and political essays.[1] He published his translations in the first decades of the twentieth century as materials accompanying his literary studies and underpinning his cultural orientation. Besides a few pieces of modern prose, the majority of texts he translated were selections from English medieval poetry rendered from the Old and Middle English originals. These he included to illustrate his account of the development of Old and Middle English literature in the two volumes of his *Dějiny literatury anglické v hlavních jejích proudech a představitelích* (History of English Literature in Its Main Currents and Representatives),[2] which examined poetry, prose and drama up to the end of the fifteenth century in their historical context,

---

[1] Josef Vachek, "Vilém Mathesius," Vilém Mathesius, *Jazyk, kultura a slovesnost* (Language, Culture and Literature) (Prague: Odeon, 1982) 455-64; Libuše Dušková, Jan Čermák, "Život a dílo Viléma Mathesia" (The Life and the Work of Vilém Mathesius), Vilém Mathesius, *Paměti a jiné rukopisy* (Memoirs and Other Manuscripts), ed. Josef Hladký (Prague: Karolinum, 2009) 9-34.

[2] Vilém Mathesius, *Dějiny literatury anglické v hlavních jejích proudech a představitelích I. Doba anglosaská* (The History of English Literature in Its Main Currents and Representatives: I. The Anglo-Saxon Period) (Prague: self-published, 1910). *II. Zápas o národnost* (II. The Struggle for National Identity) (Prague: G. Voleský, 1915).

and in his scholarly study of English ballads and their criticism (1915).[3] Later he also translated and separately published two selections from Geoffrey Chaucer's *The Canterbury Tales* (1927).[4]

In comparison with the previous Czech works in the field, his *History* was an original and pioneering book. His account combines chronology with a discussion of genres and includes translated selections from the Old English poems ("Waldere," "Finn," "Deor," "Widsith," "The Seafarer," "The Wife's Lament," "The Dream of the Rood," "Exodus," "Elene," "Judith," "The Phoenix," "The Battle of Maldon" and includes several riddles, charms, etc.), Middle English poetry (Layamon's *Brut*, *The Owl and the Nightingale*, *Sir Gawain and the Green Knight*, Chaucer's *House of Fame*, *The Legend of Good Women*, etc.) and other works of English literature. He also published several theoretical papers on the general as well as topical questions of translation and presented his ideas on translation in the notes accompanying his selection from *The Canterbury Tales*.[5]

As a literary historian Mathesius stressed the continuity of the development of English literature since its very beginnings. Besides the positivistic presentation of numerous facts and plot outlines, in his analyses of the individual works of literature one can see a trend which later culminates in Structuralism. In his studies he focused primarily on medieval and Renaissance literature and drama (John Wycliffe, Thomas Malory and William Shakespeare) but he also published stimulating essays on Daniel Defoe, Henry Fielding, John Galsworthy, G.B. Shaw and H.G. Wells, aptly characterizing the authors and their works, and taught a course on modern English literature. His lectures on sixteenth- to

---

3   Vilém Mathesius, "Problém anglických lidových balad" (The Problem of English Folk Ballads), *Věstník České akademie císaře Františka Josefa pro vědy, slovesnost a umění* 24.6,7 (1915): 245-71, 327-42.

4   Geoffrey Chaucer, *Výbor z Canterburských povídek Geoffreye Chaucera* (A Selection from Geoffrey Chaucer's The Canterbury Tales) (Prague: J. Laichter, 1927).

5   "O problémech českého překladatelství" (On the Problems of Czech Translations), *Přehled* 11.49 (1912-13): 807-808; rpt. in Mathesius, *Jazyk, kultura a slovesnost* 225-26. "Poznámky o překládání cizího blankversu a o českém verši jambickém vůbec" (Notes on the Translation of Foreign Blank Verse and on the Czech Iambic Verse in General), *Slovo a slovesnost* 9.1 (1943): 1-13; rpt. in Mathesius, *Jazyk, kultura a slovesnost* 227-41.

eighteenth-century English literature were edited by his disciples.[6] He also published numerous reviews of foreign and Czech scholarly books, in particular on medieval literature and Shakespeare[7] and practised interconnected studies of language and literature, from which both disciplines profited.

In the period of the Czech National Revival and in the second half of the nineteenth century only a small number of translations and informative articles concerning medieval English literature were published in literary journals, anthologies and encyclopaedias. In the third volume of Josef Bojislav Pichl's (1813-1888) anthology *Společenský krasořečník český* (Declamatory Verse in Czech for Social Occasions),[8] which is a representative selection from Czech translations published in the period of the National Revival since the beginning of the century, the Earl of Surrey and Walter Raleigh are the earliest authors translated. The anthology includes, besides Shakespeare and Milton, mainly pre-Romantic and Romantic poems by Thomas Gray, Walter Scott, Thomas Moore, P.B. Shelley, Lord Byron and several others. The selection opens with Ossian's "medieval" poems, but these are presented as writings by James Macpherson, the perpetrator of the Ossian literary fraud. In the course of the nineteenth century, the most widely translated genre of medieval English literature was the ballad. Several medieval ballads and their pre-Romantic and Romantic imitations by David Mallet, Thomas Percy, Oliver Goldsmith and Walter Scott were published by Bohuslav Tablic (1769-1832), Vojtěch Nejedlý (1772-1844), Simeon Karel Macháček (1799-1846), Josef Hollmann (1802-1850), František Ladislav Čelakovský (1799-1852), his son Ladislav Čelakovský (1834-1902) and Josef Václav Sládek (1945-1912). Ladislav Quis (1846-1913) then published the first annotated anthology of ballads in 1900.[9]

6 Vilém Mathesius, *Dějiny anglické literatury. Od zavedení knihtisku až po realistický román 18. století* (The History of English Literature. From the Introduction of Book-Printing to the Eighteenth-century Realistic Novel) (Prague: Spolek posluchačů filosofie Karlovy university, 1933).
7 See Emanuel Macek, "Soupis díla Viléma Mathesia" (The Bibliography of Vilém Mathesius's Writings), Mathesius, *Jazyk, kultura a slovesnost* 473-525.
8 Josef Boleslav Pichl (ed.), *Společenský krasořečník český III* (Declamatory Verse in Czech for Social Occasions, III) (Prague: Jaroslav Pospíšil, 1853) 205-70.
9 See Bohuslav Mánek, *Překlady anglické a americké poezie v období Máje. II. Bibliografie* (Czech Translations of English and American Poetry in the Period

In the first half of the nineteenth century, no articles about medieval literature in English were published, most attention being paid to the Ossianic poems, Shakespeare, Pope and Byron. As late as 1855, a relatively extensive article on English literature by Václav Zelený (1825-1875) in the magazine *Obzor* (Horizon) 1855[10] begins with John Wycliffe and Geoffrey Chaucer and presents a short outline of *The Canterbury Tales*. Short articles on, e.g., *Beowulf,* Caedmon, Chaucer or John Gower are scattered in the items of the *Slovník naučný* (Encyclopedia, 1860-1874, 1890),[11] written by Edmund Břetislav Kaizl (1836-1900), Jiljí Vratislav Jahn (1838-1902) and probably also by Jakub Malý (1811-1885). A relatively extensive and informed survey of the beginnings of English drama was published by Julius Zeyer (1841-1901) in the literary magazine *Lumír* (1875).[12] Some information on Chaucer, the Arthurian cycle, etc. was included in František Věnceslav Jeřábek's (1836-1893) *Stará doba romantického básnictví* (The Old Age of Romantic Poetical Writing, 1883),[13] a loose compilation covering medieval romance in Germanic literatures as well as in Czech (the work was submitted as a *Habilitationsschrift* at Charles University and refused). A larger, more detailed and better-informed survey of English medieval literature is found in the section devoted to English literature in *Ilustrované dějiny literatury všeobecné* (An Illustrated History of General Literature, 1881) by Václav Petrů (1841-1906),[14] another compilation including some translated selections. Václav Emanuel Mourek's (1846-1911) *Přehled dějin literatury anglické* (An Outline of the History of English Literature, 1890)[15] and his entries for

of the Almanac May. II. Bibliography), doctoral dissertation, Charles University in Prague, 1984, 7-105.

[10] Václav Zelený, "Literatura anglická" (English Literature), *Obzor* 1.2,6 (1855): 151-56, 468-71.

[11] F.L. Rieger, J. Malý (eds.), *Slovník naučný* (Encyclopaedia), 12 vols. (Prague: I.L. Kober, 1860-1874, 1890).

[12] Julius Zeyer, "Počátky anglického divadla" (The Beginning of English Theatre), *Lumír* 3.4 (1875): 41-44, 66-69.

[13] František Věnceslav Jeřábek, *Stará doba romantického básnictví* (The Old Age of Romantic Poetry) (Prague: Matice česká, 1883).

[14] Václav Petrů, *Ilustrované dějiny literatury všeobecné II* (An Illustrated History of General Literature II) (Pilsen: Vendelín Steinhauser, 1881).

[15] Emanuel Mourek, *Přehled dějin literatury anglické* (An Outline of the History of English Literature) (Prague: J. Otto, 1890).

Ottův slovník naučný (Otto's Encyclopedia, 1888-1909)[16] are predominantly purely factual, presenting names of authors and titles of works.

Mathesius was critical of the mimetic form of translation, i.e., translation preserving the meter and rhyme scheme of the original, which was required for and practised in most translations in Czech literature since the beginning of the nineteenth century. This method often deformed the Czech language and spoiled the aesthetic qualities and style of the original. In his theoretical statements and translations he proposed other techniques. Mathesius viewed the practical and theoretical aspects of translation in a broad historical and cultural context and emphasized the relationship between the function of translations and the historical development of a particular literature. He formulated his theoretical approach simultaneously with his work on his translations in his study "O problémech českého překladatelství" (On the Problems of Czech Translations):

> There is no reason why we should refuse translations on principle. The present author has come to this conclusion by examining the importance which translations have had in the development of our literature. I would add that the usefulness of translations is just part of a more fundamental question: the usefulness of foreign influences. This issue is also hotly debated in this country and the results of these debates vary. I think that the opponents to foreign influences should be referred to the study of history. How praised the originality of English literature is! Nonetheless, its greatest works grew in those days when the atmosphere was full of foreign motifs and ideas – at the end of the Middle Ages, in the Renaissance and after the French Revolution. The issue is not to fight off foreign influences but to conquer them by one's own force. It is not possible to hide oneself away from foreign truth, either scientific or artistic. It is necessary to receive it, to comprehend it fully and to transform it. It is therefore useless to meditate how to suppress the chase for translations – the issue is how to manage not to live only on them but more on our own riches. [...] Let us remember that the equation between the translation and the original is calculated with the use of artistic, not

---

[16]   *Ottův slovník naučný* (Otto's Encyclopedia) (Prague: J. Otto, 1888-1909).

philological, quantities. [...] The work of art has its harmony which must not be broken, and has its own fragrance which must be captured. [...] A perfect translation is sometimes called poetic recasting. When analyzing the technical meaning of this term, we find that the proper substance of poetic recasting is the effort to produce an artistic effect even with the use of different literary means than those utilized in the original. [...] [V]ery often the identical – or approximately identical – means produce different effects. The principle that an equivalent artistic effect is of more importance than the identical artistic means is important particularly in translations of works of poetry. [...] [N]ot even verse forms can be always transferred directly from the original to the translation. A harmony and individuality of translation should be valued more than the precision of details: art should be rated more than philology.[17]

---

[17] "Není, proč bychom se měli brániti překladům ze zásady. K důsledku tomu autor dospívá rozborem důležitosti, jíž měly překlady ve vývoji našeho písemnictví. Dodal bych, že užitečnost překladů je jen úsekem otázky větší: užitečnosti cizích vlivů. I o té se často u nás prudce debatuje a výsledky debat se měnívají. Myslím, že je dlužno odkázati odpůrce cizích vlivů ke studiu dějin. Jak se velebívá rázovitost literatury anglické! A přece největší její díla vyrůstala tehdy, kdy vzduch byl plný cizozemských motivů a myšlenek – ke konci středověku, v renesanci a po revoluci francouzské. Nejde o to, jak se obrániti cizím vlivům, jde o jejich překonání vlastní silou. Není možno se skrývat cizí pravdě, ať vědecké, či umělecké. Dlužno ji přijmout, proniknout a přetvořit. A proto je marno přemýšleti, čím potlačovati shon po překladech, – otázka je, jak dokázati, abychom nežili tolik z nich, nýbrž více z bohatství vlastního. [...] Pamatujme, že rovnice mezi překladem a originálem se počítá veličinami uměleckými, a ne filologickými. [...] Umělecké dílo má svou harmonii, jež nesmí být porušena, a má svou vůni, jež musí být zachycena. [...] Dokonalému překladu říkává se přebásnění. Analyzujeme-li technický význam tohoto termínu, dojdeme k poznání, že vlastní podstata přebásnění je o úsilí o vzbuzení uměleckého účinku i třeba jinými literárními prostředky, než jakých bylo užito v originálu. [...] [Č]asto stejné – nebo přibližně stejné – prostředky docilují účinků různých. Zásada, že důležitější je rovnost uměleckého účinku než stejnost uměleckých prostředků, jest důležita zejména při překládání děl básnických. [...] [A]ni útvary veršové se nedají přenášeti vždy přímočaře z originálu do překladu. [...] Harmonii a výraznost překladu je tedy ceniti výš než detailní přesnost, umění jest klásti nad filologii." Mathesius, "O problémech českého překladatelství" 225-26. My translation.

In this article Mathesius distinguishes three methods which have been used in nineteenth-century Czech literature in translation to solve the problems caused by differing semantic density[18] in English and Czech verse: first, preservation of the length of the original line and adding the number of lines, which often resulted in verbosity, second, the use of monosyllabic words, whose frequency, however, is considerably higher in English than in Czech, and third, omissions of individual words or even phrases in the Czech translation. Mathesius recommends a different, and yet unpractised, method: extending the length of the line. This approach was often employed later, e.g., by Jan Vladislav in his well-known translations of Shakespeare's *Sonnets*, in which he replaced the iambic pentameter with hexameter.[19]

Mathesius was thus well aware of the prosodic differences between the two languages and devoted much attention to the theoretical problems and practical employment of Czech rising metres, in particular the iambic lines both in translated and original Czech poetry and drama. He did not propose a theoretical hypothesis: his conclusions were based on the examination of the existing texts. Later he developed his ideas in an extensive three-part essay "Poznámky o překládání cizího blankversu a o českém verši jambickém vůbec" (Notes on the Translation of Foreign Blank Verse and on the Czech Iambic Verse in General).[20] In greater detail he discussed and compared J.V. Sládek's and E.A. Saudek's translations of Shakespeare's *Hamlet* and Bohumil Mathesius's translation of Goethe's *Torquato Tasso*, and the original Czech blank verse in the writings of Jaroslav Vrchlický and Julius Zeyer. He focused on key linguistic aspects and historical contexts of the development of Czech literature, and also paid attention to the performance of the iambic lines by actors, examining the extent to which it preserved the style of the original.

In his own translations, Mathesius moreover strove to preserve the most important stylistic features of the original, avoiding the deformation of the Czech language by the strict observance of the above-mentioned

---

[18] The Czech term is "obsažnost."

[19] William Shakespeare, *Sonnets – Sonety*, trans. Jan Vladislav (Prague: SNKLHU, 1955).

[20] Mathesius, "Poznámky o překládání cizího blankversu a o českém verši jambickém vůbec" 227-41.

mimetic approach. His method can be illustrated by his translation of a selection from "The General Prologue" of Chaucer's *Canterbury Tales*:

Když duben záplavou svých vlahých dešťů
březnovým suchem do kořenu vnikne
a každé vlákno vykoupe v té vláze,
z nichž silou plodivou se rodí květy,
když také Zefyr líbezným svým dechem
v lese i v poli všude popožene
výhonky křehoučké a mladé slunce
v souhvězdí skopce proběhne svou půlku
a ptáčkové se dají do zpívání,
jímž příroda tak pobuřuje srdce,
že celou noc spí s okem otevřeným:
tu touží lidé na pouti se vydat
a putovníci k cizím jíti břehům,
k dalekým svatým, známým v různých zemích;
a obzvláště z končin každičkého hrabství
z Anglie celé jdou do Canterbury,
k svatému pomodlit se mučedníku,
který jim pomohl, když přišla nemoc.
V tu právě dobu jedenkrát se stalo,
když v Southwarku jsem meškal „U kabátce"
jsa hotov na svou pouť se také vydat
do Canterbury s myslí velmi zbožnou,
že do hospody té navečer přišlo
pospolu dvacet devět různých lidí,
kteří jen náhodou se byli sešli,
a do jednoho poutníci to byli,
jejichžto cílem bylo Canterbury.[21]

In conformity with his theoretical statements he substantiated his approach as follows:

> The translation maintains the metre and rhythm of the original lines, but uses unrhymed verses instead of couplets. As can be demonstrated in the majority of Czech rhymed translations, the

---

[21] Chaucer, *Výbor z Canterburských povídek* 9-10.

reason is that considerations of rhyme make it nearly impossible to casually and fluently translate the stylistic subtleties characteristic of the original. Chaucer's masterful and finely graded style is really more important for the colour of his work than his rhyme.[22]

In his translations and theoretical opinions he paved the way for modern Czech translation techniques which began to develop in the 1920s and 1930s. Mathesius's translations represent an intermediate step because the development of Czech language and literature in the twentieth century made it possible for the following generations of translators to render both the style and the rhyme scheme, which can be illustrated by František Vrba's (1920-1985) translation of the same verse paragraph. His versions of *The Canterbury Tales* (1941, 1953, 1956, 1970) are all rhymed, demonstrating both the progress in the translator's art and the ongoing strong general trend toward mimetic translation in this country:

> Když duben vniká v šumných přeprškách
> až do kořání pod březnový prach
> a vlahou lázní v každém vláknu vznítí
> plodivou sílu, z které pučí kvítí,
> a když i Zefýr v lesíku a stráni
> líbezným dechem k růstu popohání
> výhonky něžné a když jaré slunce
> na dráze Skopcem dorazilo k půlce,
> když drobné ptáčky příroda tak vzbouří,
> že ani v spánku oka nezamhouří
> a na své šalmaje si vyhrávají,
> zatouží lidé po dalekém kraji
> a dálném břehu; každý světa kout
> má svého svatého a má svou pouť.

[22] "V překladu jsou podrženy rozměry a rytmus originálního verše, ale místo sdružených rýmů je užito veršů nerýmovaných. Stalo se to proto, že ohledy na rým téměř znemožňují, jak může dokázati převážná většina českých rýmovaných překladů, nenucené a plynulé přetlumočení stilistických jemností pro originál charakteristických. A Chaucerův mistrný a jemně odstínovaný sloh je opravdu mnohem důležitější pro barvu jeho díla nežli jeho rýmy." Chaucer, *Výbor z Canterburských povídek* 62. My translation.

A v Anglii se táhnou všemi směry
z každého hrabství k městu Canterbury,
za mučedníkem blahoslaveným,
jenž v nemoci a strázni pomoh jim.[23]

Mathesius had already used the technique of unrhymed lines in 1915 when translating several fragments from Chaucer's *Troilus and Criseyde* which was originally written in the more complex Chaucerian stanza (or rhyme royal, *ababbcc*):

Pandarus nazítři hned ráno přišel
k neteři své a pěkně pozdraviv ji
pravil: "Dnes celou noc tam pršelo tak, běda,
že bojím se, že vy, má sladká neti,
jste málo jenom mohla spát a sníti.
Po celou noc ten déšť tak probouzel mě,
Že leckoho z nás, myslím, bolí hlava.[24]

He also used this approach in translating several medieval ballads to illustrate his views in an article entitled "Problém anglických lidových balad" (The Problem of English Folk Ballads, 1915).[25] On the basis of Francis James Child's collections, from which he translated his selections, the paper discussed numerous theories about the genre. One of the selections was the ballad "The Hunting of the Cheviot" (also called "The Ballad of Chevy Chase," Child 162):

Percy z Northumberlandu
　Bohem se zařekl,
že v horách cheviotských bude
　honiti ve třech dnech
na vzdory statečnému Douglasu
　a všem, kdož s ním byli.

---

[23] Geoffrey Chaucer, *Canterburské povídky* (The Canterbury Tales), trans. František Vrba (Prague: Odeon, 1970) 7.

[24] *Troilus and Criseyde*, III.223, trans. Vilém Mathesius, *Dějiny II* 203. In his translation of a shortened version of the poem, Zdeněk Hron managed to use the rhyme royal: Geoffrey Chaucer, *Troilus a Kriseida* (Prague: BB art, 2001).

[25] Mathesius, "Problém anglických lidových balad" 245-71, 327-42.

Nejtučnější jeleny ve všem Cheviotu
pobít a odnést chtěl.
„Na mou věru," řekl zas statečný Douglas,
„té honbě zabráním, budu-li s to."[26]

The faults he criticized in previous nineteenth-century translations can be illustrated by an extract from the same ballad translated by Ladislav Čelakovský in 1855:

Z Northumberlandu Percy
Slib nebi učiní,
Že v Cheviatských horách
Chce honit po tři dni,
Statnému Duglasu na vzdor,
I všem, kdož při něm dlí.

Tam srnce nejtučnější včil
Že zabiv, odvleče jim.
Na mou čest', na to statný Duglas dí,
To mu bohdá překazím.[27]

In all probability, both translations are based on the text first printed in Thomas Percy's *Reliques of Ancient English Poetry* (1765).[28] An exception confirming the rule is Mathesius's translation of the famous rhymed couplet usually attributed to John Ball (c. 1338-1381):

26 "Balada o honu na horách cheviotských," Mathesius, "Problém anglických lidových balad" 249.
27 "Hon Cheviatský" ("The Ballad of Chevy Chase"), trans. Ladislav Čelakovský, *Časopis muzea království českého* 29.2 (1855): 207.
28 The Persè owt off Northombarlonde,
      and a vowe to God mayd he,
    That he wold hunte in the mountayns
      off Chyviat within days thre,
    In the magger of doughtè Dogles,
      and all that ever with him be.

    The fattiste hartes in all Cheviat
      he sayd he wold kill, and cary them away:
    "Be my feth," sayd the dougheti Doglas agayn,
      "I wyll let that hontyng yf that I may."
    Francis James Child, *English and Scottish Ballads VII* (Boston: Little, Brown and Company, 1860) 29. Thomas Percy, *Reliques of Ancient English Poetry I* (London: J.M. Dent, 1932) 67.

When Adam delved and Eve span,
who was then the gentleman?

Když Eva předla a Adam ryl,
kde tehdy jaký šlechtic byl?[29]

Similarly, Mathesius attempted to capture the character of alliterative poetry of Old English literature. His translation of *Caedmon's Hymn* from the Old English version can be compared with the first Czech prose translation by Václav Petrů of the Latin version in Bede's *Historia ecclesiastica gentis Anglorum* (731):

Oslavujme nyní nebes ochránce,
Tvůrcovu moc a jeho myšlenku,
dílo velebného Otce, jak on divu každému,
věčný Vládce, začátek vymezil.
On nejdřív nebesa stvořil,
střechu synům lidským, svatý Stvořitel;
zemi potom, ochránce zástupů,
věčný Vládce, vytvořil zase,
půdu pro lidi, všemohoucí Pán.[30]

Chvalmež nyní původu říše nebeské, moc stvořitelovu a radu jeho, skutky otce slávy, jak učinil, věčný pán, každého zázraku počátek. Nejprve stvořil dětem lidským nebe za střechu, stvořitel svatý, pak učinil zem, strážce pokolení lidského všemohoucí.[31]

These translations may seem less demanding, but there are some obstacles as well. Dialects of Old English are practically a foreign language not only for foreigners, but for modern native speakers of English as well. English and American translators have to solve similar problems as Czechs when translating the Old Germanic accentual metre into contemporary English accentual-syllabic metre. North, Crystal and Allard in the introduction to their book on medieval English and Old Icelandic literature expressed

---

[29] Mathesius, *Dějiny II* 147.
[30] Mathesius, *Dějiny I* 87.
[31] Petrů, *Ilustrované dějiny literatury všeobecné* 15:21-22.

the predicament as follows: "[...] all translators suffer from the fact that modern English verse does not carry the same semantic charge with the same symmetry and within the same tightly compacted space."[32] Both the contemporary Czech and English languages make it possible to use alliteration for more than three syllables in a line, and also sound figures, i.e., the repetition of certain consonants or vowels, are employed as a kind of skeleton. Archaic vocabulary, postponed adjectives, etc. then suggest the time interval from the past. In addition, contemporary Czech translators, besides alliteration, also emphasize the caesura graphically by a long blank space:

> Stoupal tu stěží královského rodu syn
> po příkrých skalách, pěšinách úzkých,
> těsných stezkách, tajemnými cestami,
> přes srázné útesy, útulky oblud.[33]

> Zdolal pak rek   rodu vznešeného
> srázná skaliska   soutěsky, kudy jen
> jeden prosmykne se,   neblahé prostory,
> příkré ostrohy   nad doupaty příšer.[34]

Mathesius preferred meaning and fluency to formal considerations, and sparingly used alliteration even in his translations of Middle English alliterative verse, as can be seen in this extract from the Prologue of William Langland's *Piers Ploughman*:

> V letní době, když slunce mile hřálo,
> v hrubý jsem se oblékl šat, jako bych ovčák byl;
> v oděvu poustevníka nesvatého činy

---

32 Richard North, David Crystal, and Joe Allard, "Why Read Old English Literature?" Richard North and Joe Allard (eds.), *Beowulf & Other Stories: A New Introduction to Old English, Old Icelandic and Anglo-Norman Literatures* (Harlow: Pearson-Longman, 2007) 23.

33 *Béowulf,* ll. 1408-11, Mathesius, *Dějiny I* 16.

34 *Béowulf,* ll. 1408-11, *Béowulf,* trans. Jan Čermák (Prague: Torst, 2003) 130. See also Jan Čermák (ed.), *Jako když dvoranou proletí pták. Antologie nejstarší anglické poezie a prózy, 700-1100* (Like a Bird Flying through the Hall: An Anthology of the Oldest English Poetry and Prose, 700-1100) (Prague: Triáda, 2009).

do světa jsem se vydal, abych divy slyšel.
Než v jitru májovém na vrších malvernských
div se mi jednou stal, zdálo se to kouzlem.
Znaven jsem byl poutí a šel si odpočinout
pod širokou stráň ku břehu potoka,
a jak jsem ležel a opíral se a na vodu se díval,
zdříml jsem spánkem – znělo to tak mile.
Tu sníti jsem počal sen velmi podivný.[35]

Later translators, for instance Ladislav Cejp (1910 1960), emphasize alliteration, sound figures and the layout on the page even more:

Svitlo světlé léto, Slibně hřálo slunce,
Odřeným šatem oděn, Jak ovčákem bych byl,
Měl jsem hrubý šat mnicha, Málo svatého díla,
Daleko do světa šel jsem Divy a zázraky hledat.
Míjelo májové jitro, Malvernské vršky se skvěly,
Div se mi zvláštní zdál, Zázraky jsem snil.
Byl jsem už hodně ušlý, Úlevy oddechu hledal
Při břehu prostorném, Kde potok plaše šuměl.
Dlouho jsem teskně dumal, Do vod se díval,
Až jsem upadl v snění, Tak úlisně to znělo.
Po tom jsem počal snít, Podivuhodný sen. [36]

Mathesius's translations of medieval poetry are not purely philological exercises, but also an artistic achievement that is still readable (it should be mentioned that Mathesius wrote poems in his youth).[37] His linguistic erudition was happily combined with his aesthetics, which can be seen even when the principles of the alliterative verse are not fully implemented:

---

[35] William Langland, "Vidění o Petru Oráči, Prolog" (*Piers Plowman*, Prologue, ll. 1-11), Mathesius, *Dějiny II* 154-55.

[36] William Langland, "Vidění Vilémovo o Petru Oráči, Prolog" (*William's Vision of Piers Plowman*, ll. 1-11), Ladislav Cejp, *Metody středověké alegorie a Langlandův Petr Oráč* (Methods of Medieval Allegory and Langland's *Piers Plowman*), *Acta Universitatis Palackianae Olomucensis. Facultas philosophica 8 – Philologica* (1961) 57.

[37] Mathesius, *Paměti a jiné rukopisy*.

Křičeli ptáci bitevní, boje žádostiví,
s rosou na křídlech, nad mrtvolami.
Spěchal milovník zdechlin, zpívali vlci
hroznou píseň večerní v naději žrádla,
zvířata nelítostná, na vraždění hbitá,
čekala ve stopách nepřátel na pád vojska:
křičeli strážci pochodů prostřed noci,
prchal duch smrtí poděšený, lid byl stísněn.
Chvílemi ze šiku toho rekové chlubní
hrdě měřili cesty kopyty hřebců.[38]

It must be added that Mathesius's attention was not only academic and limited to the past: he also strove to contribute to the social and cultural progress of the newly established republic, trying to introduce into Czech society and culture some British elements which he judged likely to exert a positive influence. This is patently clear from a reading of the book of his original essays entitled *Kulturní aktivismus. Anglické paralely k českému životu* (Cultural Activism: English Parallels to Czech Life)[39] and the selection of the essays and lectures he translated. These last included a lecture delivered at Charles University in Prague in June 1921 by James Alton James (1864-1962), an American educator and historian, an essay by George Peabody Gooch (1873-1968), a British historian, journalist and Liberal Party politician[40] and several essays by H.G. Wells (1866-1946). Both his original and translated essays have contributed to the cultivation of the original Czech essay.

In his translations of modern prose, Mathesius follows the order of the ideas expressed and the sentence structure of the original as closely as it is possible in the target language in order to fluently render the meaning and the author's original style. For example:

---

[38] From *Exodus,* Mathesius, *Dějiny I* 94.
[39] Vilém Mathesius, *Kulturní aktivismus. Anglické paralely k českému životu* (Cultural Activism. English Parallels to Czech Life) (Prague: G. Voleský, 1925).
[40] The latter translation was allegedly printed in the journal *Naše doba* in 1924. Although this item is listed in Macek's bibliography ("Soupis díla Viléma Mathesia"), it has not been found in the above-mentioned volume of the journal.

Of all the great personifications that have dominated the mind of man, the greatest, the most marvellous, the most impossible and the most incredible, is surely the People, that impalpable monster to which the world has consecrated its political institutions for the last hundred years. It is doubtful now whether this stupendous superstition has reached its grand climacteric, and there can be little or no dispute that it is destined to play a prominent part in the history of mankind for many years to come.

Ze všech velkých zosobnění, ktcrá kdy ovládala mysl lidskou, největší, nejúžasnější, nejnemožnější a nejneuvěřitelnější je jistě lid, ten nehmatatelný netvor, jemuž svět zasvěcoval své politické instituce v posledních sto letech. Je teď pochybno, zdali ta ohromující pověra dosáhla svého hlavního kritického bodu, a nemůže být sporu nebo jen málo sporu o tom, že je souzeno, aby ještě po mnoho budoucích let hrála vynikající úlohu v dějinách lidstva.[41]

The quoted passage is from one of the essays Mathesius translated for the volume *Angličan se dívá na svět* (1922), the complete translation of the collection of essays *An Englishman Looks at the World* (1914) by H.G. Wells. Wells was one of the authors Mathesius highly valued for his combined and related literary and social activities, which he appreciated in his preface to the book, titled "H.G. Wells jako myslitel" (H.G. Wells as Thinker):

Wells the novelist and Wells the thinker interpenetrate and supplement each other in such a way that any judgement based on his works of fiction – and only they are known in our country – is false. For that matter, a judgement based only on his purely reflective books would also be false, as it is difficult to decide who supports whom, whether a thinker trained in scientific analysis and induction supports the novelist, or the novelist, endowed with sharp insight into the uniqueness of the real, supports the thinker.

[41] H.G. Wells, "Is There a People?," *An Englishman Looks at the World* (Leipzig: Bernhard Tauchnitz, 1914) 241; "Existuje lid?," *Angličan se dívá na svět*, trans. Karel Randé and Vilém Mathesius (Prague: G. Voleský, 1922) 135. The other essays in the book were translated by Karel Randé (1880-1942), a librarian and translator from English and German.

The book's blurb includes the following prophetic words: "Get to know the way of thinking and the character of the nation which will soon have a say in the destiny of our country!"[42]

To conclude, Mathesius's translations and theoretical concepts pertaining to translation are closely related to his linguistic and literary studies and his idea of culture and its promotion. He attempted to render the contents as accurately as possible and at the same time to preserve the principal stylistic features of the original. In contrast to the common practice of most nineteenth- and early twentieth-century Czech translators, he refused to preserve the formal elements of the source text at the expense of stylistic nivelization and deformations of language in the target text. The development of translation techniques of poetry and prose into Czech in the twentieth century can be characterized as efforts to continue in this trend, and in addition to cope with both the content and form of the originals. The present essay has attempted to show that the verse translated by Vilém Mathesius represents an important turning point as well as a specific intermediate stage in this development, i.e., the process of refining mimetic translations.

BIBLIOGRAPHY OF VILÉM MATHESIUS'S TRANSLATIONS

1910

Vilém Mathesius, *Dějiny literatury anglické v hlavních jejích proudech a představitelích. I. Doba anglosaská* (The History of English Literature in Its Main Currents and Representatives. I. The Anglo-Saxon Period) (Prague: self-published, 1910). The study includes many short or longer passages from various Old English texts translated from the originals by the author.

---

[42] "Wells romanopisec a Wells myslitel se tak navzájem prostupují a doplňují, že jakýkoli úsudek stavěný pouze na Wellsově díle beletristickém – a to je u nás vlastně dosud jedině známo – je křivý. Stejně křivý by byl ostatně i úsudek opírající se výhradně o jeho knihy ryze úvahové, neboť těžko je rozhodnouti, kdo koho podpírá víc, zda myslitel, školený ve vědecké analysi a indukci, romanopisce, či romanopisec, nadaný bystrým zrakem pro jedinečnost reality, myslitele." "Poznejte myšlení a charakter národa, který bude jednou spolurozhodovati o osudu naší vlasti." Vilém Mathesius, "H.G. Wells jako myslitel" (H.G. Wells as Thinker), *Angličan se dívá na svět* (Prague: G. Voleský, 1922) 5.

1915

Vilém Mathesius, *Dějiny literatury anglické v hlavních jejích proudech a představitelích. II. Zápas o národnost* (The History of English Literature in Its Main Currents and Representatives. II. The Struggle for National Identity) (Prague: G. Voleský, 1915). The study includes many short or longer passages from various Middle English texts translated from the originals by the author.

Vilém Mathesius, "Problém anglických lidových balad"(The Problem of English Folk Ballads), *Věstník České akademie císaře Františka Josefa pro vědy, slovesnost a umění* 24.6,7 (1915): 245-71, 327-42. The study includes the translations of the following ballads: "Balada o lordu Randalovi" ("Lord Randal," Child 12 A), "Balada od třech havranech" ("The Three Ravens," Child 26), "Balada o junáckém Georgi Campbellovi" ("Bonnie George Campbell," Child 210 C), "Balada o honu na horách cheviotských" ("Chevy Chase or The Hunting of the Cheviot," Child 162), "Balada o Robinu Hoodovi a fráteru zahradníkovi" ("Robin Hood and the Curtal Friar," Child 123 B).

1920

H.G. Wells, "Lidské dobrodružství" (The Human Adventure), *Československá republika* 241.272 (1920): 2-3 (2 October 1920), rpt. in H.G. Wells, *Angličan se dívá na svět* (An Englishman Looks at the World) (Prague: G. Voleský, 1922) 201-206.

1921

James Alton James, "Několik význačných rysů v historii Spojených států v posledním čtvrtstoletí" (A lecture delivered at Charles University in Prague in June 1921; the title can be back-translated as Some Distinguished Features in the History of the United States in the Recent Quarter of the Century), *Naše doba* 29.1,2 (1921-22): 16-21, 87-95.

1922

H.G. Wells, *Angličan se dívá na svět. Poznámky o současných* otázkách, trans. Vilém Mathesius and Karel Randé (Prague: G. Voleský, 1922). (*An Englishman Looks at the World; being a series of unrestrained remarks upon contemporary matters*, London: Cassell and Comp. Ltd., 1914; Leipzig: Bernhard Tauchnitz, 1914). V. Mathesius translated: "Odpoutaní" (Off the Chain) 11-17, "Současný román" (The Contemporary Novel) 107-122, "Plat za mateřství" (The Endowment of Motherhood) 123-28, "Lékaři" (Doctors) 129-34, "Existuje lid?" (Is There a People?) 135-40, "Několik možných objevů" (Some Possible Discoveries) 191-200, "Lidské dobrodružství" (The Human Adventure) 201-206.

1924

G(eorge) P(eabody) Gooch, "Jednota lidstva a státní suverenita" (The Unity of Mankind and State Sovereignty). Not identified; allegedly in *Naše doba* 31.9 (1923-24): 556-58. This item is listed in Emanuel Macek's "Soupis díla Viléma Mathesia" (The Bibliography of Vilém Mathesius's Oeuvre) in Vilém Mathesius, *Jazyk, kultura a slovesnost* (Language, Culture and Literature) (Prague: Odeon, 1982) 509, but it has not been found in the above-mentioned volume of the journal or in the volumes 26 (1918-1919) to 34 (1926-1927) inclusive.

1927

Výbor z Canterburských povídek Geoffreye Chaucera (A Selection from Geoffrey Chaucer's The Canterbury Tales), "Obecný prolog"(The General Prologue) 9-33,"Vyprávění kněze jeptiščina" (The Nun's Priest's Tale) 34-60 (Prague: J. Laichter, 1927).

1938

William Shakespeare, *Večer tříkrálový nebo Cokoli chcete* (Twelfth Night, or What You Will), trans. Erik Adolf Saudek, revised by Vilém Mathesius (Prague: F. Borový, 1938).

A STRUCTURALIST HISTORY OF ZDENĚK VANČURA

Pavla Veselá

Definitions of literature and literary history have fascinated critics for centuries; Russian Formalists and Prague Structuralists[1] notwithstanding. Formalist/Structuralist novelties regarding these issues include, famously, an emphasis on form over content, the notion of estrangement, the belief in literature's partial autonomy and the view that literary history is to a great extent self-propagating. The story of the rise and fall of Formalism and Structuralism in the East is also well-known; while in the first decades of the twentieth century their impact was significant, in the Soviet Union especially after Stalin's consolidation of power (and throughout Eastern Europe after World War II), the Formalist/ Structuralist approach was systematically suppressed. Without denying these facts, the following pages do not highlight merely ruptures but also continuities and emphasize the persistence of Formalist/Structuralist methodology even in the changed post-1948 climate. Moreover, it is also clear that certain aspects of the approaches to literature that became dominant in the East in the second half of the twentieth century may be

[1] Throughout this article, "Formalism" and "Structuralism" refer to *Russian* Formalism and *Prague* Structuralism. Also, while I am aware of the differences between, as well as the varieties within, the two theoretical schools, for the purpose of sketching the background of Vančura's early work I consider Formalism and Structuralism unified by basic principles. I would like to thank Prof. Martin Procházka for his advice and insightful comments on the manuscript of this article.

discerned in the pre-1948 attitudes of the Formalists and Structuralists themselves. To that end, the work of Zdeněk Vančura – an early proponent of Structuralism, who survived in Czech academy even after 1948 – is highly illustrative.

Preliminary Observations: Formalism and Prague Structuralism on Literature and Literary History

Writing about Russian Formalism, Peter Steiner proposed that

> with all hope lost of establishing [its] intrinsic definition [...], we might at least discover extrinsic criteria of identity for the movement. For instance, there seems to be a distinct pattern in the way the Formalists characterize their collective enterprise. Again and again they speak of the novelty of their approach, or their deliberate departure from previous modes of literary studies.[2]

Departing from Steiner's observation, we may argue that in the area of literary criticism, Formalist and Prague Structuralist approaches had an analogous function to that of Russian Futurism and Czech Surrealism in the artistic sphere, where the works of writers such as Victor Khlebnikov, Vladimir Mayakovsky, Vítězslav Nezval or Toyen represented "new forms of art [that could] bring back to man his experience of the world, resurrect things and kill pessimism."[3] The dominant interpretative methodologies that Formalism and Structuralism opposed were the biographical, economic, sociological and metaphysical criticism of literature; that is, approaches that focused on the content of literature and that emphasized the impact of extra-literary phenomena. In contrast, the Formalists and Structuralists prioritized the form, and they insisted on literature's relative autonomy and its largely immanent 'development.'

---

2   Peter Steiner, *Russian Formalism: A Metapoetics* (Ithaca: Cornell University Press, 1984) 24-25.
3   Victor Shklovsky, *Voskreshenie slova*, Jurij Striedter and W.-E. Stempel (eds.), *Texte der russischen Formalisten* (Munich: Wilhelm Fink, 1972) 12, quoted in Steiner, *Russian Formalism* 49.

The reason for parenthesizing the word 'development' is because, it has been commonly argued, Formalists and Structuralists did not recognize development as, for them, literary history was static. When, for example, René Wellek (a member of the Prague Linguistic Circle since 1934) criticized the attempt to apply Hegelian dialectics and schematized evolutionary views to literature, he asked: "Does evolution in fact proceed always in the opposite direction? And what is the opposite? Is the lyric the opposite of the epic as Hegel assumed? Is accentual meter the opposite of syllabic? Is metonymy the opposite of metaphor?"[4] Drawing on Yury Tynyanov and Roman Jakobson's "Questions of the Study of Literature and Language," the Czech-American critic emphasized the significance of old forms, arguing that a work of art is not merely a reaction to its immediate past – it is not "simply a member in a series, a link in a chain" – but rather "it may stand in relation to anything in the past."[5] Like a mind, it may reach into its "own remote past or into the remotest past of humanity."[6]

Critics such as Terry Eagleton could therefore conclude that in the Formalist/Structuralist conception, "at any given point some forms and genres were 'dominant' while others were subordinate," and the history of literature consisted merely of "shifts within this hierarchical system, such that a previously dominant form became subordinate or vice versa [...]; nothing ever disappeared, it merely changed shape by altering its relations to other elements."[7] Moreover, if nothing disappeared, nothing was truly new – it merely functioned as an estranging novelty. So Roman Jakobson, when writing about contemporary Czech poetry, argued that the rhythmic tradition of the nineteenth century was invalidated by its being co-opted by the world of commerce, but that the rhythms of the Middle Ages still possessed a vital estranging impulse, worth regenerating.[8]

---

4   René Wellek, *Concepts of Criticism* (New Haven and London: Yale University Press, 1963) 49.
5   Wellek 51.
6   Wellek 51.
7   Terry Eagleton, *Literary Theory: An Introduction* (Minneapolis: University of Minnesota Press, 1998) 96.
8   Roman Jakobson, "Konec básnického umprumáctví a živnostnictví" (An End to Applied Poetry and Poetic Business Mentality, 1925), *Z korespondence* (Selected Letters), ed. and trans. Alena Morávková (Prague: Paseka, 1997) 84.

Even a seemingly "novel" form was not new and "the history of literature was [...] the history of the assembling, disassembling, and reassembling of devices (the same devices!)"[9] Both Jakobson and Tynyanov are adamant that "The hierarchy of works in a given age is decisive."[10]

Formalist/Structuralist theorists had their immediate as well as distant predecessors, some of whom they acknowledged. In his 1928 lecture at the Prague Linguistic Circle, as Steiner recalled, the Russian critic stated that it would be wrong to "assume that the new school rejected the entire heritage of Russian scholarship. If it sometimes opposed Veselovsky's and Potebnya's ideas, it did so merely to emphasize its own independent stance"; nevertheless "the new school is obligated to these two predecessors and [...] it borrowed many of its basic concepts from them."[11] And in the Czech context, Steiner also pointed out, the past was evoked in order to counter the argument that Prague Structuralism was a mere import from Russia. Jan Mukařovský, for example, when reflecting on the Prague School in the early 1940s, emphasized that the roots of structural aesthetics "can be found in the relatively distant past, especially in esthetics, then philosophy, and finally linguistics; up to now the most elaborated branch of semiotics. An important antecedent was provided by the Czech adherents of Herbartian esthetics, Josef Durdík, Otakar Hostinský and his pupil Otakar Zich."[12]

9   I.R. Titunik, "The Formal Method and the Sociological Method (M.M. Baxtin, P.N. Medvedev, V.N. Vološinov) in Russian Theory and Study of Literature," V.N. Vološinov, *Marxism and the Philosophy of Language* (1929), trans. L. Matejka and I.R. Titunik (Cambridge, MA: Harvard University Press, 1986) 184.

10   Roman Jakobson and Yury Tynyanov, "Voprosy izuchenia literatury i jazyka" (Questions of the Study of Literature and Language), *Novy Lef* 12 (1927): 26-37, quoted in Wellek 50.

11   Boris Tomaševskij, "Nová ruská škola v bádání literárně-historickém" (The New School of Literary History in Russia), *Časopis pro moderní filologii* 15 (1929): 12-13, quoted in Steiner, *Russian Formalism* 27.

12   Jan Mukařovský, "Strukturalismus v estetice a ve vědě o literatuře" ("Structuralism in Aesthetics and in Literary Studies"), *Kapitoly z české poetiky* (Chapters from Czech Poetics), 2nd ed. (Prague: Svoboda, 1948), trans. by Peter Steiner in his *The Prague School: Selected Writings, 1929-1946* (Austin: University of Texas Press, 1982) 78.

The Formalist/Structuralist conception of literary history therefore seems static; the past is a source of "novelty" and the question is which elements have an estranging function in the present. A new epoch is a mere redistribution of the same elements. What prompted this redistribution was a subject of debate, but particularly here, the Formalists and Structuralists formed their opinions in relations to other prominent schools of criticism such as the biographical and sociological: for them, a new economic system, for instance, would not generate new artistic forms; rather, a 'new' form would emerge primarily in reaction to other forms. Let us now turn to the oeuvre of Zdeněk Vančura and consider his views on literature and literary history in this context.

Vančura in the Prague Linguistic Circle

Vančura contributed to the Formalist/Structuralist debates in the 1930s and early 1940s with several articles devoted to Renaissance and Baroque prose. Having finished his studies of Czech, English and Romance languages and literatures at the Faculty of Arts at Charles University in Prague, he spent two years at various academic institutions in the United States, where he dedicated himself to the study of Anglo-American literature. Among other things, he attended Morris W. Croll's seminar at Princeton, which motivated him to explore the concept of the Baroque. The second impulse in Vančura's youth came from the Prague Linguistic Circle, of which he became a regular member. While working at the Business School of the Czech Technical University, Vančura established himself through his Structuralist discussions of literature, including "Theories of the Origin of Euphuism" ("Teorie o původu eufuismu," 1931), "An American 'Euphuist,' Nathaniel Ward" and "The Curt Style in English Seventeenth-Century Prose" ("Úsečný styl v anglické próze sedmnáctého století"), both from 1932, "Baroque Prose in America" (1933) and finally two texts from the 1940s, "The Beginning and the End of the Baroque" ("Počátek a konec baroku," 1943) and "On the Method of Renaissance Poetry" ("K metodě renesanční poezie," 1945).[13] None of

---

[13] Vančura published in both English and Czech. My article uses the English version of "An American 'Euphuist,' Nathaniel Ward" and "Baroque Prose in

these studies, with the exception of "The Beginning and the End of the Baroque," is explicitly devoted to the definition of literature and literary history, but each reveals an aspect of Vančura's conception, largely congruent with the views of the Formalists and Structuralists.

A recurrent concern in the early literary-historical studies by Vančura is, naturally, the focus on the form of a particular literary work, and the critic has here extended the project of humanistic philology with its emphasis on a rhetorical analysis of style. Under the influence of Structuralism, however, he contributed to the transformation of humanistic philology. His approach was functionalist; in his study of Euphuism, for example, Vančura showed how certain rhetorical figures changed their function when they were transported from Medieval Latin to modern languages. He also commented upon how selective Lyly was: "Lyly encountered his glistening sentences and examples wherever he could, but he chose only subjects and forms that he considered suitable for being transported home."[14]

In these early articles of Vančura, there is also a notable emphasis on the survival of old forms alongside 'new' ones; therefore historical periods, individual authors and texts appear as hybrids composed of the old and the 'new.' The aforementioned "Theories of the Origin of Euphuism," for example, begins by surveying a number of theories about the origins of Euphuism, the peculiar style of John Lyly's *Euphues* (1578) and *Euphues and his England* (1580); namely the efforts to locate Euphuism's roots in Italian literature (John Morley), in Spanish *estilo alto* (Friedrich Landman, Clarence G. Child), and in the rhetoric of Antiquity (Eduard Norden, Albert Feuillerat). Vančura finally accepted the theory of his Princeton tutor, Croll, who located the origins of Euphuism in Medieval Latin prose, considering Euphuism an old form that survived alongside humanism: for Croll, according to Vančura, humanism was "merely one of the many forms of cultural life. Alongside humanism,

America," and the Czech version of all the remaining articles. Most subsequent quotes from Vančura's work are therefore my translations (with the exception of the two aforementioned English originals).

14 Zdeněk Vančura, "Teorie o původu eufuismu" (Theories of the Origin of Euphuism, 1931), *Pohledy na anglickou a americkou literaturu* (Views of English and American Literature), ed. Zdeněk Stříbrný (Prague: Odeon, 1983) 14.

there existed other, older forms of knowledge and taste, which at times even began to flourish again due to rejuvenated interest."[15] Euphuism was just such a renovated old form; "the last flourishing of ancient stylistic tradition," one that survived in tension with the prominent 'new' Ciceronian stylistics of the sixteenth century.[16]

The same logic underlies "The Curt Style in English Seventeenth-Century Prose," another article from the early 1930s in which Vančura (again referring to Croll) differentiated between two competing Baroque styles: the epigrammatic "curt" and the sprawling "loose." Vančura observed that in the second half of the seventeenth century, the "curt" style was suppressed by the rambling "loose" type and as a consequence, Classicist writing of the eighteenth century was not directly descended from it but was instead, like Euphuism, a renovated older form.

The struggle between different styles, however, was not limited to these centuries and places only, a fact which Vančura demonstrated in his study of Baroque prose in America. In *The Simple Cobler of Aggawamm in America* (1647), by the Puritan clergyman Nathaniel Ward, Vančura identified traces of surviving Medieval Latin forms alongside the newly fashionable Baroque style (in its rambling "loose" as well as "curt" types); that is, while conforming to the novel Baroque pattern, Ward also followed "the unbroken tradition of Latin devotional prose."[17] Finally, in another article on Baroque prose in America, Vančura pointed out that half a century later, one of Ward's spiritual relatives, Cotton Mather, came to represent "the last development of English literary Baroque" due to his insistence on cultivating the Baroque style as late as the eighteenth century, when it was outdated even in America. At the same time, however, Mather used the newly dominant Classicist style in his non-religious texts.

Drawing on the above considerations, we may observe that in Vančura's view literary history was not a mere chain of events evolving towards a clear objective, but rather a system in which, recalling Wellek's and Eagleton's words, anything in the present could "stand in

---

[15] Vančura, "Teorie o původu eufuismu" 12.
[16] Vančura, "Teorie o původu eufuismu" 12.
[17] Zdeněk Vančura, "An American 'Euphuist,' Nathaniel Ward," *Charisteria: Gvilelmo Mathesio Qvinqvagenario* (Prague: Prague Linguistic Circle, 1932) 138.

relation to anything in the past,"[18] and in which change was a matter of "shifts within this hierarchical system, such that a previously dominant form became subordinate or vice versa [...]; nothing ever disappeared, it merely changed shape by altering its relations to other elements."[19] Historical epochs, authors and texts were hybrid composites of the old and the 'new' (the newly regenerated old, like Medieval Latin in Lyly). There was no consideration here of literary history as evolution and progress, as there was for example in the work of the aforementioned predecessor of the Formalists, Alexander Veselovsky (loved and hated in equal measure), whose conception of literary history drew on Herbert Spencer.[20]

Even if Vančura's early articles were consistent when describing the evolution of literary history, they were less conclusive about its motivation; that is, when the critic discussed what motivated the regrouping of elements from which a certain hybrid was composed. At times Vančura seems to see transformation occurring spontaneously, as in the opening paragraph of "Baroque Prose in America" where we learn that the term *barocco* "appeared [...] to denote something ridiculous, absurd, bizarre" and "in this way the age of sober classicism expressed its contempt for irregular design and excessive ornamentation."[21] Elsewhere in this article, the sentence subject is either the "age" (as in the above-cited sentence) or "prose" and "style," so implicitly, Vančura either did not consider any concrete agency or literary forms which changed by themselves, in reaction to other forms. As he explained:

> many theories have been put forward to explain what historical circumstances, what ways of action and reaction conditioned the character of the *Baroque epoch* and its style. Literary scholarship should not disregard parallel research in the departments of art and history, yet it should concentrate on forming its own methods,

18 Wellek, *Concepts of Criticism* 51.
19 Eagleton, *Literary Theory: An Introduction* 96.
20 Wellek, *Concepts of Criticism* 47.
21 Zdeněk Vančura, "Baroque Prose in America," *Příspěvky k dějinám řeči a literatury anglické od členů anglického semináře Karlovy university v Praze / Studies in English by Members of the English Seminar of the Charles University, Prague, Vol. 4* (Prague: Faculty of Arts, Charles University, 1933) 38.

for instance approaching the prose and poetry of that time with stylistic analysis.[22]

Finally, in another article, "On the Method of Renaissance Poetry," Vančura was equally dismissive of psychology and biography. In response to the debates surrounding the authorship of Shakespeare's works, he went as far as to argue that for his approach, it is of no importance who wrote the text since its critical analysis would not differ.

Yet, in addition to presenting literature as self-propelling and autonomous, Vančura considered the impact of the psychology of individual authors, and of politics and economy in other articles from this early period. In one of the aforementioned discussions of Baroque prose, Vančura admitted that some authors "according to their temper and their chosen models, strove after conciseness, some after ingenious subtlety; others sought somber gravity."[23] The same emphasis on individual inclination appears in Vančura's above-mentioned discussion of Cotton Mather, whose quaintness, we learn, "was intentional" and who it is claimed "belonged to a new generation of Americans who did not confine their interest to religious and moral questions only." Vančura is distinctly laudatory in his description of Mather's personality, asserting that: "He was possessed of an insatiable thirst for knowledge, prided himself upon being a scientist and sent communications to the Royal Society in London."[24] According to Vančura, Mather was therefore a part of his milieu, but it was his individual character – this "insatiable thirst for knowledge" and "pride" – that influenced his work.

The impact of institutional politics and economy on literature was most explicitly addressed in Vančura's first article on Euphuism. The Czech critic's model, Croll, asserted that "the occurrence of Euphuism was stimulated by the joy of employing worn-out Latin forms in a new medium, in the domestic language, where they had the beauty of novelty."[25] However, rather than agreeing with this view of literary development, Vančura concluded by drawing attention to the work of

[22] Vančura, "Baroque Prose in America" 39.
[23] Vančura, "Baroque Prose in America" 42.
[24] Vančura, "Baroque Prose in America" 54.
[25] Vančura, "Teorie o původu eufuismu" 13.

C.H. Conley, who observed that the first Tudor translations of the Classics were politically motivated (going as far as to call these translations "planned propaganda" of the Protestants). When the court turned away from the Classics towards Italian and Medieval literature, the stylistic taste changed, thus clearing space for Euphuism. Here, Vančura's literary history was not autonomous of politics and economy but instead was strongly conditioned by them.

To conclude, we may observe with Zdeněk Stříbrný that Vančura's early stylistic and periodization studies "provided the fundamentals for differentiating between Medieval, Renaissance and Baroque styles";[26] this enabled him to characterize historical epochs through their forms rather than their subject matter. Moreover, aware of the difficulty of establishing clear boundaries between historical periods, Vančura instead conceived of epochs, individual authors and even single texts as hybrid composites of various styles. Finally, 'new' form in Vančura's theory is in fact a rejuvenated old one. All these tenets were consistent with those sketched in my introductory characterization of Formalism and Structuralism. However, the Czech critic remained unclear when discussing the agency of literary history and he offered at least three possibilities: self-propelling development, individual psychology, and politics/economy. Although his digressions into extra-literary contexts were relatively marginal, he did not completely differ here from the critical schools that the Formalists and Structuralists opposed.

Interlude: After 1948

Wellek, who left Czechoslovakia in 1939, recalled in an interview with Peter Demetz his visit to Prague in 1957. In a private conversation, Vančura admitted to him that he envies his former colleague, Václav Černý, whom the authorities removed from his post at Charles University. The reason, Vančura explained, was that Černý

> doesn't have to lie, and I have to lie every day. There is a spy
> sitting in on my lectures and reporting on me, and it's not only

---

[26]   Zdeněk Stříbrný in Vančura, *Pohledy na anglickou a americkou literaturu* 336.

that I cannot attack the Marxist interpretation, but I have to interpret everything according to the official line or else get rebuked when I deviate in the slightest way. I find this double life terribly demoralizing, and it weighs on my conscience. Nothing else is that important; I don't mind poverty, little food, bad food, or other things which do not concern me, but this double life of lies is the worst.[27]

At that time, Vančura's career was on the rise. He returned to his Alma Mater; in the years 1950-1961 he was the Head of the Department of English and German and he served twice as the Dean of the Faculty; in 1962, he moved to the Czech Academy of Sciences, where he worked in several departments until his death in 1973. Leaving aside several translations, he published two historical surveys of early English and American literature (1951, 1953), a monograph on Walt Whitman (1955), two longer studies of G.B. Shaw (1956, 1958), and two histories: *The Pilgrim Fathers and the Beginnings of American Literature* (1965) and *Twenty Years of the English Novel: 1945-1964* (1968 in Russian, 1976 in Czech). Through numerous short essays, prefaces and afterwards, Vančura left few then-canonical authors untouched, especially from American Literature: he wrote about Poe, Hawthorne, Melville, James, Faulkner, Twain, Hemingway, Stevens, William Carlos Williams, and several times about Dreiser. All these texts emerged in the restrictive atmosphere that Vančura described to Demetz. Were they mere lies?

To answer this question, Vančura's writing must now be viewed through the optic of the Formalist/Structuralist conception of literary history as already discussed. We will observe the modifications of the critic's approach to literature, but we will also be attentive to continuities, ultimately considering it (and the post-1948 era in general) as a hybrid composed of previously existing elements that were regrouped: while some lost in their intensity, others gained in relative significance.

---

[27] Peter Demetz, "Second Conversation with René Wellek," *Cross Currents* 10 (1991): 236, online, accessed 15 October 2012.

Negations

As has been argued already, in the series of articles published from the 1930s and into the early 1940s, Vančura abided by the strictures of Formalism/Structuralism, characterizing epochs and literary works through their forms and devices. His digressions to the world outside of literature were noticeable, but they were relatively marginal and infrequent, and his concern with the author's life and psychology was minimal. As a result many works that the critic produced after the socio-political changes in the East of Europe appear as negations of these early studies.

A number of articles that Vančura published after 1948 manifest the dominant concern of Marxist literary criticism with content rather than form, and with the relationship of literature and the extra-literary world. Even if some Marxists consider literary forms to a certain degree autonomous, a more generally accepted conviction of Marxist literary critics derives from Fredric Jameson's dictum that "form is itself but the working out of content in the realm of the superstructure"[28] – which is a direct reversal of Kruchenykh's words: "Once there is a new form, a new content follows; form thus conditions content."[29] This expresses the generally accepted conviction of Marxist literary critics. Likewise, even if for some Marxists, literature (as any part of the superstructure) is not simply determined by the base, the relationship between the base and the superstructure is fundamental; in fact, "'reflectionism' has been a deep-seated tendency in Marxist criticism, as a way of combating formalist theories of literature which lock the literary work within its own sealed space, marooned from history."[30] Thus there is little consideration of what Wellek called "the separate enterprise of literary history."[31] Finally, for Marxists, history has an objective; its movements being generated by class struggle.

---

[28] Fredric Jameson, *Marxism and Form* (Princeton, NJ: Princeton University Press, 1971) 329.

[29] Jameson, *Marxism and Form* 329.

[30] Terry Eagleton, *Marxism and Literary Criticism* (Berkeley: University of California Press: 1976) 49.

[31] Wellek 7.

Vančura's *Walt Whitman: A Poet of Democracy*, which was published by The Czechoslovak Association for the Dissemination of Political and Scientific Knowledge in 1955, demonstrates most of these Marxist attitudes. The contrast between the critic's early work and his post-1948 studies is evident from the first pages, where the collection *Leaves of Grass* is introduced completely externally: we learn where the book was displayed as well as what the author's shirt, hat and beard looked like on the cover photograph. Further, there is no consideration of the autonomy of literature and literary history; instead, Whitman's poetry appears as produced by its author's social background, the era's politico-economic conditions and the progress of history: on page 56, for example, we read that "historical process enabled Whitman to speak."[32] Entire sections of the monograph are devoted to the struggle of the abolitionists in the nineteenth century and to party politics. Whitman's life and his personality are extensively described, but he is at the same time viewed as a representative who "never saw himself as an exception to be elevated above others, but rather merely as a person who felt, and thought through, more profoundly what could be common to all."[33]

When Whitman's poetry is discussed, it is largely its content, and even though the critic concerns himself with the form (to which I am going to return in the section on Vančura's continuities), the critic goes as far as to argue that the form itself is insignificant: "Whitman came to defend democratic ideas in a verbal form that was not indispensable for expressing this idea, and democratically-thinking poets did not necessarily need to accept it as their model."[34] In other words, here it is argued that the content of *Leaves of Grass* could have been expressed in

---

[32] The critic expressed this point again in his article on D.H. Lawrence's novelistic writing, where he argued that the impetus for the stylistic changes characteristic of Modernism was extra-literary: "the new, subjective manner typical of novelistic narratives related to the sudden and revolutionary changes, which objectively took place in the entire social sphere and which had to have their impact even in the world of art." Zdeněk Vančura, "Lawrencův autobiografický román" ("D.H. Lawrence's Autobiographical Novel," 1962), *Pohledy na anglickou a americkou literaturu* 174.

[33] Zdeněk Vančura, *Walt Whitman, básník demokracie* (Walt Whitman: A Poet of Democracy) (Prague: Orbis, 1955) 22.

[34] Vančura, *Walt Whitman* 64.

any other form (not merely in Whitman's idiosyncratic free verse); that the form itself was insignificant.

The contrast between Vančura's early articles and his post-1948 study of Whitman is also evident from the critic's style and his treatment of literary history. Again from the very outset, the prose is emotionally charged and there is an emphasis on conflict and progress: Whitman is repeatedly credited with "scandalizing" American society, in which democracy was an "inflammatory and subversive" word; the ideology of the ruling classes needed to be "defeated."[35] While before 1948, Vančura described the coexistence of different forms and styles in a particular epoch/text/author in a detached manner, here he emphasized struggle and, through the frequent use of superlatives and exclamation marks, he celebrated the victor: *Leaves of Grass* was eventually appreciated by "the whole world as the greatest poetic work from the American continent."[36] The entire text in fact traces the development of Whitman's poetics; his personal growth is analogical to the greater vision of historical progress that informs the monograph. Finally, another feature that is also evident in the above-cited sentence is the aspiration towards totality and wholeness; eventually Vančura praises Whitman's desire for a universal collective grounded in love, fraternity and equality.[37]

When we consider Vančura's oeuvre, *Walt Whitman: A Poet of Democracy* is a somewhat extreme example from the midst of the 'dark' 1950s; nevertheless, it illustrates the rupture between the critic's early Structuralist approach to literature and those post-1948 studies in which he abandoned the emphasis on style, focusing instead on the content of literary works and on the socio-political context that supposedly produced art. Literature no longer emerged in relation to literature. Finally, Vančura's static view of literary history was replaced with a (supposedly) dynamic one, which was fully subservient to dogmatic, Soviet-style Marxism. Rather than considering literary history as the history of "the assembling, disassembling, and reassembling of devices (the same devices!),"[38] he focused on the growth of Whitman on the background of a schematically evolving history.

---

35 Vančura, *Walt Whitman* 3.
36 Vančura, *Walt Whitman* 5.
37 Vančura, *Walt Whitman* 52.
38 Titunik 184.

Continuities

As initially claimed, Vančura's oeuvre may not be characterized merely by ruptures, this final section will discuss some continuities. They are of two kinds. Firstly, I will return to the pre-war period in order to draw a more comprehensive picture of the critic and of the Prague Linguistic Circle. Secondly, I will argue that the negations discussed in the previous section were not the only tendencies discernible in Vančura's post-1948 writing.

Considering the first type of continuity, we may argue that to insist on a complete partition of the Formalists and Structuralists from the rest of society would only serve to reproduce a myth. To a degree, we have relied on this myth in order to identify the 'movement,' but neither in life nor in thought were the Formalists and Structuralists enclosed in 'the ivory tower' of criticism. In the Czech case, Jan Mukařovský is often cited as an example of a critic who began to argue against the autonomy of literature and literary history, but Mukařovský, who eventually turned into a Marxist, may be an exception. At the same time, as for example F.W. Galan argued, the Prague School in general was more open to admitting the impact of extra-literary phenomena on literature (and we have seen traces of that already in Vančura's studies of Renaissance and Baroque prose) as well as to considerations of literary content.

Prague Structuralists also had an interest in literature's social function. Vančura wrote that "[t]he interest of Mathesius in social problems has stimulated several of his pupils to the theoretical study of socialism,"[39] and although it may be tempting to discard this statement as one of the fabrications the critic was forced to produce in the 1950s, there is a grain of truth in it. In the early 1920s, the would-be members of the Prague Linguistic Circle, for example, wrote a series of studies about H.G. Wells – and not always unfavourable ones. Otakar Vočadlo, to whom I return below, welcomed the first Czech translation of Wells's *A Modern Utopia* in 1922, noting that the Englishman's pragmatic, considered and efficient utopia may not gratify the "Slavic heart";

---

[39]   Zdeněk Vančura, "K naší literárně-vědné práci v moderní filologii za posledních deset let" (Regarding our Literary-Scientific Work in Modern Philology during the Past Ten Years), *Časopis pro moderní filologii* 37 (1955): 66.

nevertheless, at least Wells did not idealize a society "governed by chance, reckless functionaries and the iron fist of capital" nor by the "Slavic communism of the hungry."[40]

Vančura's first published article from 1928 (which partially drew on his MA thesis of 1925), discussed the philosophy of evolution in the works of H.G. Wells and G.B. Shaw. Even though the text is largely descriptive and non-judgmental, Vančura quite clearly disapproves of those aspects of Wells that demonstrate nihilism, religious dogmatism or intolerant and brutal Darwinian materialism. At the same time, he praises Wells's collectivist and humanitarian aspects: the moments when Wells did not exclude the "unfit" from his utopian designs; when he illustrated that "in the universal scheme of all things, even the smallest particle has its important function. Strength, weakness, virtues and errors are important and they complement one another";[41] when his objective was a harmonious collective synthesis achieved first on the level of culture through education (and only afterwards on the level of the economy).[42]

In the periods immediately before and after the war, apart from his Structuralist studies, and apart from a number of English textbooks and a factual history of Anglo-American countries (1947), Vančura published translations, including of such less-known authors as Rachel Field, Will Levington Comfort and Younghill Kang. In several brief essays and reviews, he approached literature in a similar way as he did after 1948 – that is, he addressed its content and function rather than merely the

---

40 Otakar Vočadlo, "Wellsova Moderní utopie" (*A Modern Utopia* by H.G. Wells), H.G. Wells, *Moderní utopie*, trans. Ludmila Vočadlová (Prague: Gustav Voleský, 1922) 7.

41 Zdeněk Vančura, "Filosofie vývoje u H.G. Wellse a G.B. Shawa" (The Philosophy of Evolution in the Work of H.G. Wells and G.B. Shaw), *Příspěvky k dějinám řeči a literatury anglické od členů anglického semináře Karlovy university v Praze / Studies in English by Members of the English Seminar of the Charles University, Prague, Vol. 3* (Prague: Faculty of Arts, Charles University, 1928) 6.

42 When Vančura returned to Wells after World War II, he praised similar values, although especially in the preface to the 1959 translation of *The History of Mr. Polly*, his style was different, more congruent with the official rhetoric. But he still admired Wells's collectivist ideals, his belief in knowledge and education, as well as his wariness of technology.

form, and he discussed literature as a part of, or even a product of, its environment. For example in his 1929 "American Survey," Vančura wrote: "Something new is happening in America. Until now, ruthless individualism of American civilization, along with the raw novelty of that continent, did not provide a fertile ground for art." Only now, the critic continued, are Americans becoming aware of their culture, which they piece together – like Carl Sandburg does his portrait of Lincoln – from "the spring in the prairie, from boastful folk humour, the turmoil of election meetings, and the details of everyday pioneer work; from faiths, prejudices and hopes of the age."[43]

To conclude, regarding the first form of continuities considered in Vančura's oeuvre, I would like to reproduce the words of Břetislav Hodek, who wrote on the occasion of Otakar Vočadlo's seventy-fifth birthday the following:

> It may look like a fantastic embellishment of *kádrový posudek* [an assessment of everyone's private and public activities made under the totalitarian regime by communist party officials], but it remains to be a fact that Associate Professor Vočadlo was for many years a member of The Workers' Educational Association and that every weekend, he lectured for free in various industrial towns, for example, to workers on strike in Coalville, textile workers in Bradford, industrial workers in Sheffield, unemployed dock labourers in Birkenhead at Liverpool, and elsewhere.[44]

Vočadlo, who in the 1940s lectured at Cambridge and who received an honorary degree from the university, was asked to leave The Faculty of Arts in 1950. With the status of a dissenter, his past social activities indeed began to look like a fantastic embellishment (and Hodek's own embellished account of the facts certainly contributed to it). But my point is that the Structuralists did not live enclosed in their circle. Of course they were critical of many practices in the Soviet Union and later in Eastern Europe as a whole, and they suffered from the dictatorial

---

[43] Zdeněk Vančura, "Angloamerický přehled" (Anglo-American Survey), *Rozpravy Aventina* 13-14 (1929): 162.
[44] Břetislav Hodek, "Univ. Prof. Dr. Vočadlo sedmdesátiletý" (The Seventy-Fifth Birthday of Prof. Otakar Vočadlo), *Časopis pro moderní filologii*, 52 (1970): 212.

measures that governed the system. But they were not indifferent to social injustice and they had their own, somewhat utopian, visions. Moreover, even in methodological terms, the Structuralists were not always exactly Structuralist. In the above-mentioned studies, neither Vočadlo nor Vančura extensively analysed the form of a literary work; instead, they discussed its content, its cultural and pedagogical value, and its position within the greater social whole (rather than within an autonomous literary space).

The second form of continuity in Vančura's oeuvre concerns Structuralism, which he never entirely abandoned. Even in his 1950s study of Whitman, where Vančura claimed that the democratic message of *Leaves of Grass* could have appeared in another form, his evidence pointed to the contrary. The critic argued that the profound complexity of feeling generated in Whitman the need to search for new forms of expression[45] and that he could have hardly achieved the desired objective "in rigid and regular verse."[46] In these passages of his monograph, Vančura went as far as to emphasize the role of the form in the construction of the meaning of Whitman's poems: "Already the concept of the 'catalogue' draws attention to the generic affinity of the listed items as well as to their individual differences."[47] Such observations contradict those that the critic presented elsewhere in the same text.

So, even though in his post-1948 writing, Vančura tended to treat literature in accordance with the dominant approach, he found an opportunity to discuss literary form and technique (e.g., in his studies of William Carlos Williams, John Dos Passos, Ernest Hemingway, Herman Melville and especially of Emily Brontë's *Wuthering Heights*). Much of his prose, moreover, maintained its past pensiveness and richness; it was picturesque and descriptive, rather than didactic and argumentative. And in thought, even in the articles that include tendentious formulations, Vančura's voice was consistently notable for its forgiveness, tolerance and the willingness to pay attention to, and to accept, a variety of human experiences and ideas. His entire life seems to

[45]   Vančura, *Walt Whitman* 34.
[46]   Vančura, *Walt Whitman* 65.
[47]   Vančura, *Walt Whitman* 65.

have been informed by the same ethical values that he held already at the age of twenty-five, when he praised the ability of H.G. Wells to value the importance of every detail "in the universal scheme of all things."

Conclusion

When Vančura published his Structuralist articles in the 1930s, he relied on a theory that could be applied to his own life and oeuvre. Like Cotton Mather, the critic became a hybrid composed of a number of approaches and styles. Besides a clear Formalist/Structuralist line of thought, Vančura maintained a lifelong interest in literature's content and its social function. Moreover, in addition to these two tendencies, another biographical approach becomes increasingly dominant. Neither Formalists nor Structuralists, and certainly not Marxists, were inclined to study a literary work in relation to its author's life and psychology. The former, as Victor Erlich put it, "were impervious to all theories locating the *differentia* in the poet rather than the poem, invoking a 'faculty of mind' conducive to poetic creation. The Formalist theoretician had little use for all the talk about 'intuition,' 'imagination,' 'genius,' and the like. The locus of the peculiarly literary was to be sought not in the author's or reader's psyche, but in the work itself."[48] Marxists did not significantly differ regarding this point; for them, literature was never "mysteriously inspired, or explicable simply in terms of the authors' psychology."[49] Contrary to this, Vančura paid attention to the writer's life and his/her psychology, and he interpreted literary works in relation to the personal, idiosyncratic struggles of the authors. Writing about *The Picture of Dorian Gray*, for example, Vančura described Wilde's internal torment and subsequently concluded that the "fear of the depths into which he [Wilde] had fallen is mirrored in this gracious but painfully restless text."[50] A similar tendency is evident in Vančura's 1971 article about Hemingway, in which the shortcomings of the American's late work are attributed to the writer's old-age and nostalgia. In this way, we could

---

[48] Victor Erlich, "Russian Formalism," *Journal of the History of Ideas* 34 (1973): 628.
[49] Eagleton, *Marxism and Literary Criticism* 6.
[50] Zdeněk Vančura, "Oscar Wilde – poslední romantik" (Oscar Wilde – The Last Romantic, 1958), *Pohledy na anglickou a americkou literaturu* 172.

perhaps conclude, Vančura compensated for the disregard for the human subject that both Formalism/Structuralism and Marxism exemplified during this era.

Finally, Vančura's life and work, which stretch over two distinct periods in terms of politics and economy, demonstrate that in the sphere of culture, there were not only ruptures, but also continuities. It has been argued that after 1948, Structuralism vanished in the East; Jakobson lamented that "the Prague Linguistic Circle had to declare and publish a series of repentances and to disavow its ties with Western scholarship and with its own past, to repudiate structuralism and to rally around the banner of dialectical materialism and Marr's doctrine."[51] Nevertheless, as Vančura himself pointed out, "The replacement of one ideology or sensibility with another one, their mixing or conflicts, tend to be a long-term process."[52] Moreover, we may add, that this process is incomplete. No era – totalitarianism included – has ever succeeded in becoming monolithic; there has always been variety and dissent, even if not clearly recognized as such. Literary history itself remains unsettled; as another member of the Prague Linguistic Circle, Felix Vodička, wrote: "even a literary period is a structure made rich by the dynamic tension of its components, so that a current conception is only one of many ways of concretizing it."[53]

[51] Roman Jakobson, "Notes on General Linguistics: Its Present State and Crucial Problems," mimeographed (New York, Rockefeller Foundation: 1949), quoted in Steiner, *The Prague School* 66.
[52] Zdeněk Vančura, "Shakespeare – čí současník?" (Shakespeare – Whose Contemporary?, 1966), *Pohledy na anglickou a americkou literaturu* 127.
[53] Felix Vodička, "Literárně historické studium ohlasu literárních děl: Problematika ohlasu Nerudova díla" (A Literary-Historical Study of the Reception of Literary Works: The Problem of the Reception of Neruda's Works), *Slovo a slovesnost* 7 (1941), quoted in Steiner, *The Prague School* 130.

JAROSLAV HORNÁT'S CRITICAL METHOD IN HIS STUDIES OF CHARLES DICKENS

Zdeněk Beran

Jan Mukařovský, a leading figure of Czech Structuralism and founding member of the Prague Linguistic Circle, defined one of the goals of Structuralist aesthetics to be examination of "the *aesthetic object*, i.e., the work of art conceived [...] as an external manifestation of non-material structure, i.e., of a dynamic equilibrium of forces, represented by [its] individual constituents."[1] This dynamic character of the artistic structure, continues Mukařovský, results from the fact that

> one group of its constituents always preserves the state which is given by the conventions of the most recent past while the other part transforms this state, which brings about a tension calling for balance, i.e., for new and further changes of the artistic structure. Although every work of art is a structure *per se*, the artistic structure is not limited to a single work but, like a continuum in

---

[1] "[E]stetický objekt, tj. umělecké dílo, pojaté [...] jako zevní projev nehmotné struktury, tj. dynamické rovnováhy sil, představovaných jednotlivými složkami." Jan Mukařovský, "Strukturální estetika" (Structural Aesthetics), an entry in *Ottův Slovník naučný nové doby* (The Otto Encyclopaedia of the Modern Age), Part VI, Vol. 1 (Prague: Jan Otto, 1940). Reprinted as the second part of "Strukturalismus v estetice a ve vědě o literatuře" (Structuralism in Aesthetics and Literary Criticism, 1941), *Kapitoly z dějin české poetiky* (Chapters from the History of Czech Poetics), 2nd ed. (Prague: Svoboda, 1948) 1:16-17. All translations from Czech are mine.

time, passes from work to work, ever modifying its own character; these modifications consist in an incessant reshaping of relations between and comparative significance of the constituents, among which those are of primary importance that are aesthetically foregrounded, i.e., that contradict the actual state of the artistic convention. The other group, which comprises of those constituents that submit to the convention, makes up a background where the foregrounding of the first group is reflected and made felt.[2]

This idea of the dynamic processes characterizing any work of art as a product of its specific context seems to be central to Mukařovský's conception of Structuralism, recurring in his early as well as later texts.[3]

It was Mukařovský's disciple and follower, Felix Vodička, who, in his study "Literární historie, její problémy a úkoly" (Literary History, Its Problems and Tasks, 1942) published soon after Mukařovský's succinct definitions in Otto's *Encyclopaedia*, attempted to elaborate this theoretical conception in more practical terms and to show what it would mean when applied to the analysis of poetry and fiction, especially from the perspective of literary history. For Vodička, the ultimate goal of a literary historian is to study the principles on which the constituent parts of a literary work are organized and the way this organization in texts reflects the basic tendencies of development (be it the development of an individual writer, of national literatures, or of movements such as Romanticism). Vodička's key term here is *aesthetic function*: to be able to

---

[2] "Dynamičnost umělecké struktury má původ v tom, že jedna část jejích složek zachovává po každé stav daný konvencemi nejbližší minulosti, kdežto druhá tento stav přetváří; tím vzniká napětí, vyžadující si vyrovnání, tj. nové, další změny umělecké struktury. Třebaže je každé umělecké dílo strukturou samo v sobě, není umělecká struktura záležitostí jen díla jediného, nýbrž trvá v čase, přecházejíc jeho postupem od díla k dílu a stále se přitom proměňujíc; proměny záleží v stálém přeskupování vzájemných vztahů a poměrné závažnosti jednotlivých složek; v popředí stojí vždy ty z nich, které jsou esteticky aktualizovány, tj. které jsou v rozporu s dosavadním stavem umělecké konvence; druhá skupina, skládající se z oněch složek, jež se dosavadní konvenci podřizují, tvoří pozadí, na kterém se aktualizace skupiny první odráží a je pociťována." Mukařovský, *Kapitoly* 17.

[3] See, e.g., Mukařovský, *Kapitoly* 30-31; Jan Mukařovský, *Studie z estetiky* (Studies in Aesthetics) (Prague: Odeon, 1966) 109-114; Jan Mukařovský, *Studie z poetiky* (Studies in Poetics) (Prague: Odeon, 1982) 788.

understand the character of a work of art we must analyse its constituent parts and also the processes which organized these parts so as to achieve the desired aesthetic function. Such an analysis, however, cannot be limited to a work of art in isolation; on the contrary, to be able to discover all the aesthetic properties of the given work of art, we must study it in its historical context and compare it with other works. Meaningful analysis is not possible without a constant consideration of what Vodička calls "literary tradition"; only in this way can we understand and view a literary work as a manifestation (or, in a broad sense of its unstable cultural role and meaning, *concretization*[4]) of the dynamically developing structure.[5]

It is clear then that Vodička accentuates what we may call the dual perspective of the Structuralist approach: a Structuralist critic sees a work of art both in its internal context (as a specifically organized entity) and in its external context (as an entity whose structure relates organically to structures of a higher order, i.e., to its organic, non-arbitrary contexts or tradition),[6] but at the same time regards these two aspects as inseparable. In this way he also predicts his own role in literary studies: to analyse the historical processes which produce specific works of art

4   A term Vodička borrowed from Roman Ingarden's *Das literarische Kunstwerk* (The Literary Work of Art, 1931). See Felix Vodička, *Struktura vývoje* (Structure of Development) (Prague: Odeon, 1969) 41.

5   See Vodička, *Struktura vývoje* 13-53, particularly 17-23.

6   In his monograph, Tomáš Kubíček explains the significance for Vodička of this broadly conceived context (*kontext vnější*) since "every phenomenon of any plane can convey a meaning of large consequence. To understand such a meaning, it is necessary to activate the context in which the given work originates and which it enters." What is vital, however, is the fact that, according to Kubíček, a critic can regard not just any context but always that one "which is attracted by the text's activity" ("každý jev z kterékoli roviny [se může stát] nositelem dalekosáhlého významu"; "[kontext,] který je přivoláván aktivitou textu"). Tomáš Kubíček, *Felix Vodička – názor a metoda. K dějinám českého strukturalismu* (Felix Vodička: A View and a Method. Towards the History of Czech Structuralism) (Prague: Academia, 2010) 121. These two contexts, the internal one (*kontext vnitřní*) and the external one (*kontext vnější*), can also be understood as microstructural and macro-structural contextualizations, though I have not come across these terms in the Structuralist writings outside purely linguistic studies.

and to decide how these works of art or dynamic structures define the historical periods that condition them.

Among the post-war generations of Prague scholars specializing in English Studies, Jaroslav Hornát (1929-1990) seems to carry on the legacy of Structuralism most effectively. A student of English and Czech at Charles University, Hornát attended lectures of both Jan Mukařovský and Felix Vodička. Although the time when he studied at Charles was highly unfavourable (if not openly hostile) to Structuralism – it was a period of "total chaos," to use the words of Robert Kalivoda[7] – Hornát's critical work clearly shows at least partial methodological dependence on the basic tenets of the Structuralist analytical approach. During the first post-war decade, but also in later years, several attempts were made to defend Structuralism as a method which is very close to, or even identical with, Marxist critical principles. Mukařovský himself tried to harmonize Structuralism with Marxism in his article "K pojmosloví československé teorie umění" (Towards the Terminology of Czechoslovak Theory of Art), written for the Polish journal *Myśl współczesna* (Contemporary Thought) in 1947, where he stresses the dialectical character of the structure and introduces the idea of "noetic materialism" (*noetický materialismus*), i.e., the objective existence of the structure independent of the perceptive subject. Much later, in a 1971 interview, he felt it again necessary to defend the dialectical character of the structure and thus of the Structuralist critical method.[8] Yet Structuralism was always looked down on by the most radical Marxist critics and it was not easy or even safe to present oneself as a proponent of Prague Structuralism during the communist era; this is perhaps why Hornát

---

[7] Robert Kalivoda, "Dialektika strukturalismu a dialektika estetiky" (The Dialectics of Structuralism and the Dialectics of Aesthetics), *Struktura a smysl literárního díla* (Structure and Meaning of the Literary Work of Art), eds. Milan Jankovič, Zdeněk Pešat and Felix Vodička (Prague: Československý spisovatel, 1966) 13.

[8] See Mukařovský, *Studie z poetiky* 788-89. Though he uses Marxist terminology, and even Marxist clichés, one cannot miss the irony with which Mukařovský comments upon the Hegelian and Marxist (revolutionary) dialectic thought, implicitly on its primitive form which was used to discredit Structuralism in the 1950s. Vodička disparaged these tendencies more fiercely in his introduction to *Struktura vývoje* 7-12.

never spoke of himself explicitly as a Structuralist although he admitted the influence of Structuralism on his critical method. So even if he tended, on the whole, to avoid the critical apparatus of the Prague Structuralist school, he introduced a modified terminology of his own which enabled him to pursue in his studies what others suggested in theory: to analyze literary texts from both Structuralist and Marxist points of view and to harmonize the two critical methods.[9]

The period of total chaos around Structuralism ended, according to Kalivoda, in 1958. It is not without interest that this is the year in which Vodička published his seminal book-length study *Cesty a cíle obrozenecké literatury* (The Ways and Objectives of the Literature of the Czech National Revival). Yet it is even more significant that ten years before, at the very dawn of the chaotic period, Vodička presented his first substantial monograph on early nineteenth-century Czech literature, *Počátky krásné prózy novočeské* (The Origins of Modern Czech Fiction, 1948), in which he applied the Structuralist method, as he defined it in "Literary History," to the large canvass of a distinct cultural period. That same year, Hornát began his studies at Charles University; which he graduated from in 1952 and where he defended his doctoral thesis a year later. We can thus say, though not without a pinch of salt, that Vodička's books symbolically mark the beginning of Hornát's own critical career. At the same time, it is necessary to stress that this career was dramatically affected by political developments in Czechoslovakia, especially following the Russian invasion of the country in the late 1960s. Up to this point Hornát worked as a researcher in the Czechoslovak

---

[9] In the article he wrote in the mid-1970s for Professor Ada B. Nisbet's ambitious but never published collection of critical essays mapping the reception of Charles Dickens worldwide, Hornát characterizes the method he uses in his introductions to the Czech edition of Dickens as "a sustained attempt to develop a Marxist critical view of Dickens's work." What he means by this is explained a few lines below where we learn that "Hornát seeks in his critical studies to combine the approach of *aesthetic and structural analysis* with that of constant regard for the social relevance of the novel discussed." Jaroslav Hornát and Ian Milner, "Dickens in Czechoslovakia," *Prague Studies in English* 19 (1991): 37 (my emphasis). I will try to prove that his first Dickens essay, accompanying *Nicholas Nickleby*, was also one of the first texts in which he made use of Mukařovský's and Vodička's critical approach at length.

Academy of Sciences and Humanities and taught at Charles University but from the early 1970s, due to his refusal to be loyal to the new political régime, he was only allowed to take a teaching position at the School of Dramatic Arts (DAMU) in Prague (an institution providing tertiary education for future actors, directors, etc.) and could only return to Charles in the very last years of his life, when he also habilitated as Associate Professor (docent). This all means that his 'official' academic output culminates with *Anglická renesanční próza* (English Renaissance Prose, 1970), a Czech-language monograph on Euphuism, which summed up his research output of the previous years.[10] Nevertheless, Hornát's critical work can by no means be reduced to his academic publications only, since the essays he wrote for various Czech editions of English and American authors usually retain the same high critical standard and this is something he continued to do, due to the favour of publishers, until his early death.[11] We can thus identify two basic areas of interest which found consistent attention in Hornát's writings: the work of Charles Dickens (and other modern classics such as Henry Fielding or Mark Twain) on the one hand, and Elizabethan prose and drama on the other. It will be a matter for the following pages to see how the legacy of the Prague school of Structuralism is discernible in Hornát's interpretations of Dickens.

As stated, one of the first texts to which Hornát applied his knowledge of the Structuralist approach in full was his essay accompanying the (as yet) singular Czech translation and edition of *Nicholas Nickleby* in 1957. This essay also marks the beginning of his Dickens criticism since it was at this point that he took over editorship of the prestigious series of the Collected Works of Charles Dickens, launched in 1952, for which he was to write insightful critical introductions from then on (eight essays altogether, some of them being extended and substantially revised versions of previous essays

---

10   For bibliographic details, see Zdeněk Beran, "Bibliography of Doc. PhDr. Jaroslav Hornát, CSc. (1929-1990)," *Litteraria Pragensia* 20.40 (2010): 134-45.

11   Late in 1989 he began to prepare material for his critical study on *Our Mutual Friend*, the last novel in the series of Dickens's *Collected Works*, and with undiminished enthusiasm worked out a proposal for a four-volume edition of R.L. Stevenson, for which he planned to translate *Treasure Island*.

accompanying different editions outside the series; the one volume he did not introduce was *Dombey and Son*, 1964). These essays are, at the same time, the most important and most consistent contributions of Czech post-war scholarship in terms of critical writing on Dickens.

It was, however, another former student of English at Charles, Josef Škvorecký, who very likely provided Hornát with inspiration as far as critical reading of Dickens is concerned. A year before the publication of *Nickleby*, his own essay introduced a tiny paperback edition of *The Chimes*, one of Dickens's Christmas Books. The circumstances under which Škvorecký's essay appeared may seem odd: the tale, translated by Jaroslav Albrecht, came out three times in a relatively short time span, in 1948, 1949 and 1956, each time with a different publisher, each time with a different critical text accompanying the translation. Popularity of the tale granted, the publishing policy under which this title was offered to the Czech reading public is still rather exceptional and can be understood only when the conditions of the period (chaotic not only with regard to Structuralism) are taken into account. For the first edition, published by the private firm of Vilém Šmidt, a short concluding note was written by the translator himself; the accent was put on biographic and aesthetic parallels between Dickens and his younger Czech contemporary, Jan Neruda, with an apparent effect of endearing Dickens yet further with Czech readers. The following edition was prepared by *Svoboda*, a publishing house owned directly by the Central Committee of the Communist Party and specializing mostly in political literature; this edition included an introduction written by Vladimír Smrž (who was to become the first editor of the Collected Works a few years later), in which Dickens was recommended as a sharp critic of social conditions in the capitalist world but the text of the tale was not discussed at all.

Škvorecký's essay was thus the first of the three which attempted to identify specific features of Dickens's method of writing, distinguishing it from that of his contemporaries. So while in the 1949 edition it was apparently not possible to retain the previous account underlining the unique atmosphere of Christmas (which all Christian peoples, including the Czechs and the English, share), its one-sided, ideologically biased portrayal of Dickens was no more tenable for the following, 1956 edition.

The text which replaced it was actually a step towards Hornát's own critical reading of Dickens.

"We used to emphasize and admire Dickens's acute view of the social reality of his times," writes Škvorecký. He elaborates, saying that

> Dickens's novels are tendentious works in the best sense, written to assist in ameliorating the conditions and intended directly to become the tools of reform. Yet in their times they are not exceptional as such. Their author was only one of many men of letters, even if one of the best and most influential, who since the end of the eighteenth century had lent their pen to the attempts at eliminating social injustice.[12]

What made Dickens so outstanding, Škvorecký asserts, was the way in which "the common ideas of political radicalism of the mid-nineteenth century make up an organic part of his art, how they are transformed into images, characters, figures and actions, and how, in the context of the work of art, their appeal grows due to this very fact."[13] The author is then at pains to show how intricately Dickens works with seemingly banal motifs, in particular with the motif of eating, which in his hands and imagination acquire an all-important function as a means of social commentary. Škvorecký's introduction to *The Chimes*, together with Hornát's earlier essays on Fielding and other modern classics, are texts by the young, post-war generation of English students clearly indicating that modern criticism cannot do without structural text analysis.

---

[12] "Zvykli jsme si zdůrazňovat a obdivovat Dickensův ostrý pohled na sociální skutečnost jeho doby... Dickensovy romány jsou díla v nejlepším slova smyslu tendenční, jsou psány s úmyslem napomáhat k zlepšení poměrů, jsou přímo zamýšleny jako nástroje reformy. Tím však nejsou ve své době ničím výjimečným. Jejich autor byl jen jedním, i když jedním z nejlepších a nejvlivnějších z celé řady literátů, kteří od konce osmnáctého století dávali svá pera do služeb snah po odstranění sociální nespravedlnosti." Josef Škvorecký, "Umělec Dickens" (Dickens the Artist), Charles Dickens, *Zvony novoroční* (The Chimes), trans. Jaroslav Albrecht (Prague: SNKLHU, 1956) 11.

[13] "[J]ak běžné myšlenky politického radikalismu poloviny devatenáctého století tvoří organickou součást jeho umění, jak jsou přetavovány v obrazy, charaktery, postavy a děje a tím nabývají v kontextu uměleckého díla zvýšené působivosti." Škvorecký 15.

Hornát's interpretation of *Nicholas Nickleby* has two thrusts: first, to show the principles on which the novel is constructed, and second, to identify its position in the context of Dickens's work and the history of the English Realistic novel in general. The two aspects are very closely connected: the novel's structure is determined by the fact that it combines the characteristic elements of the traditional novel of travel and adventure with those of a more modern form, the social novel of character. This combination results in two opposite tendencies concerning composition: while the first half of the novel manifests a divergent tendency to expand the main story-line by use of many digressions, the second half is based on a convergent principle, in which all motifs, no matter how disparate, work towards one single goal: a dénouement of the basic conflict. This particular structure stems directly from the initial contention between Nicholas and his uncle Ralph, which was ignited by their antagonistic natures: a feature that, according to Hornát, significantly distinguishes *Nicholas Nickleby* from Dickens's previous novel, *Oliver Twist*, where the traits of the protagonist's character do not determine the plot, whereas in *Nickleby* they do. The dual strategy in plot construction is then reflected in the dual thematic plane: the first, divergent, half is motivated socially; the second, convergent, half is motivated morally. Hornát concludes: "[T]he picture of objective reality, which inspires him, provides him with models for his characters and is also a basis of his social scenes imbued with critical and reforming tendencies, intersects or runs parallel with a subjective moral point of view, which makes an inseparable part of Dickens's understanding of the real world."[14]

Hornát's analysis of the construction techniques and thematic planes of the novel demonstrates how intrinsically these two factors are interconnected, mutually deterministic and conveying the meaning of the work in an inseparable unity. Even more importantly, it implies that

[14] "[O]braz objektivní skutečnosti, z níž vychází, z níž čerpá pro svou kresbu charakterů a na níž buduje i své sociální výjevy s kritickou a reformní tendencí, se kříží nebo se paralelně prostupuje se subjektivním hlediskem morálním, které Dickens nerozlučně spíná se svým viděním reálného světa." Jaroslav Hornát, "Mikuláš Nickleby" (Nicholas Nickleby), Charles Dickens, *Mikuláš Nickleby* (Nicholas Nickleby), trans. Emanuel Tilsch and Emanuela Tilschová (Prague: SNKLHU, 1957) 479.

the specific character of the organization of constituent parts stems from a broader, "external," context, i.e., from Dickens's effort to modify traditional forms of the novel and to find such a mode of expression which would suit his goals most appropriately. This complex view is in full accord with Vodička's theoretical imperative:

> We regard every work and every series of works as a unit aiming at a definite goal, which we learn by analysis of the relations between the components of the structure; so the individual components are used as means towards this goal, which is immanently present in the work. Hence the functional view, which enables us not only to recognize how the structure is organized at a particular moment (a single work), but also to explain functionally how the individual constituents move with respect to the tendencies of literary development.[15]

In its complexity, the *Nickleby* essay represents a new, more mature phase of Hornát's critical writings. This is very apparent especially when compared with his earlier study which is appended to the opening volume of Fielding's Works, *Tom Jones* (1954). Despite being another obvious attempt at a structural analysis, the appropriate passage focuses predominantly on the three types of contrasts which constitute the "thematic core" ("thematické jádro") of the novel, dealing thus with one particular constituent of the structure in its "internal context" and reducing all other aspects to passing remarks at the most. The "external context" is reflected only in brief comments on the difference between *Tom Jones* and *Joseph Andrews*. Moreover, this structural analysis[16] is strikingly distinct from what was perhaps intended as a Marxist critical method but which instead reads like a rather conventional social

---

[15] "Na každé dílo i na soubor děl se díváme jako na celek směřující k určitému cíli, jejž poznáme vnitřním rozborem vztahů složek struktury, takže jednotlivých složek v díle je užito jako prostředků k cíli, obsaženému imanentně v díle. Odtud funkční hledisko, jež umožňuje nejen poznat organizaci struktury v daném okamžiku (jednotlivé dílo), ale i funkčně vysvětlit pohyb jednotlivých složek vzhledem k vývojovým tendencím literárním." Vodička, *Struktura vývoje* 19-20.

[16] Jaroslav Hornát, "Fieldingovo dílo mistrovské" (Fielding's Masterpiece), Henry Fielding, *Tom Jones*, trans. František Marek (Prague: SNLHU, 1954) 470-74.

critique.[17] Whether Hornát was instructed to insert this concluding part by the publisher or not, the fact is that this early essay exemplifies how difficult it was for him to find a way in which to harmonize Structuralist and Marxist discourses convincingly. In this regard, Škvorecký's essay can be seen as a part of a tantalizing trail of breadcrumbs he later encountered.[18] Hornát's combination of Structuralist and Marxist critical methods, which he consistently applied in his Dickens criticism up to the late 1980s, modifies Vodička's ideas of literary analysis considerably. Vodička, for example, puts great stress on language analysis, following Mukařovský's concept as it was expressed in his study "O jazyce básnickém" (On the Language of Poetry, 1940). That Hornát avoids this in his essays for the Czech edition of Dickens is understandable: not only does he realize that such comments would hardly be justifiable in the books intended for a broad readership, especially in translated books, but is also aware of the fact that language and sound organization plays a much more important role in poetry than in Realistic fiction. Nevertheless, this does not seem to be the only reason: in his book-length study of Euphuism, *Anglická renesanční próza*, he dedicates some passages to language analysis, especially to the use of rhetorical figures and complex sentence construction (see, e.g., the chapter on "Pettie, a Euphuist before *Euphues*"[19]), but even here he is apparently more fascinated by the higher planes of analysis – in particular by those which Kubíček identifies as "the level of thematic planes" ("rovina tematických plánů"), consisting in "clusters of motifs or even larger wholes."[20] So if for Vodička these are just one part of a critic's concern, however significant, for Hornát they are central.

No other essay on Dickens documents this fact more patently than "Oliver Twist – svět chudoby a zločinu" (*Oliver Twist*: A World of Poverty and Crime, 1966). After a detailed examination of the social, political and

---

17 Hornát, "Fieldingovo dílo mistrovské" 474-78.
18 On the other hand, Hornát's essay written for the Czech translation of *Amelia* (1959) is the finest example of his structural analysis of Fielding's novels in its attempt to distinguish *Amelia* typologically from the author's previous work.
19 Jaroslav Hornát, *Anglická renesanční próza* (English Renaissance Prose) (Prague: Charles University, 1970) 19-27.
20 "[Z] motivických trsů a popřípadě i větších celků." Kubíček 99. Vodička uses the term "motivická řada" (a series of motifs).

literary causes which led Dickens to parallel in the novel two basic thematic fields, the world of a provincial workhouse and the metropolitan underworld of crime, Hornát sets out to demonstrate how rich the novel is in echoing various motifs that connect different situations and different "worlds" (including the world of Oliver's rich relatives). In this way he progresses from the "outer interrelatedness of the two fields (common atmosphere) to their deeper affinities, which could be called a 'paradoxical relation of missing contrast and a cause-effect relation.'"[21] Quite unusually, this passage abounds with examples.

What Hornát does here is in fact a modest, succinct variant of Vodička's detailed, one-hundred-page long analysis of Josef Linda's *Záře nad pohanstvem* (A Radiant Light over the Heathens, 1818), the first Czech historical novel of sorts.[22] Several strikingly similar points can be found between the two texts, Hornát's and Vodička's. For instance: while Vodička shows how Linda has discarded conventions of historical writings that were retained even in the novels of Sir Walter Scott, Hornát tries to explain how Dickens has transformed the traditional way of representing the criminal world in the novels of the eighteenth century. Where Vodička identifies two opposite contexts, the world of Paganism and the world of Christianity, Hornát speaks of the aforementioned two thematic areas ("tematické okruhy"). But most importantly, Vodička also lists a number of examples of dominant motifs which appear recurrently in the text of *Záře* and create an intricate web of central meanings, similar to the motivic echoes in *Oliver Twist*. Vodička's conclusion can almost apply to Hornát's analysis too: "Abandoning a *sujet* mode of motivation, [Linda] was not left with a work broken into solitary and isolated parts where any intrinsic semantic relation is suppressed, but by organizing dominant motifs or situations and their repetition, by framing

---

21 "[O]d vnější spojitosti obou okruhů (příbuzná atmosféra) k jejich hlubším souvislostem, jež bychom mohli nazvat paradoxním vztahem chybějícího kontrastu a vztahem příčiny a následku." Jaroslav Hornát, "Oliver Twist – svět chudoby a zločinu" (*Oliver Twist*: A World of Poverty and Crime), Charles Dickens, *Oliver Twist*, trans. Emanuel Tilsch and Emanuela Tilschová (Prague: Odeon, 1966) 470-71.

22 Felix Vodička, *Počátky krásné prózy novočeské* (The Origins of Modern Czech Fiction) (Prague: Melantrich, 1948) 157-258.

and arranging the theme he effectively managed to intensify and accentuate the semantic unity of the whole."[23]

This is not to say that Hornát was uncritical of Vodička; on the contrary, he was inspired by what he found productive in his own criticism, such as the thematic planes, and left aside what was not applicable for him, that is the lower planes of textual organization. In this way his interpretation of Dickens is based on two focuses: on the function of motifs and their distribution and mutual relations within a text, and on the principles of construction which arrange themes and motifs in a specific way. These two aspects are hard to separate in Hornát's essays, they often appear simultaneously as the cornerstones of his argumentation, yet they are distinguishable as distinct tendencies. We can notice that an emphasis on the first aspect prevails in his studies of *Oliver Twist*, *Bleak House* (1980) or *The Posthumous Papers of the Pickwick Club* (1983), while the second aspect dominates his essays introducing *Nicholas Nickleby*, *Great Expectations* (1972) and *Barnaby Rudge* (1986). It should also be noted that the essays written for *Hard Times* (1968) and *The Old Curiosity Shop* (1976) are the ones least affected by the Structuralist legacy.

What especially distinguishes the two tendencies is the attention paid to the external context or, in other words, to the fact that the structure is, according to Vodička, "a fictive, non-material whole consisting of all its literary constituents and manifested concretely in a specific arrangement in individual works."[24] This external context actually determines Dickens's decisions about how to construct his novels, an idea that exactly corresponds with Vodička's concept of evolution in literature ("the immanent causes of evolution").[25] In his last Dickens essay, "Dickensův první historický román" (Dickens's First Historical Novel)

---

23 "Neboť opuštěním sujetového způsobu motivace nerozpadlo se mu dílo v osamocené a isolované části s potlačenou vnitřní významovou souvislostí, ale organizováním výrazných motivů nebo situací, jejich opakováním, rámcováním a rozvrhem thematu dovedl významovou jednotu celku účinně posíliti a zdůrazniti." Vodička, *Počátky* 252.
24 "[P]omyslný, nehmotný celek daný souborem všech literárních složek a projevující se konkrétně v určitém uspořádání v jednotlivých dílech." Vodička, *Struktura vývoje* 18.
25 Vodička, *Struktura vývoje* 18-19.

Hornát very neatly compares Scott's *Heart of Midlothian* with *Barnaby Rudge* to prove how with this novel Dickens moved away from the picaresque tradition of the eighteenth century and how readily he embraced Scott as a new source of inspiration; but at the same time he in fact shows what use Dickens made of a concrete structure (as "a fictive, non-material whole") or, to use Vodička's terminology once more, how Dickens dealt with a tradition.[26]

A detailed analysis of one of the two above aspects, or of both of them, also secures for Hornát the possibility of formulating the meaning of the analysed work as accurately as possible. This fact implies that the meaning is encoded in the work itself, in its organization.[27] Believing in this tenet, Hornát actually disregards what the Prague Structuralists, and Vodička in particular, considered to be an important factor of the process in which the meaning is generated, namely concretization as critical response to the work in different periods. How this idea was applied in Structuralist criticism can be demonstrated in the studies of another member of the Prague Linguistic Circle, Zdeněk Vančura, who was Hornát's professor of English and American Literatures in the English Department. When Hornát commenced his work on Euphuism, he claimed dependence on Vančura's two earlier essays, "Teorie o původu eufuismu" (Theories of the Origin of Euphuism, 1931) and "Euphuism and Baroque Prose" (1932).[28] Nevertheless, Vančura's critical method is

---

[26] "With regard to literary tradition, which the poet knows, his effort or work is related to it in two possible ways: either he identifies with it, or, striving for a new, individual kind of work, he deviates from it." ("Vzhledem k literární tradici, kterou básník zná, má jeho úsilí nebo dílo dvojí možný vztah: buď se s ní ztotožní, nebo ve smyslu úsilí o novou, individuálně odstíněnou tvorbu se od ní odchýlí.") Vodička, *Struktura vývoje* 25.

[27] In his early essay "O současné poetice" (On Contemporary Poetics), Mukařovský called this organization "form," distinguishing it thus from "material," that is language. See Mukařovský, *Studie z poetiky* 24-25. Hornát does not use this term in relation to meaning.

[28] These essays are discussed in Pavla Veselá's chapter in the present volume. In a footnote to his study of Robert Greene's Euphuistic stories, Hornát expresses his gratitude as follows: "It should be mentioned here by way of an introductory note at least that it was Prof. Zdeněk Vančura – to whom this paper is dedicated – who first put 'euphuistic' studies on a scientific basis in Czechoslovakia. [...] I also wish here to acknowledge my indebtedness to Prof.

very different from Hornát's because in both his texts he presents recent interpretations of Euphuism (by German scholars mostly) and only after refuting their validity he arrives at his own definition of Euphuism as a style using different rhetorical means than Baroque prose. For Vančura, meaning originates from a dialogue with other attempts to establish this meaning – a strategy Hornát scarcely, if ever, uses.[29] For him, other critics' views are useful mostly to support his own ideas and only exceptionally to play the role of contrastive material.

The Marxist critical approach is reflected in Hornát's essays when he analyzes the social and economic conditions in which Dickens's novels were written. These contexts are important for the Structuralists too but Hornát's emphasis is stronger, his sources including, among others, Dickens studies by Marxist critics such as Arnold Kettle or V.V. Ivasheva. But where he somewhat departs from both the Structuralists and Marxists is in his belief in purely personal causes playing a significant role in the rise of a work of art. This is patent especially in his treatment of Dickens's later novels such as *Bleak House* and may be a sign of Hornát's own genuine humanism, which did not allow him to neglect the sphere of private feelings and experience. While for Vodička the poet first of all "knows the tradition," for Hornát it was indisputable that Dickens also projected ideals of his own emotional life into his fiction (for instance the character of Esther Summerson is interpreted as a tribute to Georgina Hogarth, his wife's sister and "good soul" of their common household). Vodička's tendency to suppress such personal concerns in the process of literary creation is very clearly reflected in his discussion of Jungmann's translation of Chateaubriand's *Atala*, where he expands on the reasons why Jungmann, who liked Voltaire most of all French Enlightenment writers, decided to translate a work so different from

Vančura, who actually aroused my interest in this sphere of literary research." Jaroslav Hornát, "Two Euphuistic Stories of Robert Greene: *The Carde of Fancie* and *Pandosto*," *Philologica Pragensia* 6 (1963): 21.

[29] It would indeed be interesting to see his reading of such special kinds of concretization as, e.g., František Langer's dramatic adaptation of *The Pickwick Papers* (1930). For my comments on Langer's method, which united the disparate parts of Dickens's first, loosely constructed novel, see Zdeněk Beran, "Monumental Presence: More About Czech Reception of Charles Dickens," *Prague Studies in English* 25 (2010): 17-19.

those of Voltaire. Vodička asserts that Jungmann wanted to introduce into Czech literature a work that would illustrate his theory of poetic language and therefore he preferred an author who was not so dear to his heart; his personal predilections simply giving way to a programme.[30] This is how Hornát sees the Dickens of the late 1830s and early 1840s; in later works he more and more allows privacy to rule his intentions. For Hornát, a work of art is not just a child of its time but a child of its progenitor, the author who can under certain conditions be independent of his own times. Modifications such as this one attest to the fact that Hornát not only followed a certain critical tradition but at the same time did not hesitate to extend the scope of its potential.

Taking the above as granted, Hornát's critical forte is showcased in the manner in which he capitalized on the legacy of Prague Structuralism, in particular in his emphasis on analyzing the relationship between the *fabula* and the *sujet* (or in Hornát's more complex terms, *plán dějový* and *plán naddějový*) concepts adopted by the Structuralists from the Russian school of Formalism. The attention Hornát paid to the way in which meanings can be arrived by way of attempting to understand the organization of motifs, something that he often described as "contrasting parallelism" – has remained to this day one of the most inspirational moments in Czech critical methodology.

---

[30] Vodička, *Počátky* 53-54.

2. CONTEXTS AND OUTCOMES: FROM PRAGUE STRUCTURALISM TO RADICAL PHILOLOGY

STRUCTURALISM AND THE PRAGUE LINGUISTIC CIRCLE REVISITED

Robert J.C. Young

No one nowadays seems to have a good word to say about Structuralism: it was, apparently, ahistorical, masculinizing, objectivizing, totalizing and universalizing. Given the summary dismissals prevalent today, one is tempted to ask, how was everyone at the time so duped by its limitations and now so self-evident ideological parameters? At the same time, it remains the case that contemporary theory has been in many ways its historical product, at the very least as a result of the critiques of Structuralism if not of Structuralism itself. In that context, the objection sometimes made against postcolonial theory about its reliance on, or contamination by, European theory, or rather non-Marxist European theory of the kind usually described under the sobriquets Structuralism and Post-structuralism, has always, I have felt, required a re-examination of its relation to them. This in turn requires some rethinking of what such theory involved and what it was seeking to achieve in its own time. Although influential in Western Europe and North America since the 1960s, Structuralism and Post-structuralism were both intellectual movements which genealogically and geographically came from outside Western Europe and which were, in their inception, formulated as anti-Western strategies. They were also taken up outside Europe as anti-ethnocentric discourses just as international Modernism was adopted by writers and artists in the earlier part of the twentieth century as offering an escape from imperial ideologies.

Structuralism

Structuralism came from the East, Post-structuralism from the South: the two collided in Paris in the 1960s.[1] With respect to the latter, many French intellectuals, some of them labelled Structuralists or Post-structuralists or both, either came from Algeria or experienced the war in Algeria directly in one form or another: Louis Althusser, Pierre Bourdieu, Jacques Derrida, Frantz Fanon, Abdelkadir Khatibi, Jean-François Lyotard, Albert Memmi, Jean-Paul Sartre, were all either in or of Algeria in some way. But if Post-structuralism could even be described as Franco-Maghrebian theory as I have suggested,[2] what of Structuralism – a body of thought that seems on the face of it to be as high and as abstract a European theory as they come? But theory always has a history too, produced by particular people as a particular strategy for particular circumstances. Structuralism was developed in the 1920s by some of those associated with the Prague school not only as a literary methodology relating to grammar, phonology and stylistics (as in the work of Vilém Mathesius and Jan Mukařovský) but also as a broader cultural project in a self-conscious anti-Western strategy, directed against the hierarchical imperialist cultural and racialist assumptions of European thought. To that degree it can be affiliated, I want to suggest, to the huge body of anti-colonial thought that was developed round the world during the first half of the twentieth century and which now forms the basis of Post-colonial Studies, as well as to the broad anti-imperialist thrust of international Modernism that was adopted in Japan and elsewhere. Valentin Mudimbe, to take just one example, opens *The Invention of Africa* with a testimony to the significance of Claude Lévi-Strauss's Structuralism for enabling post-colonial African thought to begin to free

---

[1] For an outstanding account of Structuralism's Eastern origins see Patrick Sériot, *Structure et totalité. Les origines intellectuelles du Structuralisme en Europe centrale et orientale* (Paris: Presses Universitaires de France, 1999). See also Françoise Gadet and Patrick Sériot (eds.), *Jakobson entre l'Est et l'Ouest, 1915-1939. Un épisode de l'histoire de la culture eureopéene* (Lausanne: Université de Lausanne, 1997).

[2] Robert J.C. Young, *Postcolonialism: An Historical Introduction* (Oxford: Blackwell, 2001) 414.

itself from colonial representations of Africa.[3] It was not a coincidence that Mudimbe found Lévi-Strauss's Structuralism so enabling. It was for comparable theoretical and ideological reasons that Structuralism was seized upon by radical French intellectuals such as Lévi-Strauss, Roland Barthes and Louis Althusser – not forgetting the Bulgarian émigrés, Tzvetan Todorov and Julia Kristeva – who were disenchanted with, and trying to challenge, the universalist assumptions of French culture in the wake of the violence and mass slaughter that preceded the defeats of the French in Indochina and Algeria in the 1950s and 1960s.

The historical significance of Structuralism as a cultural theory was that it was the first anti-ethnocentric general theory to put all cultures, high/low, west/cast/south, on a level playing field, arranged synchronically through a differential non-hierarchical structure. Instead of the conventional historical anthropological view of languages, races, cultures and economies, in which some were regarded as more advanced or developed than others, Structuralism placed them all beside each other as equal but different players in the world system. Structuralism was inherently egalitarian, and cheerfully unconcerned with the aesthetic criteria of value, taste, discrimination that have always been deployed in the West to shore up claims of superiority, whether of class, culture or race. Without even thinking about it, post-colonial theory assumes its radical central presupposition, namely that all cultures should be treated in a homologous way, and that the criteria for evaluation should focus on issues such as form, representation and representativeness, rather than aesthetic evaluations driven by the partiality of individual taste. This shift of criteria away from Western aesthetic value has enabled post-colonial literary analysis to develop as a mode of cultural studies that has now affected almost every discipline in the humanities and social sciences, from Medieval Iberian Studies to Theology, and therefore to move out of, and in doing so challenge, the traditional norms of the Western literary milieu.

---

[3]   Valentin Y. Mudimbe, *The Invention of Africa: Gnosis, Philosophy, and the Order of Knowledge* (London: James Currey, 1988) 19-36.

Structuralism and Phonology

In the history of European imperialism and the growing material and intellectual resistance to it, the Bolshevik's seizure of power in 1917 represented a pivotal historical turning point. In its own way, the Russian Revolution itself had emerged from a context of anti-imperialist resistance, particularly to the Russification programme of the authoritarian, centralized imperial administration of Alexander III from the 1880s onwards.[4] One of the most significant results of the Russian revolution internationally was that for the first time in modern history a major state was anti-imperialist, and this dramatically changed the dynamics of global politics. Structuralism emerged at the historical moment when Marxism's political triumph was at its height. The politics of Structuralism, I want to argue, were in certain ways developed in sympathy with the Comintern's, and the revolutionary Bolshevik government's, policies with regard to nationalistic self-determination and anti-colonialism. In some respects, Structuralism proved more radical than Soviet Marxism, at least with respect to its critique of Eurocentrism.

In the context of Lenin's revolutionary anti-imperialism, his hostility to the cultural, linguistic and political chauvinism of the powerful imperial nations, and of the extraordinary complexity of the minoritarian, cultural, linguistic and ethnic diversity within the USSR which the Bolsheviks struggled to conceptualize and realize in an adequate political form,[5] I want to consider the work of two Russian émigrés associated with, though never central to the Prague School, whose ideas developed to some extent in sympathy with the ideas of the Soviet revolution. The first of these was a Russian diplomat, who was sent to Prague in 1920 as part of the Soviet diplomatic mission. The second

---

[4]   Hugh Seton-Watson, *The Russian Empire 1801-1917* (Oxford: Clarendon Press, 1967).

[5]   Broadly speaking, their policy involved allowing a degree of national or local autonomy, officially recognizing 150 languages for example, at the same time as establishing Russian as a "first among equals" across the whole state. See Michael G. Smith, *Language and Power in the Creation of the USSR, 1917-1953* (Berlin: Mouton de Gruyter, 1998) 4.

was a Russian prince, who went into exile and always preserved a loyalty to autocratic forms of government. However, his friendship and close intellectual collaboration with the Russian diplomat suggests that his politics were by no means simplistically to the right. The names of these two men were Roman Jakobson and Nikolai Troubetzkoy.

Jakobson and Troubetzkoy together are often considered responsible for formulating the method, and perhaps even inventing the name, of Structuralism. Among the founders of the Prague Circle, despite the emphasis on collectivity, Vilém Mathesius is more correctly credited with inventing the functional method, while Bohumil Trnka is associated with the formation of Structuralism in terms of structural linguistics.[6] It was, however, through Jakobson, and through him Troubetzkoy, that Structuralism was developed in Europe and North America. In this context it is significant that Jakobson and Troubetzkoy came as outsiders to the Prague Circle, with a rather different political agenda. The conceptual basis of Structuralism was created by Jakobson and Troubetzkoy in part as a form of émigré culture, underpinned by a form of Russian nationalism. Although they are best known today as linguists, both had much wider interests and developed a synthesis of cultural, political and social thinking: Troubetzkoy like many linguists of his time was also an ethnologist and anthropologist, folklorist and dialectologist. As an ethnologist, he participated in the contemporary movement critical of evolutionism in anthropology and ethnology, associated particularly with the Americans Alfred Louis Kroeber and Franz Boas, and in the Soviet Union with Borisovich Aptekar.[7] Like Boas, Troubetzkoy took his anti-ethnocentric views across into linguistics.[8] Jakobson, though known

6   Rostislav Kocourek, "On Trnka on Linguistics and Signs," *The Prague School and Theories of Structure*, eds. Martin Procházka, Markéta Malá and Pavlína Šaldová (Göttingen: V+R UniPress, 2010) 63.

7   The Marrist Valerian Borisovich Aptekar argued that "it was created by priests, missionaries, merchants, slave-owners and travellers who founded colonies." Quoted in Ronald Grigor Suny and Michael D. Kennedy, *Intellectuals and the Articulation of the Nation* (Ann Arbor: University of Michigan Press, 1999) 249.

8   Jindřich Toman, "Troubetskoy Before Troubetskoy," *Papers in the History of Linguistics*, eds. Hans Aarsleff, Louis G. Kelly and Hans-Joseph Niederche

in the West today primarily as a linguist, also wrote on comparative mythology as well as Czech cultural nationalism. The two men first met in Moscow in 1914 but developed their significant work, the creation of Structuralism in linguistics, after the Russian Revolution as members of the Prague Linguistic Circle, which had been founded by Mathesius in 1926.

Arriving in Prague in 1920 as a Soviet Diplomat, Jakobson was widely assumed to be a Soviet spy;[9] in 1939 he fled the country, pursued by the Nazis, and after travelling through Denmark, Norway and then, smuggled in a coffin, to Sweden, he arrived in New York, where he was pursued by the CIA on suspicion of being a communist and threatened with deportation (he was saved by the intervention of Boas). As a result, and especially during the McCarthy period, Jakobson was careful to downplay his political past. His influence was enormous; he created a living, strategic connection between the avant-garde Russian Formalists of the beginning of the century, the development of structural linguistics in the Prague Circle, and the French/American Structuralism of the 1960s and 70s. While in Moscow, Troubetzkoy was never an enthusiast for Formalism or the avant-garde, nor even primarily for linguistics,[10] and this signals a difference between the two men that would continue to be played out in their work.[11] When the October Revolution occurred, Troubetzkoy was in the South; as an aristocrat, and with a father who was reviled by Lenin, he had little option but to migrate with the White army, wandering in the Caucasus and arriving in Baku in March 1918 at the time of the Muslim rebellion against Soviet power. After further peregrinations he ended up teaching at the university in Sofia, Bulgaria, where he remained for two years before moving to Vienna. Despite not being based in Prague, Troubetzkoy became the acknowledged

(Amsterdam: John Benjamins,1987) 630; Roman Jakobson, *Selected Writings*, 8 vols. (The Hague: Mouton de Gruyter, 1962-1986) 2:483.

9   Jindřich Toman, *Letters and Other Materials from the Moscow and Prague Linguistic Circles, 1912-1945* (Ann Arbor: Michigan Slavic Publications, 1994) 41.

10 Toman, *Letters and Other Materials* 31-32.

11 For an extended discussion of their similarities and differences, see Boris Gasparov, "The Ideological Principles of Prague School Phonology," *Language, Poetry and Poetics. The Generation of the 1890s: Jakobson, Trubetzkoy, Majakovskij*, eds. Krystyna Pomorska, Elżbieta Chodakowska, Hugh McLean and Brent Vine (Berlin: Mouton de Gruyter, 1987) 49-78.

intellectualforce behind the Prague school, which centred much of its work on the principles of phonology. When the Nazis arrived in Vienna in March 1938, Troubetzkoy was in hospital. Largely as a result of his public statements against racism and anti-Semitism which Troubetzkoy objected to on the grounds of their determinism and, he argued, illogicality,[12] the Nazis seized his papers and interrogated him as soon as he was allowed out of hospital. He died shortly afterwards on June 25, 1938, aged 48.[13] Troubetzkoy's famous *Principles of Phonology* was published posthumously in 1939.[14]

From the time of the International Congress of Linguists in the Hague in 1928, the intellectual centre of the Prague circle focussed around Troubetzkoy's newly invented sub-discipline of phonology concerned with the universal systematic organization of speech sounds. Phonology provided common structural concepts and came to serve as a model not only for other aspects of linguistics, but also for other disciplines. The basic principle of homology, which eventually allowed Structuralism to be translated into almost every other discipline in the humanities and social sciences, was actively developed from the first. The concept of structure that the Circle employed was predicated on the idea of language as a system, a systematic whole. This was not in itself an original perception (earlier examples can be found in linguistics, philosophy and sociology). What differentiated the Prague school approach, however, was their concept of how the system was internally organized. Although they followed Saussure in seeing the different elements in the system as possessing a differential, formal rather than material and substantial identity, they were critical of his assumption that difference in itself produced meaning outside any specific structural

[12] N.S. Troubetzkoy, *The Legacy of Genghis Khan and Other Essays on Russia's Identity*, ed. Anatoly Liberman (Ann Arbor: Michigan Slavic Publications, 1991) 277-87. Further references are given in parentheses in the text.

[13] Despite working feverishly on the project in his final months, Troubetzkoy died before *The Principles of Phonology* had been completed. On Troubetzkoy's hostility to anti-Semitism, see Gasparov, "The Ideological Principles" 60-62.

[14] N.S. Troubetzkoy, *Principes de phonologie* (Grundzüge der Phonologie, 1939), trans. J. Cantineau (Paris: Klincksieck, 1949). The original was posthumously published in Prague.

relation. The key, as Karcevskij among others realized,[15] was not so much difference in itself, for disjunction in itself does not produce meaning or identity: it needs to be positioned in a specific relation with another significant element, as Saussure himself latterly acknowledged by moving from an emphasis on difference to opposites, though the nature of these oppositions remained unformulated. In "Die phonologischen Systeme" Troubetzkoy argued that there can be no differential identity in general, only significant marked differences.[16] Troubetzkoy had first formulated his concept of the logic of oppositions, what the American linguist Edward Sapir referred as "the difference between,"[17] in a letter to Jakobson of July 1930. Jakobson responded (on 26 November 1930):

> Your idea that correlation is always a relationship between a marked and an unmarked series is one of your most brilliant and productive thoughts. I think that it will be of importance not only for linguistics, but also for ethnology and the history of culture, and that historico-cultural correlations such as life-death, freedom-lack of freedom, sin-virtue, festive days-workdays, etc., always reduce to relationships of the type *a/non-a*, and that it is important to establish for each epoch, group, nation, etc., what precisely constitutes the marked series.[18]

It was thus Jakobson who saw the logical corollary of Saussure's theory of difference, refined by Troubetzkoy, as a way of characterizing identities outside language, and developed the idea into a systematic basis for Structuralism. Toman comments: "Whereas Troubetzkoy's remarks were restricted to a linguistic discussion, Jakobson's reply is almost shocking in the way it demonstrates his unrestrained readiness to

---

15 Jindřich Toman, *The Magic of a Common Language: Jakobson, Mathesius, Trubetzkoy, and the Prague Linguistic Circle* (Cambridge, MA: MIT Press, 1995) 146-47.

16 N.S. Troubetzkoy, "Die phonologischen Systeme," *Travaux du Cercle Linguistique de Prague* 4 (1931): 96-116; Françoise Gadet, "La genèse du concept de marque (1926-1931)," *Cahiers de l'ILSL* 5 (1994): 81-92.

17 Edward Sapir, letter to Troubetzkoy dated 18 March 1930; see Toman, *Letters and Other Materials* 141.

18 Roman Jakobson, *N.S. Trubetzkoy's Letters and Notes* (The Hague: Mouton, 1975) 163; quoted in Toman, *The Magic of a Common Language* 149.

transpose linguistic notions to a general level, to raise linguistic methodology to a general mode of research."[19] Note that while Jakobson sees culture as operating according to the terms of marked series, he regards this as fluid and subject to challenge and change. If Jakobson was able to envisage how Troubetzkoy's concepts could be extended elsewhere, the Prague Circle was itself already characterized by its ability to utilize models and insights from other disciplines, by its emphasis on an activist, committed scholarship in which each detailed insight was potentially of use in the analysis of another field, and by its opposition across a range of to what was seen not merely as an outmoded form of thinking but one devalued by its implicit political ideology.

Eurasia

What is less well known outside Slavic academic circles is the degree to which Jakobson's and Troubetzkoy's development of the structural method for linguistics was advanced alongside a political and cultural programme that was based on a critique of the ethnocentric culture of Europe, the product of a revolutionary Russia trying to disengage itself from Western cultural assimilation and colonization.[20] The corollary of the critique of European culture was the espousal of a new kind of Russian nationalism, centring its identity in Eurasia. The Eurasian movement, of which Troubetzkoy was the acknowledged leader in the 1920s, was predicated on the argument that Russia was a discrete, autonomous region, geographically situated between Europe and Asia, incorporating distinct but inter-related ethnic groups, culturally closer to the Asiatic cultures of the steppes than to Europe. The word "Eurasia" was used to describe this region, a geographical term used in English since the late 1860s for the great central plain spreading between Europe and Asia.[21] As a compound word itself, Eurasia involves hybridity

---

[19] Toman, *The Magic of a Common Language* 150.
[20] Gasparov remains the most substantial treatment of the links "that existed between the theoretical researches of the two linguists [...] and the ideological, psychological and social processes at work in the world around them." Gasparov, "The Ideological Principles" 50.
[21] Somewhat confusingly, in English the term Eurasian had been invented in India in the 1840s by the Marquess of Hastings to describe people of mixed

at every level. The movement was formally initiated with the publication in Sofia in 1921 of a collective volume entitled *Exodus to the East. Forebodings and Events. An Affirmation of the Eurasians*, which heralds the decline of the West and the imminent rise of the East to replace it as the centre of world civilization.[22] This book has recently been republished in English, a marker of the revival of interest in the Eurasians, or in neo-Eurasianism, in post-Soviet Russia today.[23]*Exodus to the East* opens with an announcement by the geographer P.N. Savitskii that "[p]recisely because Russia is not merely 'the West' but also 'the East,' not only 'Europe' but also 'Asia,' and even not Europe at all, but 'Eurasia' – precisely because of that, there is added in the case of the Russian Revolution [...] a certain different essence which has not yet revealed itself on a full scale [...]."[24] According to Troubetzkoy, here following Savitskii, "Eurasia represents an integral whole, both geographically and anthropologically," an autarky first made into a single state by Genghis Khan and embodied in the institution of the Russian Orthodox Church. Its geographical scope also more or less corresponded to the much reduced boundaries of Russia after the Brest-Litovsk treaty and the declarations of independence by the regional states in 1917-18. Importantly, its language was "Turanian" (the prototype of which was

Indian and European descent, though they are generally now referred to as Anglo-Indian. On Russian Eurasia, see Marlène Laruelle, *L'idéologie eurasiste russe, ou comment penser l'empire* (Paris: L'Harmattan, 1999).

[22] Petr Savitskii, Petr Suvchinskii, Nikolai Trubetskoi and Georgii Glorovskii, *Exodus to the East. Forebodings and Events. An Affirmation of the Eurasians*, trans. Ilya Vinkovetsky (Idyllwild, CA: Charles Schlacks, 1996).

[23] In recent years, Eurasianism has found a new life with the founding of the Eurasia Movement as a right-wing Russian political party in 2001. The leading figure, Aleksandr Dugin, has proposed a Turkic-Slavic alliance, and has criticized President Vladimir Putin for the loss of the Ukraine. However, in October 2011, the then Russian Prime Minister Putin himself called for a "Eurasian Union" of former Soviet republics. Cf. the following news item: http://www.bbc.co.uk/news/world-europe-15172519, accessed 6 January 2013. For contemporary Eurasianism in Russia, see Laruelle, *L'idéologie eurasiste russe*; Dmitry Shlapentokh (ed.), *Russia Between East and West: Scholarly Debates on Eurasianism* (Leiden and Boston: Brill, 2007) and Dmitry Shlapentokh, *Global Russia: Eurasianism, Putin and the New Right* (London: Tauris, 2013).

[24] Savitskii et al. 6.

Turkic) rather than Indo-European.[25] Eurasian people were made up of an eclectic "cultural conglomerate" of genetically unrelated different ethnic groups – Eastern Slavs, Finns, Turks, Mongols, Caucasian and Paleo-Asiatic peoples, all of whom had converged through centuries of sharing the same geographical zone.[26] These people and their culture were very different from those of Western Europe. The mistake of Peter the Great, the Russian Imperial Government and eventually even the Bolsheviks, according to Troubetzkoy, had been to try to Europeanize Russia, and to force the non-European peoples indigenous to the rest of the Russian empire to submit to a process of "Russification." In this Troubetzkoy was later followed by Iurii Lotman, one of the founders of structural poetics in the 1960s, who in an influential essay written with P.D. Uspenskii, "Binary Models in the Dynamics of Russian Culture," argued that it was Peter the Great who had introduced a fundamental dichotomy, or ambivalence, into the basis of Russian culture between Europhiles and Slavophiles that was to endure to his own time.[27] For Troubetzkoy, Eurasianism offered a way of reconceptualizing the whole basis of a divided Russian culture as a hybrid mixed, but at the same time through the historical effects of geographical proximity an organically coherent society, while at the same time allowing him to reject its chauvinist imperialist tendencies.

While Troubetzkoy was concerned to define Eurasia as a discrete, autonomous nation with its own individual culture, after he arrived in Prague Jakobson began to develop similar historical ideas about the newly restored Czech nation. In his comprehensive history of the Prague Linguistic Circle, *The Magic of a Common Language,* Jindřich Toman writes:

[25] The national Russian cultural "type," according to Troubetzkoy, who all the same did not fully subscribe to the nineteenth century notion of a national psychology, was neither Turanian nor Slavic but their organic fused product: "which is in essence not pure Slavic but 'Slavo-Turanian'" – or Eurasian. Shlapentokh, *Russia Between East and West* 39.

[26] Gasparov, "The Ideological Principles" 53.

[27] Iurii Lotman and Boris A. Uspenskii, "Binary Models in the Dynamics of Russian Culture (to the End of the Eighteenth Century)," *The Semiotics of Russian Cultural History: Essays by Iurii M. Lotman, Lidiia Ia. Ginsburg, Boris A. Uspenskii Translated from the Russian,* eds. Alexander D. Nakhimovsky, and Alice Stone Nakhimovsky (Ithaca, NY: Cornell University Press, 1985) 30-66.

Jakobson emerges in his Czech historiography as an author of an emancipatory narrative designed to remind the West that it, the West, is not the center of the World, neither in the present days, nor in the past. In this sense, Jakobson is akin to his colleague and friend N.S. Troubetzkoy, who expounded a similar idea very explicitly in his Eurasian writings.[28]

This work continued after Jakobson left Czechoslovakia: in 1943 in New York he published *The Wisdom of the Ancient Czechs* which asserted the continuity of the Cyrillo-Methodian (i.e., Slavic) legacy. In this work, which remains uncollected and untranslated in English, he claimed that the decision to choose a Slavic liturgy comprehensible to all church participants amounted to an early example of democratic national self-determination. More than that, by its example, it represented the first assertion of the doctrine of human and cultural equality:

Right at the dawn of history, a principle was spelled out, in a simple manner and once and for all, of the equality of all languages, all nations, and all members of a nation – an egalitarian principle, an earthshaking slogan of equality, and a revolutionary Czechoslovak innovation. This happened in the 860s, nine centuries before the French Declaration of Human Rights.[29]

Jakobson reaffirmed this argument in 1945 when he wrote that "Equal rights – both of nations and of languages – is the leading principle of the Great Moravian spiritual heritage."[30] This spiritual heritage was itself a hybrid, a composite of Czechoslovak innovation and the Byzantine East (just as elsewhere Jakobson would describe the Prague Circle as a symbiosis of Russian and Czech linguistics).[31] Czechoslovakia functions as a bridge between East and West, itself belonging to neither:

[28] Just as in Troubetzkoy's case, Jakobson's discourse is activist historiography, something entirely compatible with the ideas of scholarship of the period under consideration. Jindřich Toman, "Jakobson and Bohemia / Bohemia and the East," Gadet and Sériot (eds.), *Jakobson entre l'Est et l'Ouest* 237.

[29] Quoted in Toman, "Jakobson and Bohemia" 240.

[30] Roman Jakobson, "The Beginnings of National Self-Determination in Europe," *Selected Writings* 6:119.

[31] Jakobson, *Selected Writings* 2:544.

The very location of the core of the Czech (and Russian) states provides an imperative prerequisite of the familiar slogan – Neither West, nor East. The entire history of the Czech and Russian states is determined by an oscillation between two poles – surges towards the West constantly repeat, as do the counterreaction.[32]

In making such assertions, Jakobson was drawing on the ideas of the Czech logician, sociologist and first President Tomáš Garrigue Masaryk, together with Foreign Minister Eduard Beneš, that drove the foreign-policy of the pre-war Czechoslovak state, which looked towards its Slavic neighbours to the East (including Russia) as a defence against German expansionism. Although in many ways close to the ideas of its main proponents, Jakobson differs from them in that he avoids any genetic definition of Slavdom, characteristically renouncing any legacy of consanguinity through culture, common anthropological or ethnological characteristics, apart from linguistic community. For Jakobson, the Slavic community was based on determinate choice rather than race; its form we might say was synchronic rather than diachronic, associative rather than genetic.[33]

---

[32] Quoted in Toman, "Jakobson and Bohemia" 244.

[33] In Jakobson, Toman observes, the "slavic commonalty was dehistoricized"; it represents "a community based on a choice, on a decision to act together – eine *Entscheidungsgemeinschaft*," that is a decision/determination-community as opposed to a *Blutegemeinschaft*, a blood or racial community ("Jakobson and Bohemia" 243). Here Jakobson comes close to Otto Bauer's notion of a nation as bound together by a common destiny, as well as to Troubetzkoy's ideas about Eurasia, which, with a mixed ethnic basis, is also ultimately an *Entscheidungsgemeinschaft*. The difference is that for Troubetzkoy in the last resort its coherence is one of spiritual essence, and it is this that separates him from the materialism of the Bolsheviks and which made Eurasianism so popular in Russian émigré and resistance cultures. See René Fülöp-Miller, *The Mind and Face of Bolshevism: An Examination of Cultural Life in Soviet Russia*, trans. F.S. Flint and D.F. Tait (London, G.P. Putnam's Sons, 1927) 262-64. For a recent and more penetrating reflection of political and aesthetic aspects of Eurasianism in relation to Marxism and Formalism see Galin Tihanov, "Seeking a 'Third Way' for Soviet Aesthetics: Eurasianism, Marxism, Formalism," *The Bakhtin Circle: In the Master's Absence*, eds. Craig Brandist, David Shepherd and Galin Tihanov (Manchester: Manchester University Press, 2004) 44-69.

Although Troubetzkoy was hostile to the imperial policy of Russification, indeed any attempt by one culture to dominate another, he was not at all hostile to the idea of cultural mixture – indeed Eurasia itself is defined as the product of a mixture. He was rather opposed to any attempt to force a mixture by means of dominant power through an artificial policy of assimilation rather than to allow a "national tradition of fraternization" that "happened naturally, without force or oppression." (165; 206-207) Troubetzkoy thus sets up the possibility of two forms of mixture, one "natural" and organic, constituting "the essence of Russia-Eurasia" (207), the basis of Russia's unique national identity, the other artificial, and based on Russia's imperial power relation and the coercion of a stronger nation upon indigenous peoples. The latter he regards as secondary and inferior, remaining an unassimilated mixture, to the former which creates a new totality. This formulation is remarkably similar to Mikhail Bakhtin's later distinction between the two forms of what he calls "organic" and "intentional" hybridity.[34] Troubetzkoy's distinction, together with his criticisms of Russian imperial chauvinism and ethnocentrism, suggests that like Bakhtin he continued to work within the intellectual context of revolutionary ideas developing in Russia, despite his reservations about the regime. Though he was no pan-Slavist, Troubetzkoy took over many of pan-Slavism's anti-Western ideas, together with an ambivalence about European culture fundamental to Russian intellectuals such in the nineteenth century.[35]

Although it would become identified with the general perspective of the Eurasians, Troubetzkoy's critique of Western culture was first made in the remarkable pamphlet, *Europe and Mankind*, published soon after his arrival in Sofia in 1920. Troubetzkoy begins his essay with a persuasive

---

[34] M.M. Bakhtin, *The Dialogic Imagination: Four Essays*, trans. Caryl Emerson and Michael Holquist (Austin: University of Texas Press, 1981) 358-59.

[35] In this context, Riasanovsky has suggested that a major influence on Troubetzkoy was also the philosopher Vladimir Solovyov: around the time of the First World War, an eschatological Scythianism allowed assimilation of Solovyov's ideas while reversing the perspective of his anti-Asian "pan-Mongolism." Nicholas V. Riasanovsky, "Prince N.S. Trubetskoy's *Europe and Mankind*," *Jahrbücher für Geschichte Osteuropas, Neue Folge* 12.2 (1964): 217-20. Nicholas V. Riasanovsky, "The Emergence of Eurasianism," *California Slavic Studies* 4 (1967): 57. Cf. Gasparov, "The Ideological Principles" 54.

attack on the theory of assimilation that lay behind the programme of Russification – a Russian colonial project which he identifies with the ideology of European imperialism. Using the systematic logic that would become so central to the creation of structural linguistics, Troubetzkoy demonstrates why the doctrine of assimilation, according to which one nation is expected to assimilate the culture of another, is impossible. The argument against the doctrine of assimilation was not in itself a radical position – indeed, as in the case of Léopold de Saussure, Saussure's brother, it could be the mark of a right-wing racialism, of the wish to preserve distinction between unequal cultures.[36] What distinguishes Troubetzkoy's analysis, however, and demonstrates the consistency of his anti-racialism, is that he relies on the power of logical argument rather than racial and linguistic biology and psychology as in the case of de Saussure. He argues that even in a situation where nation A borrows the entire cultural products of nation B, the remainders of its existing common stock of cultural assets, living on in the national memory, will mean that its new traditions will be altogether different from those of nation B. Even if nations A and B merge "anthropologically" through cross-breeding, the cultural tradition produced will be different from that of B alone. Assimilation will then also necessarily operate through the differing cultural experiences of successive generations:

> While they are receiving the traditions of the new, borrowed culture [...] the younger generation also retains the traditions of their former national culture, which are passed on by the family and reinforced by its authority for a long time. They quite naturally combine both traditions and create a mixture of concepts drawn from the two distinct cultures. This mixture is created in every individual consciousness. [...]
>
> [...] when the younger generation ceases to be the receiver of culture and becomes its transmitter, it will give the next generation not the unadulterated tradition of nation B's culture, but a tradition that mixes the cultures of A and B. (41)

[36] John E. Joseph, "The Colonial Linguistics of Léopold de Saussure," *History of Linguistics 1966: Selected Papers from the Seventh International Conference on the History of the Language Sciences*, ed. David Cram, Andrew Linn, and Elke Nowak (Amsterdam: John Benjamins, 1999). Robert J.C. Young, "Race and Language in the Two Saussures," *Philosophies of Race and Ethnicity*, ed. Peter Osborne and Stella Sandford (London: Continuum Books, 2002) 63-78, 183-85.

While the entire culture of nation A will become an amalgam of those of nations A and B, that of nation B will remain homogeneous. It follows therefore that two will never share the same culture; the doctrine of assimilation produces not identity but a new composite culture in the receiving nation: as with any colonized nation, it may mimic the culture of the colonizer, but it will never be the same. In this unique analysis of the logic of the processes of inter-systemic cultural mixture and assimilation, Troubetzkoy does not consider overtly the question of the power relation between the two nations, or factor in the category of resistance, although this is presupposed in the immediate context of the attack on Russification, on the ways in which European powers relate to indigenous peoples elsewhere, his rejection of the West and his outspoken support for the emancipation of colonized peoples.

The Critique of Eurocentrism

Beyond its analysis of the processes of cultural hybridity, a primary interest of *Europe and Mankind* comes in its early critique of Eurocentrism. The whole argument is predicated on a radical critique of European culture from the point of view of the world outside Europe – where Troubetzkoy positions himself – and involves a thoroughgoing attack on the then current assumption that "progress" consists of the forced acquisition, through imperialism, of European modernity by other cultures around the world. Although the book declares grandly that "[b]y its very nature Eurasia is historically destined to comprise a single state entity" (165), Troubetzkoy's opposition to European culture was not simply a matter of Russian nationalism, as it had been for the earlier pan-Slavists or Eurasianists such as Savitskii, although he followed them to the extent that the main targets of his critique were those whom he called the "Romano-Germans," the mentality of whose cultural world he characterized as narrow-minded, positivist, historicist and imperialist. His remarkable essay constitutes not only an early critique of Eurocentrism and its relation to European imperialism, but also a powerful argument for cultural relativism and the equal value of non-Western cultures. He attacks the ethnocentric assumption that European culture is the most advanced and civilized, a presumption that was then also frequently adopted by the "cosmopolitan" ruling upper classes of non-European nations, including the comprador classes of imperial colonies. Rather than relying on a moral argument which presupposes the prior agreement of the reader, a form of preaching to the converted that is common in more recent critiques of Eurocentrism, Troubetzkoy deploys the same kind of logic that was to sustain the development of a systematic Structuralism, in order to demolish the idea of a cultural hierarchy, with Europeans (whom he characterises as "Romano-Germans") at the top, and "primitive" cultures at the bottom. For hierarchical difference, Troubetzkoy substitutes a more equitable synchronic relation: "There is neither higher nor lower. There is only [the] similar and dissimilar."[37] He objects that the very concept of the primitive simply "joins the most diverse of the world's peoples together on the basis of a single characteristic, namely, the extreme cultural differences that separate them from contemporary Romano-Germans," concluding:

> There are and can be no objective proofs of the superiority of Europeans over 'savages,' because in comparing various cultures to one another, Europeans know only one criterion: what resembles us is better and more perfect than anything that does not resemble us. But if Europeans are not more advanced than 'savages,' then the evolutionary scale or ladder [...] collapses. If its top rung is no higher than the base, then it is obviously no higher than the other rungs between the top and the bottom. Rather than a ladder, we obtain a horizontal plane; rather than the principle of arranging peoples and cultures according to degrees of perfection, we obtain a new principle of the equal worth and qualitative incommensurability of the cultures and peoples on this earth. (28, 34)

The Structuralist comparison of the value of different cultures is always at the same time marked by what Jean-François Lyotard would later call the *différend*, their "qualitative incommensurability" or their untranslatability.[38] European knowledge, Troubetzkoy contends, in a move that anticipates that of Edward W. Said, is deeply marked by its own ethnocentric prejudices and assumptions. To date, he argues, disciplines

---

37 Quoted in Toman, "Troubetskoy Before Troubetskoy" 631.
38 Jean-François Lyotard, *Le différend* (Paris: Éditions de Minuit, 1983).

such as ethnology, anthropology and cultural history "are at best a means to deceive people and to justify in the eyes of Romano-Germans and their henchmen the imperialistic, colonial policies and the vandal-like cultural "mission" of the Great Powers, Europe, and America." (35) Or to put it the other way round: there is an internal contradiction between the lifeblood of the European powers, "moved only by militarism, imperialism, and capitalist exploitation," and "the hypocritical profession of entirely different ideals such as humanism and civilization that is still considered 'good taste' there." (211)

Troubetzkoy always held to this anti-imperialist perspective, which remains consistent throughout his work. As a result he found himself in many ways sympathetic to the Bolshevik world view even if at another level his own politics were very different. In his preface to the Russian translation of H.G. Wells's *Russia in the Shadows* (1920), he wrote approvingly that Bolshevism's "sharp point is directed primarily at the smug Europeans who regard the whole of non-European mankind as a mere ethnographic mass, as slaves fit only for supplying Europe with raw materials and buying European goods." (315) Although Troubetzkoy's critique of imperialism was predominantly one based on relations of power and cultural dominance (bourgeois nationalism), he shows here that this relation is predicated on its fundamental economic structure of capitalist exploitation. At the same time, he argues perceptively that the First World War has produced a decline in the prestige of the imperial nations and that liberation for the colonies is now in prospect.

> Everywhere, despised 'natives' are slowly raising their heads and beginning to criticize their masters. [...] Efforts to achieve liberation from the Romano-Germanic yoke are evident in many colonies now; and if these efforts sometimes find expression in senseless, easily suppressed armed uprisings, there are others that show signs of being very serious national movements. In the misty distance, vistas of the imminent liberation of oppressed humanity from the Romano-Germanic predators seem to be unfolding. (108)

In this vision of a world soon to be decolonized, Troubetzkoy is therefore quite happy with the Soviet Union's new historical role under the Third

International "as the leader in the liberation of the colonial world from the Romano-Germanic yoke." (108) Like Lenin, Troubetzkoy looked East to Asia for the revolutionary future. He recognized, however, that the success of the Revolution in the East was inextricably bound up with a nationalist agenda; communist arguments against western capitalism being "perceived as a nationalist attack upon Europeans and their lackeys." (108) Rather like Zinoviev, who described the colonized countries as the "proletariat nations," Troubetzkoy suggests that in the colonies the word "bourgeois" meant European, and by implication the proletariat the natives. Many Asians, according to Troubetzkoy, "now associate the Bolsheviks and Russian with the idea of national liberation and with protest against the Romano-Germans and European civilization. This is the view of Russia found in Turkey, Persia, Afghanistan, India, and to some extent in China and other East Asian countries." Russia's new historical role, therefore, he argues, is to lead "her Asiatic sisters in their common struggle against the Romano-Germans and European civilization" (109), a role that the Soviet Union did in fact begin to play in a certain way under the Comintern.[39] Troubetzkoy himself, therefore, though hostile to the Bolsheviks in terms of communist materialism, and although always signing his letters as a prince and in many respects politically conservative, was equally hostile to the westernized imperialism of the Tsarist Russian government, and therefore fully approved of the Bolshevik's policy of world revolution on the grounds of its support for national liberation: "for the first time," he remarked, "Russia recognizes herself to be the natural ally of the countries of Asia in their struggle against the imperialism of the countries of European [...] civilization." (214) The man who, with Jakobson, is commonly credited with laying the basis for Structuralism was, therefore, aggressively committed both to colonial emancipation and to a complete restructuring of the ethnocentric cultural hierarchy that operated at the foundation of western imperial civilization in the disciplinary formation of its knowledges. Only the hierarchies of gender appear to have escaped his critique and this would also emerge as one of the problems of Structuralist analysis.

[39] See Young, *Postcolonialism* 115-57.

The Prague School and the Development of Structuralism

Like any intellectual movement characterized with an "-ism," Structuralism eventually came to mean a diversity of different things, particularly as it was developed in France, where, largely because of its own analogical potential with regard to very diverse kinds of material, it was developed in a creative way in disciplines as different as literature, psychoanalysis, film, popular culture to say nothing of the remorseless theoretical analyses of Althusser. However, the contemporary assumption that theories with names ending in "-ism" involve a single coherent intellectual movement derives in part from Structuralism itself in its original form as developed by the Prague Linguistic Circle. The group initially published a Manifesto, and anyone who belonged to the group was required to sign his or her agreement to its Statues and thus to subscribe to the purpose of the Circle, namely "to work on the basis of the functional-structural method towards progress in linguistic research."[40] Any member who showed signs of being opposed to this purpose was liable to expulsion.[41] It was, as Jakobson wrote, "*a militant and disciplined organisation*" clearly inspired by the revolutionary avant-garde party of the Bolsheviks.[42] This similarity was not coincidental. In Prague, Toman comments, Jakobson "initially considered himself an intellectual emissary of Soviet revolutionary culture and did not keep this attitude secret." Jakobson was loyal to Mayakovsky and "to the culture the poet represented." In 1969, in an address in Prague he confirmed his commitment: "[Fifty years ago,] the Revolution – then genuine and pure – brought me as its diplomatic representative and faithful fighter to this marvellous country."[43] The anti-individualist ideal of collective work of the Prague School was deliberately opposed to the late nineteenth-century positivistic philosophy of European imperial capitalism with its self-rationale of linear progress and espousal of individualism in all spheres. The Prague Circle's activist, anti-individualism was mirrored in the organizing synchronic idea of Structuralism, based on the idea of looking at individual phenomena from the non-hierarchical perspective of the

---

40   Toman, *The Magic of a Common Language* 155.
41   Jakobson, *Selected Writings* 2:541.
42   Quoted in Toman, *The Magic of a Common Language* 156.
43   Toman, *Letters and Other Materials* 41.

system in which they formed a part, rather than the conventional western point of view of looking at the system from the point of view of the individual or the literary or philosophical imagination.

The Prague Circle thus developed in an activist spirit a number of shared 'dissident' themes into a syncretic goal-oriented theory that opposed contemporary orthodoxies in academic linguistic scholarship, and a set of ideas that were subsequently developed by Troubetzkoy and others into the conceptual basis of Structuralism: synchrony as opposed to diachrony, anti-psychologism, linguistic activism, concepts of language contact and convergence, homology, principles of phonology, all founded on a revision of the Saussurian concept of oppositional structure based on differential identity, importantly modulated by Troubetzkoy according to the principle of marking or significant differences. Although to some degree they seem to have been symbiotic, Troubetzkoy utilized these formal ideas developed for his analysis of the laws of the phoneme for the analysis of his cultural ideas, but he never made his cultural analysis systematic in the same way as his linguistic work on the phoneme that would provide the model for other forms of structural linguistics. It was of course the anthropologist Claude Lévi-Strauss who, having met Jakobson in New York, would remediate, or retranslate, Troubetzkoy's linguistic methodology into the cultural sphere in 1945, arguing that:

> In one programmatic statement ["La Phonologie actuelle," 1933], N. Troubetzkoy, the illustrious founder of structural linguistics, reduced the structural method to four basic operations. First, structural linguistics shifts from the study of *conscious* linguistic phenomena to study of their *unconscious* infrastructure; second, it does not treat *terms* as independent entities, taking instead as its basis of analysis the *relations* between terms; third, it introduces the concept of *system* [...] finally, structural linguistics aims at discovering *general laws*, either by induction 'or [...] by logical deduction, which would give them an absolute character.' [...] The problem can therefore be formulated as follows: Although they belong to *another order of reality*, kinship phenomena are *of the same type* as linguistic phenomena. Can the anthropologist, using a method analogous *in form* (if not in content) to the method used in structural linguistics, achieve the same kind of progress in his own science as that which has taken place in linguistics?[44]

[44] Claude Lévi-Strauss, *Structural Anthropology*, trans. Claire Jacobson and Brooke Grundfest Schoepf (London, Allen Lane, 1968) 33-34.

The history of Structuralism since that initial transference in 1945 is well known, and the radical cultural effects of its theoretical trajectory, the many subsequent critiques and developments, have been well documented. Few of those critiques, however, have taken into account its original political impulses and conceptual moves. What we might observe here is that Structuralism, by taking among its foundational principles synchrony and the principle of homology, the assumption that all languages and therefore cultural phenomena could be compared equally to each other, initiated at a theoretical level a post-war process of cultural decolonization, starting with rationalism itself, particularly in Lévi-Strauss's equation of rational with "primitive" thought in *La Pensée sauvage*, which in some sense represents a development of Troubetzkoy's own critique of the category of the primitive, current in his own day in the work of Lucien Lévy-Bruhl. The French initiative after World War II to develop Structuralism as a form of cultural analysis can also be related to the degree to which the anti-historicist methodology of the Prague School was explicitly anti-German, and designed to free Europeans and non-Europeans alike from the dominant influence of German positivist scholarship.[45] The Prague School doctrines were thus both technical and ideological: the emphasis on synchrony was deliberately opposed to the historicist Indo-European comparative linguistics of the nineteenth century that had been dominated by German historical scholarship, and which had been committed to implicitly racialist notions of linguistic hierarchy that assumed the superiority of European languages, and committed to a doctrine of the single Indo-European origin of European languages organized according to a developing family tree in which inflectional European languages represented the most advanced stage. Such comparative linguistics had allied linguistics to anthropology, ethnology, culture and religion, and had provided a corroborative linguistic basis for the racial doctrine of Aryanism and anti-Semitism.

Far from Structuralism being apolitical and ahistorical, therefore, its "ahistoricism" involved a deliberate political challenge to imperialist genetic thinking in linguistics, positing instead a structural diachronic of historical breaks comparable to the disjunctive theory of history of

45 Toman, *The Magic of a Common Language* 132.

Walter Benjamin, and more broadly opposing imperialist views on questions of cultural difference. It can therefore be regarded as taking its part in the history of what the Kenyan writer Ngũgĩ wa Thiong'o has called "the decolonization of the mind."[46] If we do now live in a post-colonial age in which peoples, cultures and languages are treated for the most part as being relatively equal, then Structuralism's task has indeed been fully achieved. Its apparent obsolescence is the mark of its success.

Convergence: The *Sprachbund*

The Prague Circle emphasis on function rather than genetic descent raises a number of significant questions. I want to conclude this chapter by considering its relation to contemporary Soviet linguistics and science. This involves another aspect of Prague Circle thinking which, like the critique of Eurocentrism, is of particular interest to those working in Post-colonial Studies, namely the ideas of convergence and hybridity. Such ideas raise questions about the relation of Jakobson, Troubetzkoy and others to contemporary Soviet science and linguistics, and thence also to the historical poetics of Mikhail Bakhtin.

The Prague Circle rejected the genetic model of linguistic history. In addition, as Troubetzkoy's discussion of cultural assimilation suggests, the Circle was particularly concerned with the historical question of language contact and merger, and with the development of common features as a result, an idea first explored in the nineteenth century by Hugo Schuchardt and Johannes Schmidt, proponents of the wave theory (*Wellentheorie*) of language according to which linguistic innovations spread out from a central point in concentric circles to the languages around them. The Circle opposed this to the prevalent comparative philological notion of genetic language development in which the relationship between languages lay exclusively in their origins on the basis of the *Stammbaumtheorie*, or genetic tree model, established in the nineteenth century by August Schleicher. The Structuralist argument was that languages, even if genetically different, can also converge through the history of a common cultural life, for example, under the influence of

---

[46] Ngũgĩ Wa Thiong'o, *Decolonizing the Mind* (London: James Currey, 1981).

a common religion.[47] This convergence paradigm was central to Troubetzkoy's work, particularly in his idea of the *Sprachbund*, linguistic alliance or language union, which he proposed in 1923 and again in 1928 in contrast to the implicitly biological basis of the *Sprachfamilie*. Enthusiastically endorsed by Jakobson in 1931, the great attraction of Troubetzkoy's *Sprachbund* was that it was able to offer a theoretical model through which to constitute the linguistic cohesion of Eurasia, where different languages with no necessary genetic or relation had converged organically as a result of their geographical contiguity, displaying similarities at the level of phonetics, morphology, syntax and lexis.[48] The obvious point of comparison in relation to comparative linguistics today would be theories of Nostratic, though this remains conceptualized according to genetic relations.[49] For its part, Troubetzkoy's language union shifts the language model from a linear to a spatial evolution, from the language tree to the linguistic chain, net or, to move to Deleuzean terms, the rhizome.

In his 1923 essay "The Tower of Babel and the Confusion of Tongues," Troubetzkoy writes:

> [I]n addition to genetic grouping, we can observe grouping of neighbouring languages not derived from the same source. Several languages belonging to a single geographic and cultural-historical region often exhibit similar features and this resemblance is conditioned by prolonged proximity and parallel development, rather than by common derivation. For groups formed on a non-genetic basis, we propose the term language unions. Not only separate languages but even families can form language unions; in such cases several genetically unrelated families belonging to a single geographic and cultural-historical zone are united by common features and form a union of language families. (153-54)

In this paradigm, relations of similarity and contiguity, to put it in Jakobsonian terminology, of genetic and non-genetic groupings, together

47 Toman, *The Magic of a Common Language* 144.
48 Helmut W. Schaller, "Roman Jakobson's Conception of 'Sprachbund,'" Gadet and Sériot (eds.), *Jakobson entre l'Est et l'Ouest* 207-11.
49 Joseph H. Greenberg, *Indo-European and Its Closest Relatives: The Eurasiatic Language Family*, 2 vols. (Stanford, CA: Stanford University Press, 1999).

make up the totality of language unions. Since there are no borders to language then logically all languages exist in an interrelated continuum:

> all the languages of the world form an uninterrupted network whose links merge into one another – something like a rainbow. Because this rainbowlike network is continuous and transitions within it are gradual, the overall system of the languages of the world, for all its motley variety, constitutes a whole, obvious though it may be only to a scholar. (155)

This model allows Troubetzkoy to deny simple nationalist identifications with languages on the European model, and to make an important distinction between language and culture: cultural zones, such as Eurasia, are formations of the same kind as language zones, but they are not necessarily to be identified with them: "The distribution and interrelation of cultures do not coincide with the grouping of languages. Native speakers of the same branch, let alone the same family, may belong to different cultures [...]." (155) Linguistic and cultural networks are never identical. Between neighbouring peoples, there will always be "cultural-historical 'zones' [...]. The boundaries of these zones intersect one another, so that cultures of a mixed, or transitional, type emerge. Separate peoples and their subgroups appropriate definite cultural types and contribute to them their own individual traits." (155)

Troubetzkoy thus offers a complex multi-layered diffusionist model of language and culture. While he separates the zones of language and culture, he stresses at the same time the formative role of language on culture so that genetically unrelated languages begin to cohere within a single geographic and cultural historical zone. In many ways, the idea of the language union solves the problem of linguistic totality that had defeated Saussure, namely how to separate languages from identifications with race or nation, acknowledge the indeterminateness of their boundaries, while at the same time provide a principle of cohesion that enables a language to operate as a self-regulating system. Saussure characterizes the principle of unity as a "social bond" but he can only define what this is by inventing a nonce-word for it, "éthnisme."[50] By contrast, the *Sprachbund* is a non-

---

50 Young, "Race and Language in the Two Saussures" 67.

national, non-racial union that binds a discrete language system. Troubetzkoy's language-union marks a functioning, idiosyncratic whole *without* fixed boundaries or totalization, continually reacting and inter-reacting, colliding and combining with other systems in its border zones, compounding "the processes of divergence (the breakdown of a language into dialects) and convergence (the rapprochement of languages in contact)" in a dialectical movement of centripetal and centrifugal forces that anticipate those of Bakhtin.[51] Such an open form of totality moreover forestalls Derrida's critique of Structuralism (how can a totality be closed?) while at the same time avoiding the linguist's implausible distinction between pure/discrete and creolized or hybridized languages and cultures.[52]

For his part, in relation to the implicit geographical dimension of the *Sprachbund*, Jakobson was also particularly enthusiastic about the anti-Darwinian thesis of Lev S. Berg, the Leningrad geographer and biologist, who argued in his *Nomogenesis, or Evolution Determined by Law*[53] that analysis of the ecological systems of individual geographic regions revealed evolutionary phenomena such as mimicry that demonstrated principles of biological convergence rather than random selection.[54] We might want to compare this with the work of Gabriel Tarde (*Les lois de l'imitation*, 1890), or with Lacan's later ideas about mimicry and camouflage,[55] or Bhabha's theory of colonial mimicry. Berg's book embodied

---

[51] Gasparov, "The Ideological Principles" 57.
[52] Jacques Derrida, "Structure, Sign and Play in the Discourse of the Human Sciences," *Writing and Difference*, trans. Alan Bass (London: Routledge and Kegan Paul, 1978) 278-95.
[53] Leo S. Berg, *Nomogenesis, or Evolution Determined by Law* (Nomogenez. Evolyutsiia na osnove zakonomernostei, 1922), trans. J.N. Rostovtsow (London: Constable, 1926).
[54] See Patrick Sériot, "La pensée nomogénétique en URSS dans l'entre deux-guerres: l'histoire d'un contre-programme," *Le discourse sur langue en URSS à l'époque stalinienne (épistemologie, philosophie, idéologie)*, ed. Patrick Sériot (Lausanne: Université de Lausanne, 2003) 183-91. Jakobson's biologism can be compared to Bakhtin's: see Ben Taylor, "Kanaev, Vitalism and the Bakhtin Circle," Brandist, Shepherd and Tihanov (eds.), *The Bakhtin Circle* 150-66.
[55] See Jacques Lacan, *The Four Fundamental Concepts of Psycho-Analysis* (1973), trans. Alan Sheridan (London: The Hogarth Press and the Institute of Psychoanalysis, 1977) 98-100 and *passim*.

the fundamental framework of ideas that were subsequently developed in Lysenko's ideological science.[56] Jakobson, arguing that "genetically unrelated languages of Eurasia can undergo a process of convergent development triggered by geographical proximity,"[57] subsequently sought to develop his own parallel linguistic version of nomogenesis.[58] Even in later life, Jakobson "repeatedly recommended this book" to others', even Noam Chomsky's, attention.[59]

As a Formalist, Jakobson was originally associated with the ideological position denounced in the realm of linguistics as well as in genetics; he was also a supporter of the brilliant Oriental linguist Yevgeny Polivanov, who was executed in 1938. In many ways, he always retained his Formalist leanings. However, as his enthusiasm for Berg indicates, in the context of the Prague Circle, Jakobson increasingly took a positive view of the Soviet orthodoxy in which the context of environment, and its influence towards a goal-oriented evolution, received primary emphasis. This is not a simple matter of Jakobson being contaminated by Lysenkism, for as Boris Gasparov has argued, the organicist view which Lysenko developed represented a general paradigm that gained ascendancy in the 1920s across the humanities and natural sciences in the Soviet Union and elsewhere.[60] The problem was rather Lysenko trying to make science correspond to social and political ideals.

---

[56] On Lysenko in this context, see David Joravsky, *Soviet Marxism and Natural Science, 1917-1932* (New York: Columbia University Press, 1961) and, by the same author, *The Lysenko Affair* (Cambridge, MA: Harvard University Press, 1970).

[57] Toman, *Letters and Other Materials* 122-23.

[58] See Patrick Sériot, "The Impact of Czech and Russian Biology on the Linguistic Thoughts of the Prague Linguistic Circle," *Travaux du Cercle Linguistique de Prague, NS / Prague Lingusitic Circle Papers* 3 (1999): 18-19. Sériot mentions Jakobson's article "Über die heutigen Voraussetzungen der Russischen Slawistik," *Slawische Rundschau* 1 (1929): 629-46. Cf. also the section "Towards the Nomothetic Approach to Language" of Jakobson's *Selected Writings* 2:367-602.

[59] Toman, *Letters and Other Materials* 123.

[60] Boris Gasparov, "Development or Rebuilding: Views of Academician T.D. Lysenko in the Context of the late Avant-Garde," *Laboratory of Dreams: The Russian Avant-Garde and Cultural Experiment*, ed. John E. Bowlt and Olga Matich (Stanford, CA: Stanford University Press, 1996) 132-50.

The Prague Circle and Soviet Linguistics: Nikolai Marr

The thesis of linguistic convergence, together with Troubetzkoy's focus on forms of cultural mixture, and his dislike of the notion of mixed or hybrid cultures and languages unless they could be viewed as organic products, puts Troubetzkoy and Jakobson in certain respects close to the position of the Soviet linguist Nikolai Marr. Marr could be said to represent for linguistics what Lysenko represents for genetics. With Marr we arrive at a politico-intellectual milieu of particular significance for post-colonial theory in that we encounter a further theoretical context for Bakhtin's concept of hybridity that has been so central to post-colonial thought. Through the mediation of Marr, it is here too that we find links between Jakobson and Troubetzkoy and Bakhtin in the context of Soviet linguistics during the 1920s and 1930s.[61] Marr was a notorious figure in Soviet linguistic science: his work dominated Soviet linguistics until Stalin himself denounced some of his ideas in the 1950s, and perhaps uniquely he has never been rehabilitated.[62] Although this is no doubt

---

[61] Recent substantive treatments of Soviet linguistics in this period that has begun to elaborate the broader context in which the major thinkers worked, and the interrelations between them, can be found in: Gisela Bruche-Schulz, *Russische Sprachwissenschaft. Wissenschaft im historisch-politischen Prozeß des vorsowjetischen und sowjetischen Rußland* (Tübingen: Max Niemeyer Verlag, 1984); Vladimir M. Alpatov, "La linguistique marxiste en URSS dans les années 1920-1930," *Le discourse sur langue en URSS* 5-22; Vladimir M. Alpatov, "Soviet Linguistics of the 1920s and 1930s and the Scholarly Heritage," *Politics and the Theory of Language in the USSR 1917-1938: The Birth of Sociological Linguistics,* eds. Craig Brandist and Katya Chown (London: Anthem Press, 2011) 17-34. See also Sériot (ed.), *Le discourse sur langue en URSS.*

[62] See Joseph Stalin, et al., *The Soviet Linguistic Controversy,* trans. John V. Murra, Robert M. Hankin, Fred Holling (New York: King's Crown Press, 1951). Cf. Marcello Cherchi and Paul H. Manning, *Disciplines and Nations: Niko Marr vs. His Georgian Students on Tbilisi State University and the Japhetology/ Caucasology Schism* (Pittsburgh, PA: University of Pittsburgh, Center for Russian & East European Studies, 2002) 6, discussing some attempts by Georgian academics in the 1980s. Apart from Lawrence L. Thomas, *The Linguistic Theories of N.J.A. Marr* (Berkeley, University of California Press, 1957), the most substantive treatments of Marr can be found in: René L'Hermitte, *Science et perversion idéologique. Marr, Marrisme, Marristes. Une page de l'histoire de la linguistique soviétique* (Paris: Institut d'études slaves,

right with respect to Marr's later Japhetidology, nevertheless other aspects of his work remain, as Patrick Sériot has suggested, a "lost paradigm";[63] in the present context what is important about his work is that from the first he championed the idea of linguistic crossing, or hybridization, as the determining factor in linguistic evolution.

Marr, himself speaking a minority language that was the object of Tsarist suppression, identified himself with the defence of linguistic minorities dominated by cultural and political oppression. Following the established lead of the Slavophile linguistic movement, Marr took strong exception to the way in which the Georgian language had been dealt with by comparative philologists in the nineteenth-century, particularly Max Müller's thesis of the isolation of Georgian from Indo-European, and put forward his own thesis of a relation between Georgian and Arabic. In larger terms, Marr then sought to develop a theory of the isolated languages indigenous to Eurasia, which he named the Japhetic languages. Many of the arguments that he made were similar to those of Troubetzkoy: both challenged the ideology of positivistic neogrammarian European linguistics and developed comparable alternative theoretical models. So according to Marr, nineteenth-century philology, which he identified particularly with Aryanism, was essentially nothing but a form of rapacious imperialism whereby Europeans attempted to claim their own branch of the Indo-European languages as the most evolved: "Indo-European linguistics [...] is the flesh and blood of obsolete bourgeois sociality, built on the oppression of the peoples of the East by Europeans and their murderous colonial policy."[64] In place of the dominant hierarchical model of linguistic evolution, specifically Schleicher's *Stammbaum* theory of the family tree of languages according to which all languages had a genetic

---

1987); V.M. Alpatov, *Istoriia odnogo mifa: Marr i marrizm* (Moscow: Nauka, 1991); Gisela Bruche-Schulz, "Marr, Marx, and Linguistics in the Soviet Union," *Historiographia linguistica* 20.2-3 (1993): 455-72; Patrick Sériot (ed.), *Un paradigm perdu: la linguistique marriste* (Lausanne: Université de Lausanne, 2005). See also Sériot, *Structure et totalité*; Sériot, "La pensée nomogénétique en URSS"; Cherchi and Manning, *Disciplines and Nations*; Brandist and Chown (eds.), *Politics and the Theory of Language in the USSR*.

[63] Sériot (ed.), *Un paradigm perdu*.

[64] N.Ya. Marr, *Izbrannye raboty* (Selected Writings), 5 vols. (Leningrad: Gosudarstvennoe sotsial'no-ekonomicheskoe izdatel'svo, 1933-35) 3:1, quoted and translated by Alpatov, "Soviet Linguistics of the 1920s and 1930s" 25.

relationship to others (though from multiple origins), Marr also developed a theory of linguistic crossing, or the hybridization of languages, based on the work of Karl Vossler, Hugo Schuchardt, Baudoin de Courtenay and others, all of whom had sought to challenge Formalist theories of linguistic development in which all change was theorized as the result of internal, structural laws. In this project, they too adapted theories from natural science according to which, languages, like plants, could give birth to new hybrid languages as a result of the interactions brought about by the social, geographical and historical environment. It was Schuchardt who had first taken issue with Friedrich Max Müller's Aryanist dictum that there are no mixed languages, asserting rather that there are no languages that are totally pure.[65]

In his so-called "New Theory of Language," Marr argued that linguistic cross-breeding and hybridization was an integral factor in the development of all languages, both between languages and within them, and that this language mixture was an effect of the history of a racial and cultural mixture. He wrote of "the hybridisation of languages" as the "basic element in the creation of speech and the proliferation of its types, connected with an inevitable grafting of different tribes."[66] Hybridity was, in a sense, originary. Marr wrote:

> It is now time to put the question whether the Japhetic languages which fused with Indo-European to create the two linguistic types of Armenia known to us were not already hybrid before the process of fusion with nonnative layers – in general before the arrival of the Indo-Europeans within the boundaries of Armenia.[67]

For Marr, the process of hybridity, or multiple grafting, constituted the basic form of the language-forming process ("glottogony"), which he envisaged as developing historically by stages. The phonological or morphological elements in any given language enabled him, he claimed, to isolate its

---

65 Daniel Baggioni, "Problematique du substrat et histoire de la creolistique (1879-1939)," Aarsleff et al. (eds.), *Papers in the History of Linguistics* 559.
66 Marr, *Izbrannye raboty* 1:254, quoted in Thomas 57.
67 N.Ya. Marr, "Astronomicheskie i etnicheskie znachenia dvukh plemennykh nazvanii armyan," *Zapiski vostochnogo otdelenia Imperatorskogo russkogo arkheologicheskogo obshchestva* 25 (1920): 230, quoted in Thomas 33.

originary ethnic source. At the same time, his work on Armenian led Marr to suggest that within individual languages, language was dependent on the social structure of the speech community. Marr therefore divided Armenian into two languages, the aristocratic and the demotic. In the late 1920s, under political pressure, Marr then generalized this to a view in which all languages were divided by the class struggle: each individual language was itself a hybrid form in its formation and in its utilization by different classes, the conflicting antithetical aspects of which were set against each other dialogically, producing what can be called, in Bakhtin's terms, intentional hybridity.

Linguists consider Marr's theories and methods to be an aberration in the history of linguistics. Troubetzkoy said it more bluntly: Marr was mad. However, the idea that language is divided by class and its forms of speech set dialogically against each other is common to most Russian linguists and literary theorists of the period; with respect to the idea of convergence, in particular, the two were in many respects similar. The difference between them is that whereas Marr saw linguistic mixture as the origin of language and its dialectical mechanism of development, eventually leading him to claim that all languages are gradually moving towards fusion and union in a single world language, Troubetzkoy maintained a Jakobsonian dialectic of similarity and dissimilarity, enabling local mutual assimilation to operate within the broader terms of multilingualism:

> As a result, we have the same rainbowlike network, unified and harmonious by virtue of its continuity and infinitely varied by virtue of its differentiation. (155-56)

This description of individual languages coexisting within the general system of languages, anticipates Troubetzkoy's central proposition of the internal organization of the system of phonology through marked antithetical pairs.[68] In Troubetzkoy and Jakobson's work, there was an emphasis on the functioning of language as a self-governing system with its own autonomous structural laws, including those relating to language

---

[68] This paradigm of harmony also contrasts with Jakobson's stress on organized violence, of confrontation and imbalance. See Gasparov, "The Ideological Principles" 68.

contact; it was, finally, their systematizing based on marked oppositions that preserved them from the unbounded mixtures of Marr. The balanced harmony of the uninterrupted rainbow of languages in Troubetzkoy's account also distinguishes him from Marr's thesis about the class character of language, with language embodying the class struggle from its very origin. Nevertheless, despite his increasingly idiosyncratic methods, in other respects, for example his attack on the *Stammbaum* model, and his thesis regarding hybridity, or the rhizomatic mixture of contiguous languages as a fundamental form of linguistic relation and development, Marr was by no means out on a limb, and in certain respects quite close to some of the positions of the Prague Circle.

The significant differences between them are nicely illustrated in Jakobson's essay on the linguistic theories of Franz Boas. Jakobson emphasizes Boas's refutation of "Indo-European imperialism" and ethnocentrism in linguistics and notes approvingly that Boas became critical of the 'genealogical tree' model in the 1920s, discovering only later that Troubetzkoy was taking up the same position.[69] In its place Boas, like Troubetzkoy and Marr, posited a relation based on contiguity and mixture: "many significant facts made it impossible to infer a common origin from any striking similarity in neighbouring languages" observes Jakobson. While Marr emphasized hybridization as the fundamental basis of linguistic formation, Jakobson here stresses the possibility of both linguistic convergence and separation in the process of linguistic development: "The more deeply Boas delved into indigenous linguistic life, the more clearly he saw that side by side with *differentiation* stands *integration*, another and opposite factor which works widely." However, even here, it could be argued that Marr in his own way also promoted the thesis of similarity and dissimilarity in his two forms of hybridity: if ethnic mixture brings languages together, the class struggle within societies pushes them apart. Jakobson notes that in "The Diffusion of Cultural Traits" (1937), Boas "appealed to an 'actual intermingling of tribes,' although nearly at the same time in *The Mind of Primitive Man* (1938) he stressed that "assimilation of cultures occurs everywhere without actual blood-mixture, as an effect of imitation" – or mimicry.[70]

[69] Jakobson, *Selected Writings* 2:481-84.
[70] Jakobson, *Selected Writings* 485.

Whereas Marr had allied linguistic hybridization to physical hybridization between different ethnic groups, and Troubetzkoy distinguishes between cultural and linguistic mixture as a natural process of the product of human interbreeding and cultural assimilation as a result of political domination, Jakobson here stresses his preferred view of hybridization as a social rather than natural or biological phenomenon, a position consonant with progressive linguistic theory since Whitney and Saussure, with Bakhtin's account of linguistic hybridity in the novel, and post-colonial theory since Bhabha. Nevertheless, it was a version of Marr's theory of these two forms of hybridity, one the "natural" process of ethnic fusion and the other the "artificial" divisive effect of the class struggle, that Bakhtin was to invoke as the antithetical forms of "organic" and "intentional" hybridity in his essay on the novel written in 1934-35. Marr, Bakhtin, and Troubetzkoy: all in different ways utilized the notion of hybridity in this period. Their exact intellectual and historical relations are only now beginning to be charted and determined.[71]

Conclusion

The main argument of this chapter has been that Structuralism was conceived not only as a method of analysis whose basis was drawn from linguistics, but as a cultural and political project whose epistemological reach formed a wide-ranging challenge to the Eurocentric presuppositions of European positivism and the forms of knowledge that had been developed under its aegis. This was particularly the case in the work of Jakobson and Troubetzkoy, but analysis of their work demonstrates close links to many others working in the general sphere of Russian linguistics and cultural analysis in the 1920s and 1930s. The overall implications of the radical thesis of convergence, in opposition to genetic forms of analysis, that was current in various forms in that period, have yet to be fully developed.

---

[71] See, for example, Craig Brandist and Mika Lähteenmäki, "Early Soviet Linguistics and Michail Bakhtin's Essays on the Novel of the 1930s," Brandist and Chown (eds.), *Politics and the Theory of Language in the USSR* 69-88.

FUNCTIONAL LINGUISTICS AS THE "SCIENCE OF POETIC FORMS": AN ABC OF THE PRAGUE LINGUISTIC CIRCLE'S POETICS

David Vichnar

I

It has become one of the better established facts of the history of the European avant-garde that Russian literary Futurism and literary-scientific Formalism were parallel developments. In René Wellek's words, "the Russian formalists [...] were closely associated with the Russian Futurist poets, and their theories, in part, were a defense of their experimentation with language."[1] Poetic theory grew out of direct engagement with poetic practice, which in turn was informed by contemporary advances in the field of Structuralist and semiotic poetics – as is corroborated by, for instance, the life-long friendship between Viktor Shklovsky, one of the founders of the St. Petersburg OPOYAZ group, and Vladimir Mayakovsky, the leader of the Futurist avant-garde. In the quote above, Wellek singles out Roman Jakobson, and for good reason, for throughout his life Jakobson cherished friendships and close collaborative relationships with a number of Russian poets and, after his 1920 move to Prague, acted as a great promoter of Russian poetry in the

[1]   René Wellek, *The Literary Theory and Aesthetics of the Prague School* (Ann Arbor: University of Michigan Press, 1969) 12.

Czech context. Vítězslav Nezval alone mentions, addresses, or salutes Jakobson directly in no fewer than three of his early-to-mid-1930s poetry collections. These include *Skleněný havelok* (A Havelock of Glass, 1932), where Jakobson is listed among the poet's "friends" and invited to transform Prague into "a miraculous city created for poetry" ("Vyzvání přátelům" – An Appeal to My Friends). In the same collection, Nezval connects Jakobson with Vladimir Mayakovsky, dedicating to him a poem "Majakovský v Praze" (Mayakovsky in Prague). In a short poem entitled "Roman Jakobson," Nezval refers to the critic's thought as corresponding to the "secret levers" of his poetry and to his faith in "poetry in its wholeness."[2] Nezval's *Zpáteční lístek* (A Return Ticket, 1933) includes a "Letter to Roman Jakobson," concluding on a note of gratitude: "Roman, thanks for everything!" And finally, the "Poříč" poem from Nezval's collection *Praha s prsty deště* (Prague with Fingers of Rain, 1936) is also dedicated to Jakobson. Nezval surely spoke on behalf of many of his colleagues when he wrote:

> In Roman Jakobson I found a friend for many years with whom I shared a deep understanding in matters of poetry. He was a friend of Mayakovsky's, Pasternak's and of Russian futurists, and his experience was interesting for us. He defended us against the artistically narrow-minded and often did so with a well-aimed blow – in polemics, he was not to be surpassed by anyone.[3]

These dedicative and commemorative gestures are, of course, relevant less as tokens of personal homage than as statements of the indebtedness of Nezval's artistic practice to Jakobson's theoretical system. As has recently been argued by Jeanette Fabian in her article detailing Jakobson's relationship with the Devětsil Artistic Federation, what is at stake here is that many of Nezval's poems "employ in their sound the linguistic principles of shifting, parallelism and other forms of

2   Vítězslav Nezval, *Skleněný havelok* (A Havelock of Glass) (Prague: František Borový, 1932), e-text by Lukáš Borovička (2004) 52, 55, 37, online, accessed 19 October 2012. My translation.
3   Quoted in Jindřich Toman, *The Magic Of A Common Language – Jakobson, Mathesius, Trubetzkoy, and the Prague Linguistic Circle* (Cambridge, Mass. and London: The MIT Press, 1995) 225.

repetition that Jakobson reconstructed and proclaimed in his phonological studies and which Nezval applies with virtuosity."[4]

However, when it comes to the subject of the Czech "wing"[5] of the Prague Linguistic Circle, the almost 'natural' connection between avant-garde literary theory and praxis seems far from obvious, and rather difficult to pinpoint. Its linguistic-semantic bent, its staple pragmatic concern with the linguistic "norm," and conceptualizations of linguistic "functionality" – all these seem to point toward a certain disregard for the contemporary poetic practice. To take but one example of an Anglophone account of Structuralism's history and evolution, the only extended mention of the "Prague School" in Jonathan Culler's influential *Structuralist Poetics* runs as follows:

> Following Saussure's example and concentrating on the system which underlies speech sounds, members of the Prague linguistic circle – particularly Jakobson and Trubetzkoy – effected what Lévi-Strauss called the "phonological revolution" and provided what was to later structuralists the clearest model of linguistic method.[6]

This and many other similar historical evaluations seem to follow Květoslav Chvatík's assessment in *Strukturalismus a avantgarda* (Structuralism and the Avant-Garde):

> Never have Mukařovský or any other prominent Czech Structuralist been the spokesmen of this or that avant-garde group, none have

4   Jeanette Fabian, "Ruku v ruce s básnictvím – Roman Jakobson a Umělecký svaz Devětsil" (Hand in Hand with Poetry: Roman Jakobson and the Devětsil Artistic Federation), *Slovo a smysl* 2.4 (2005): 88. My translation.

5   This division is elaborated upon in, for instance, Josef Vachek's "On Some Less Known Aspects of the Early Prague Linguistic School," *Praguiana: Some Basic and Less Known Aspects of the Prague Linguistic School*, ed. Josef Vachek, trans. Paul Garvin (Prague: Academia, 1983) 233-41. See for instance his assertion that "undoubtedly, the major achievements of the group were to be associated with its brilliant Russian protagonists, Nikolay Trubetzkoy, Roman Jakobson, and Sergei Karcevsky. Still, the portrait of the group would be incomplete if people like Vilém Mathesius, Bohumil Havránek, and Bohumil Trnka were omitted from that picture." (233)

6   Jonathan Culler, *Structuralist Poetics* (London and New York: Routledge, 1975) 7.

published in their magazines, none have made critical intervention in the name of this or that artistic conception. Modern art was outside their interest on the thematic level as well.[7]

Chvatík's judgment is wrong and unfair both *ad hominem* and *ad rem*. As regards Mukařovský, author of a range of studies devoted to Nezval, Vančura, avant-garde theatre, modern visual art and film (particularly under the impact of Surrealism), his interest in modern art is undeniable. Nor is it true that he eschewed publishing in avant-garde periodicals: some of his studies, e.g., "K sémantice básnického obrazu" (On the Semantics of the Poetic Image, 1946) were published in the first post-war edition of the avant-garde magazine *Kvart*, side by side with Jakobson's work.

And, as regards the *ad rem* of Chvatík's argument: although a prevalent one (see Culler above), the view of the Circle's status as a grouping of linguists with less than little interest in literature overlooks a significant widening of attention paid to social and cultural concerns from the late 1920s onward, giving rise to a vital strand in the Circle's thinking as well as their collective public intervention in perhaps the hottest linguistic debate within the Czech cultural space of the early 1930s. An easily underestimated (but indispensable) role in this widening of attention was played by the figure of Vilém Mathesius, the Circle's early driving force. This essay will focus on his importance as a source of inspiration for two of his followers in the fields of linguistics and poetics: namely, Bohuslav Havránek and the afore-mentioned Jan Mukařovský.

II

Mathesius's 1929 inaugural article on "Functional Linguistics" already attests to the close connection – in the Circle's "functionalist" approach – between linguistic and "poetic" investigation. This connection is particularly significant in that the article was to become a source of inspiration for Havránek's theorization of the "standard language" and Mukařovský's functionalist aesthetics, especially his concept of the "aesthetic function,"

---

[7]   Květoslav Chvatík, *Strukturalismus a avantgarda* (Structuralism and the Avant-garde) (Prague: Československý spisovatel, 1969) 13. All quotations from this source are in my translation.

worked out over the course of the 1930s. Mathesius surveys the past twenty years in linguistics as an age of gradual transition from what he terms the Neogrammarian School (diachronic, comparative, and proceeding from form to function) and Functional Linguistics (synchronic, contrastive, and proceeding from function to form). Mathesius's argument advances in three stages, showing how functionalism deals with the linguistic problems of the sentence (understood performatively as "a communicative utterance by which the speaker assumes an *active attitude* to some fact or group of facts"[8]), word order (restricted to the "plastic" and "elastic" Czech language), and the study of sounds (from phonetics to phonology). From the viewpoint of Functional Linguistics, for Mathesius, the study of language phenomena is again, chiefly threefold: what he terms onomatology (the activity of naming and word formation), syntax (investigation of the predicative forms of language) and the phonic/speech aspect of the language. So far, so Saussurean. It is toward the end of his paper that Mathesius's approach exceeds the confines of linguistic approach to communication only – the thorny issue of linguistic "correctness" brings him to a radical dissent with the predominantly "communicative" view on language purported by linguistic "purists":

> The function of speech is not confined to the communicative function alone, although in everyday life this function predominates. Of major importance is also its expressive function, i.e., expression for the sake of expression itself, with no regard to the hearer, and the formulatory function, i.e., accurate and detailed recording of complicated thoughts. (137)

It rapidly becomes clear that Mathesius's concern is a broadly socio-cultural one ("after all, we want a language that would meet the highest demands of cultural life in all its forms," 137-38) and not one confined to the nitty-gritty of linguistic science. Directed against the "purists," this is his rejection of their proposed substitutions for "unnecessary" words, since "banishment of such words often involves loss of fine shades of

---

8   Vilém Mathesius, "Functional Linguistics," *Praguiana* 125. Further quotations appear in parentheses in the text.

meaning, i.e., it leads to impoverishment." (137-38) It is here, in the paper's conclusion, that his project of Functional Linguistics is expressly tied in with contemporary poetics:

> In the question of language correctness the linguist who regards language from the functional point of view goes hand in hand with the linguistically creative artist. This is not incidental. This close relationship between the new linguistics and *belles lettres* proves profitable even elsewhere. The new linguistics helps to lay the foundations of the new science of poetic form and itself learns about the possibilities of linguistic expression from authors of literary works. (139)

Implementation of Mathesius's call for "the new science of poetic form" was quick in coming. Simultaneously with the presentation of Mathesius's article, the Circle – represented by the collaborative effort of Havránek and Mukařovský – worked out its ten "Theses Presented to the First Congress of Slavists Held in Prague in 1929." The third thesis, "Problems of Research into Languages of Different Functions, Especially Slavic," renders Mathesius's differentiation of linguistic functionality as a dichotomy, strictly distinguishing the *communicative* ("when it is directed towards the content of the message") from the *poetic* function ("when it is solely directed towards its form").[9] The approach to the status of the "standard literary language" is functionalist, too. While its constitution is always partly based on political, socio-economic and cultural-religious conditions, these constitute "no more than *external factors*" since they explain the *how*, but not the *why* of the differentiation from the popular language which gives rise to the linguistic norm. This differentiation – to be subsequently elaborated upon by Havránek – is "*due to its function,* particularly to the exigencies imposed upon it to a higher degree than on the popular language," for the standard literary language has the function of expressing facts of cultural and civilizational life far broader and more complex than those of the popular speech, a task which "*increases and modifies* (intellectualizes) *its vocabulary.*" (91)

---

[9]   "Theses Presented to the First Congress of Slavists Held in Prague in 1929," *Praguiana* 89. Further quotations appear in parentheses in the text.

When it comes to poetic language ("a neglected domain of linguistic research," with "most Slavic languages" having "so far hardly been examined" from this viewpoint, 93), a similar differentiation is in place: as long as standard language is to be distinguished from popular speech, then so must be the poetic function from the communicative one – a revisiting of Mathesius's distinction above. Further elaboration on the various levels of poetic language is called for – and it is here that the germ of Mukařovský's concept of *foregrounding*[10] appears:

> From the thesis stating that the poetic expression is directed towards the way of expression itself it follows that all levels of the linguistic system, which in communicative utterances play only an ancillary part, acquire in poetic utterances more or less independent values: linguistic means grouped within these levels as well as the mutual relations of the levels, both of which in communicative speech tend to become automatized, in poetic utterances, contrary to this, tend to become foregrounded. (94)

This is not the place to elaborate on the evident parallels with, if not anticipations of, the later famous Jakobsonian definition of the poetic function in terms of paradigmatic and syntagmatic axes. What is more important is how further investigation into the linguistic types of poetic foregrounding (phonic, morphological, and syntactic) reveals a profound difference, within the functioning of poetic language, from not only communicative language, but also from the standard literary language. This is most explicit, in terms of poetic vocabulary, where "unusual words (neologisms, barbarisms, archaisms) are poetically valuable by distinctly differing from current words of communicative speech by their very phonic effect" and moreover, "unusual words enrich the semantic and stylistic multiformity of the poetic vocabulary." (97) Where standardization of "literary language" demands uniformity and compliance with the norm, the foregrounding that sets off "poetic language" as different from the former is marked by "multiformity" and deviance from, if not breech of, the norm.

---

[10] Translation of the Czech term "aktualizace."

III

It was precisely the insistence on the difference between, indeed incompatibility of, the "standard" and "poetic" languages that underlay the Circle's collective role in the "purism" debate of 1932, surrounding the critique of Nezval's poetics launched in the journal *Naše řeč* (Our Speech), particularly by its then editor-in-chief, Jiří Haller. The story has been well-documented by several commentators, including both Wellek and Toman: under Haller's editorship, the journal served as a mouthpiece for Bohemists and Czech philologists promoting the most extreme purist and archaic standards of language (as exemplified by Haller's article on "Problém jazykové správnosti" ["The Problem of Language Correctness"][11]). Thus, unsurprisingly, when presented with Nezval's *Kronika z konce tisíciletí* (A Chronicle from the End of a Millennium, 1929) – an experimental text replete with morphological and syntactical neologisms and deviations from the standard norm – Haller's review launched a scathing critique of the perceived "awkwardness" of Nezval's style, the "ineptitude" of his handling of language, and the overall "defectiveness" of his first novelistic attempt (his starting point being "the age-old truth that lyrical poets tend to make for poor novelists").[12] The Circle's collective response took the form of a lecture series on the related questions of linguistic correctness, literariness and poetic function, published in the co-authored essay collection, *Spisovná čeština a jazyková kultura* (Standard Czech and Language Culture, 1932), to which all three – Mathesius, Havránek, and Mukařovský – contributed.

"O požadavku stability ve spisovném jazyce" (On the Requirement of Stability in Standard Language), Mathesius's contribution to the volume, emphasizes the difference – sidestepped in the purist campaign of Haller and co. – between linguistic purity and refinement (again, the former diachronic, the latter synchronic), the one far from presupposing or leading

---

11 Jiří Haller, "Problém jazykové správnosti," *Výroční zpráva českého státního reformovaného reálného gymnásia v Ústí nad Labem* (Annual Report of the Czech Reformed *Realgymnasium* in Ústí nad Labem) (Ústí nad Labem: České státní ref. reál. gymnasium, 1930) 1-16.

12 Jiří Haller, "Kronika z konce tisíciletí" (A review of Vítězslav Nezval's novel *A Chronicle from the End of a Millennium*), *Naše řeč* 14.7 (1930): 153-63.

to the other. Here, drawing on his lifelong expertise, Mathesius resorts to the contrastive example of the English language, claiming that "from the viewpoint of historical purity, English is a genuine bastard, and yet this bastard is a more refined language than the historically purer and more Germane German."[13] In accordance with his earlier understanding of linguistic functionality, the stability Mathesius posits is a "flexible" one, complying with the codified norm, yet non-identical with historical purity. Contrary to the purist prescriptiveness, according to which it is linguistics – rather than literature – that determines literary language, Mathesius insists that "the objection that there is no writer whose language is genuinely good is absurd. If good standard Czech is not to be found in literature, it doesn't exist."[14] Hence the "flexible" stability posited by Mathesius: "If one objects to this requirement that it effectively forbids the exact scientific determination of the correct usage, I agree and add that no living language is to be yoked by scientific principles." In effect, the sole guarantor of such flexible linguistic stability is "the language of the average of Czech literature in the broadest sense over the last half-century."[15]

Bohuslav Havránek's "Úkoly spisovného jazyka a jeho kultura" (The Tasks of the Standard Language and Its Culture)[16] picks up where Mathesius's article has left off – the necessity of developing a theory of the linguistic standard – and devotes itself to substantiating the claim that the usage of linguistic devices in popular speech and in the standard language is determined by the purpose or the function of the act of speech. The crucial factors in the functional and stylistic differentiation of language are lexical and syntactic devices, more so than phonological and

13 Vilém Mathesius, "O požadavku stability ve spisovném jazyce" (On the Requirement of Stability within Standard Language), *Spisovná čeština a jazyková kultura* (Standard Czech and Language Culture), ed. Bohuslav Havránek and Miloš Weingart (Prague: Melantrich, 1932) 16. All quotations from this source are in my translation.
14 Mathesius, "O požadavku stability ve spisovném jazyce" 24.
15 Mathesius, "O požadavku stability ve spisovném jazyce" 30.
16 Bohuslav Havránek, "Úkoly spisovného jazyka a jeho kultura" (The Tasks of the Standard Language and Its Culture), *Spisovná čeština a jazyková kultura* 32-84. Partly translated by Paul Garvin as "The Functional Differentiation of the Standard Language," *Praguiana* 143-63.

morphological ones. Havránek continues in Mathesius's functionalist repositioning of some Saussurean binaries by drawing a distinction between the inventory of devices of functional and stylistic differentiation (*langue*) and the mode of utilization of the devices (*parole*), most prominent among which are the *automatization* and *foregrounding* of the devices in terms of their functional differentiation.[17] Automatization is equated with lexicalization, "a use of the devices of the language, in isolation or in combination with each other, as is usual for a certain expressive purpose,"[18] based on which the linguistic norm is established. Foregrounding, on the other hand, is a use in which language attracts attention to itself, "and is perceived as uncommon, as deprived of automatization, as deautomatized, such as a live poetic metaphor."[19] Again, Havránek's theorization of standard language sets the poetic language off as a markedly different, as an almost self-substantial language form that needs to be treated on its own terms.

It is just such treatment that poetic language receives in Mukařovský's study, which pits "standard language" against "poetic language," viewing the latter as a special language within language which has its own rights and norms. What makes poetic language possible is a systematic violation of the norm of the standard. However, such violation is not without its commensurate effects on the standard itself; it is here that Mukařovský takes issue with Haller's insistence on excluding aesthetic valuation from linguistics – precisely because "aesthetic valuation is a very important factor in the formation of the norm of the standard." This for two reasons: because "the conscious refinement of the language cannot do without it" and more importantly, because "it sometimes, in part, determines the development of the norm of the standard."[20] Despite this "flexible" opposition, Mukařovský argues for maintaining the differences between the standard and poetic language: whereas the former subordinates foregrounding to communication, the latter does the exact opposite. In so doing, Mukařovský gainsays Mathesius's identification of the linguistic standard with literary/poetic language, insisting that as

17 Havránek 146-47.
18 Havránek 152.
19 Havránek 153.
20 Jan Mukařovský, "Standard Language and Poetic Language," *Praguiana* 175-76. Further quotations appear in parentheses in the text.

long as "poetic language is a different form of language with a different function from that of the standard," it is "equally unjustified to call all poets, without exception, creators of the standard language as it is to make them responsible for its present state." (180) Conversely, the poetic foregrounding of linguistic phenomena, "since it is its own purpose, cannot have the purpose of creating new means of communication." (181-82)

This is not to say, nevertheless, that the mutually exclusive status of the standard and the poetic language denies any significance of poetry as language art for language in general; claims Mukařovský: "the very existence of poetry in a certain language has fundamental importance for this language." (183) This not least because foregrounding brings about an effect within the linguistic standard not unlike the formalist defamiliarization – in Mukařovský's words: "foregrounding brings to the surface and before the eyes of the observer even such linguistic phenomena as remain quite covert in communicative speech, although they are important factors in language." (185) Although separate, the poetic function is active within the standard language in ways that lay bare its essence, its very functioning.

IV

In taking a collective position on the questions of linguistic norm, the Czech "wing" of the Circle opposed the prevailing sentiment among Bohemists and Czech philologists of the age and sided with Nezval's poetic experimentation. In so doing, they also acknowledged the common basis between Nezval's poetic creation and their own theoretical examination of the modern Czech standard and poetic language. In Toman's thoughtful summary:

> One of the reasons why the Circle was reaching the avant-garde artistic audience with such ease is that it had assimilated itself to avant-garde standards by its conscious emphasis on collectivism and its bellicose public appearance. Much of this attitude remained visible throughout the 1930s. The Russian pattern of a merger between scholars and the avant-garde was effective in Prague as well. The affinity was deep. The magic of a common language was accompanied by the magic of a common behaviour.[21]

---

[21] Toman 165.

As this essay has attempted to show, to portray the Prague Linguistic Circle as a group fixated with linguistic issues at the expense of engagement with the verbal arts of their day and age – a picture so common in the English-speaking world – is to reduce the Circle's heritage to its (pre-)nascent state, for the 1929 formation of its famous "Theses" and its 1932 collective development of its famed "functionalist" approach, by way of defence of contemporary aesthetics – all these laid the ground for a systematic exploration of the poetic function as a self-substantial, self-reflexive aspect of language deserving its very own, specific linguistic status. Mathesius's distinction between different functional languages and Havránek's conceptualization of the "poetic" as markedly different from the "standard" were devised to save poetry from the norms of linguists judging language by the yardstick of correctness and purity. Mukařovský's theorization of the feedback of foregrounding for the linguistic norm, as well as the aesthetic dimension of linguistic standardization, complemented this by requiring of poetry a clear commitment to linguistic innovativeness and social relevance. Together, theirs was a linguistics whose theory of language never lost sight of the peculiar problems and challenges but also of the unique enrichments made possible by the study of literature.

A GATEWAY TO A BAROQUE RHETORIC OF JACQUES LACAN AND NIKLAS LUHMANN

Erik S. Roraback

This essay will assess some distinguishing features of the ideological content and rhetorical nature of selected works by the two major twentieth-century theoreticians, the French psychoanalytic thinker Jacques Lacan (1901-1981) and the German systems theorist Niklas Luhmann (1927-1998) and, where relevant, the mediatory roles of the Prague philosopher Ladislav Rieger (1890-1958), of Edmund Husserl (1859-1938), who lectured to the members of the Prague Philosophical Circle in 1935, and of the founding member of the Circle and the first Professor of English Language and Literature at Charles University, Vilém Mathesius (1882-1945).

The double dynamic of violence and representation will also be addressed in view of the inherent violent nature of representation and the representation of violence in the work of Lacan and of Luhmann, both of whom are striking for their capacity to offer critiques of conceptual systems and ideological frameworks. In this context, Husserl's phenomenological philosophy as a critique of consciousness and perception highlights and inspires points of issue in the systems-theory of Niklas Luhmann, who adduces and builds on Husserl at many crucial points across his oeuvre including especially his notions of sense and consciousness.[1]

---

[1]   However, as Hans-Georg Moeller has pointed out: "In his later writings, Luhmann typically avoided referencing Husserl when using the term *Sinn*,

The essay moves from one cultural platform to another one, from Lacan to Luhmann, and back, where applicable, vis-à-vis the above-mentioned scholars from the Czech lands. What Lacan and Luhmann have done as culture producers is not without mention, and the following lines aspire to be an index of this in being attentive to the high rhetorical standards of their cultural texts. It is precisely the devoted efforts of the above-mentioned Prague-School figures, which will be employed to reveal some new connections with the problem of rhetoric in Lacan and in Luhmann as part and parcel of the cultural superstructure of their respective bodies of work.

The communicative function of language is a conceptual and ideological fingerprint of the Prague School. Philip A. Luelsdorff writes of the movement that "[t]he concept of behavior being functional in the sense of goal-directed, individuated, and variable reverberates throughout the literature."[2] Also, the idea of communication is interesting in terms of what is not communicated, which is truly important; for instance, why is it that Luhmann and Lacan never engaged in critical discussion as two leading theorists of our late modernity? Would that have been too unorthodox or too experimental? Although they vibrate in the same wavelength in multiple regards as philosophers of difference, their communication remains a wordless rhetoric.

Lacan and Luhmann encircle each other in a dance of rhetoric that reveals how the violence of representational power can be mitigated or made a good thing in part via the mediating soft power of their basic self-subtractional strategies such as that of Luhmann when he confesses that his theory may not be a correct one of society, but a descriptive theory of society it remains nevertheless.[3] Both corpuses of writing are part and

---

turning instead to Deleuze's *Logique de sens* [...] Luhmann's shift from Husserl's *Sinn* to Deleuze's *sens* can be understood as an indicator of what I am calling the shift from philosophy to theory. It goes along with making reason ironical." Hans-Georg Moeller, *The Radical Luhmann* (New York: Columbia University Press, 2012) 22.

2   Philip A. Luelsdorff, "On Praguian Functionalism and Some Extensions," *Praguiana: Some Basic and Less Known Aspects of the Prague Linguistic School: An Anthology of Prague School Papers*, ed. Josef Vachek, trans. Paul Garvin (Prague: Academia, 1983) xv.

3   Not only this, Luhmann's modesty may also be discerned here when Hans-Georg Moeller writes, Luhmann "has no sympathy for a 'monoculture of reason,' be it in Kantian, Husserlian, or [...] Habermasian terms. Such claims

168

parcel of a Baroque prose style, which, as William Egginton puts it, "makes a theater out of truth, by incessantly demonstrating that truth can only ever be an effect of the appearances from which we seek to free it."[4] The ideological value of this kind of rhetoric goes hand in hand with the late capitalist Baroque dynamic of which our two principal target thinkers are a part.[5] Not only this but the ideas of the early modern, of the theatrical, including not least Lacan's teaching style and use of seventeenth-century Spanish Baroque models in his rhetoric also reverberate in our conception of the Baroque.

More generally, I am interested in the interpretation of rhetoric as it pertains to the highly influential and even controversial nature of the intellectual work of Lacan and Luhmann.[6] An interesting question to ask is where rhetoric ceases to be instrumental and becomes an end in itself (for example to dramatize some statements or conclusions). Do in this context Lacan (or even Luhmann) display, on certain rhetorical occasions, an undue sum of vocational representational violence if not authoritative professional power? Or is this a more Baroque, which is to say theatrical, aspect in the conceptual persona of both of these authors?

have no place in a 'supertheory' that, after all, has to be able to include itself in itself and thus to ironically reflect on its own limitations." Hans-Georg Moeller, *Luhmann Explained: From Souls to Systems* (Chicago: Open Court, 2006) 185.

4   William Egginton, *The Theater of Truth: The Ideology of (Neo)Baroque Aesthetics* (Stanford, CA: Stanford University Press, 2010) 2.

5   Here it is worth noting that the notion of the Baroque as one origin of modernity, referred to in this essay, stems from this kind of tradition: "For Agamben, following the conceptions of both Heidegger and Benjamin, origin is not that which is dead and monumentalized in the past, but that which is dynamic and alive in the present." Leland de la Durantaye, *Giorgio Agamben: A Critical Introduction* (Stanford, CA: Stanford University Press, 2009) 35.

6   Hans-Georg Moeller writes notably here that "Luhmann offered a radical alternative to [Habermas's] normative political philosophy. He conceived of his theory as a subversive Trojan horse that, once inside the enemy's camp, might destroy them from within [...] one of the tactics employed by Luhmann to disguise this threat was his often rather convoluted writing style. By adopting the jargon of Habermas and others who constituted the academic elite of the time, Luhmann was granted entry into their Troy." Moeller x. Of course Lacan too is notorious for his own convoluted writing style and for similar reasons about what would be permissible for him to say explicitly.

Or, is this obdurate obscurity merely an occupational hazard for big name thinkers?

Or better yet, what happens to the discourses of Lacan and of Luhmann when they become a zone for delineating the interference between violence and representation? Does this even have something to do with Egginton's words, "the very *mise en abîme* that is at the heart of theatricality itself"?[7] Even if one prefers the unfinished to the polished, and the daringly experimental over the brutally orthodox, how do we begin to account for the several rhythms (and so by extension of structures if rhythm is a form of structure) running at once in the Lacanian and Luhmannian discourses? The violent and the representational, the unconscious and the suggestive, and so on and so forth.[8]

Nevertheless, the commutability and the comparability of Lacan and Luhmann should not occlude the wide gaps between their two bodies of work; nor should this interpretation underwrite normalizing assumptions about violence and representation and of their co-imbrication with the violence and representational power involved in the demarcation of disciplinary boundaries. For what makes the Lacanian rhetoric of desire and of the unconscious so potent is its multifaceted backgrounding, just as what informs Luhmann's rhetoric of contingency and autopoiesis is its capacity too for a rare kind of interdisciplinary scaffolding in its unfolding conceptual architecture. If rhetoric has an ontology, then that of Lacan and Luhmann constitutes a special science of interdisciplinary being. For instance, in Luhmann's case we read of the import of Husserl:

> Luhmann translates a whole set of Husserlian terms into the language of systems theory. He begins with 'intention' [...]. Intention [for Luhmann] is thus no longer a certain mental interest. It is now the primal operation with which any observing

---

7 Egginton 49.
8 Incidentally, Philip A. Luelsdorff avers that "the original Praguian paradigm is thus the discovery of relationship between structure and function." Luelsdorff xii. One may ask of the rhetorical challenge laid down by this formulation for a better interpretive place in the court of criticism of Lacan and of Luhmann.Here we define structure as does Lalande in his 1925 dictionary of philosophy: "a whole that contains something more than the simple sum of its parts." de la Durantaye 39.

system ignites itself [...]. In line with this functional redefinition of the concept of intention, Luhmann reformulates the Husserlian distinction between noesis and noema, between phenomena and consciousness activity, with the distinction between other-reference and self-reference.[9]

This idea, and even ideology, of the functionalization of concepts is in keeping with the propensity of the Prague School, which valorizes the concept of function in many contexts. A little further on, Moeller continues:

The functionalization and de-ontologization of Husserlian terminology, its separation from consciousness and the subject, also applies to three other tightly connected Husserlian concepts: sense, horizon, and world [...]. Luhmann then formally defines sense, in immediate connection to Husserl, as the unity of the difference between actuality and possibility – and applies it to all sense-processing systems including social systems. Sense emerges only within a context – it needs a horizon.[10]

Husserl emerges out of an ideological and intellectual world partly defined by this estimation of function with regard to one's conceptual cartography, equipment and system.

In truth, it can be argued that the Husserlian and Luhmannian approaches to sense and context were anticipated in the thought of the Prague Linguistic Circle. As Peter Steiner writes,

the "Theses of the Prague Circle" is [...] a unified text propounding a new and original view of language and linguistic phenomena (including verbal art). What unites the "Theses" is its functionalist standpoint, the recognition that language is above all a tool of communication and all its forms are in some respect connected with this goal-directedness.[11]

---

[9] Moeller 182.
[10] Moeller 183.
[11] Peter Steiner, "Introduction" to "Theses Presented to the First Congress of Slavic Philologists in Prague, 1929," *The Prague School: Selected Writings, 1929-1946*, ed. Peter Steiner, trans. John Burbank, Olga Hasty, Manfred

This well articulates certain tenets of Luhmann's theory of autopoiesis. Prague School luminary, Vilém Mathesius, himself produced a classic essay on "Functional Linguistics."[12] Moreover, Josef Vachek points out that

> [t]he functionalist approach of the Czech 'wing' was also manifested by its keen interest in the quantitative analysis of language facts, i.e. in the establishment of the degree to which the items of language are functionally utilized [...] Both [Mathesius and Bohumil Trnka] rank among the first to take up the quantitative analysis, not only in the context of the Prague group, but even in that of world linguistics. Thus, the functionalist approach indeed appears to have been the dominating factor in the Czech wing of the group.[13]

Vachek's observation innately relates to the approach of the Prague Linguistic Circle in general, and by extension also to Husserl's and to Luhmann's very functionalistically interested and vested conceptual systems; Luhmann for example cites functional differentiation as one key structural fingerprint and specification of modernity.

The overall reading sensibility of the present essay also derives from Wayne C. Booth's work on rhetoric, in *The Rhetoric of Fiction* (1961, 1983) and *A Rhetoric of Irony* (1974), in addition to Malcolm Bowie's voluminous *Freud, Proust, Lacan: Theory as Fiction* (1987), which highlights a number of essential features of the topography of Lacan's rhetoric. For instance, in Booth's *A Rhetoric of Irony* we read that, "[t]here is no real art of interpretation – only a game of competing improvisations. The critic with the most persuasive style wins, because there are after all no rules imposed by 'the work itself,' and there is no referee."[14]

Let us attempt to tease out the implications of such a statement for Lacan and for Luhmann criticism. To begin with, it seems prima facie

Jacobson, Bruce Kochis, and Wendy Steiner (Austin: University of Texas Press, 1982) 4.

[12] Vilém Mathesius, "Functional Linguistics," *Praguiana* 121-42.

[13] Josef Vachek, "On Some Less Known Aspects of the Early Prague Linguistic School," *Praguiana* 236.

[14] Wayne Booth, *A Rhetoric of Irony* (Chicago: The University of Chicago Press, 1974) 133.

that a paradoxical loop and circularity comprises the movement of the hermeneutic perspective on these works. And for example, in Bowie we read:

> The edited transcripts of the weekly seminars that Lacan conducted in Paris over two decades, and that are now in the process of publication, take us even further into his speculative workshop. Certain sections of the *Séminaire* serve to clarify the main ideas of *Écrits*, others elaborately rework them, and others still are the record of a surging glossolalia in the face of which critical intelligence falls indignantly or admiringly silent. Lacan's prose aspires perpetually to the conditions of speech. And his aims in writing like this are clear: to allow the energies of the unconscious to become palpable in the wayward rhythm of his sentences, to discourage the reader from building premature theoretical constructions upon the text and to compel him to collaborate fully in the inventive work of language.[15]

It is precisely here that Ladislav Rieger may be of help, when he writes in a pioneering essay that

> we are concerned with a text, which is not a description of 'what is' but an appeal for a mental realization of a new view with an analogous intention, an appeal for the creation of a new situation. If the whole context [...] leads us to the very act of intuition through the realization of an analogous situation, we obtain an interpretation by which it is possible to capture [...] the original movement of thought whose force is reflected in the text.[16]

This is relevant for our understanding of Lacan's statements, insofar as in the participative structure of Lacan's conceptual universe in his *Seminar*, one is continuously invited to innovate one's mental realizations with a dynamic interpretive force. One must for example fill in the gaps of Lacan's undoubted powers of evocation and suggestion in his pedagogic

---

[15] Malcolm Bowie, *Freud, Proust and Lacan: Theory as Fiction* (Cambridge: Cambridge University Press, 1987) 104-105.

[16] Ladislav Rieger, "The Semantic Analysis of Philosophical Texts," *The Prague School: Selected Writings* 99.

discourse and come to terms with the Baroque facets of Lacan's rhetorical economy described at some length by Bowie; Bowie speaks of

> the kind of thinking that 'baroque' writing encourages Lacan to perform. He abandons the language of tranquil certitude in which his colleagues and contemporaries in psychoanalysis mostly choose to write (even when describing their uncertainties), and uses instead an enraged, risk-taking language of skepticism. His writing is propelled not simply by an urge to be difficult and discontinuous, but by an urge, transmuted into a moral imperative, to be surprising.
>
> If we consider the baroque writers whom Lacan chose to name as ancestors, we find that his enthusiasm for Gracián is matched and to some extent offset by his enthusiasm for Góngora: the traditions of *conceptismo* and *culteranismo* that clashed so vigorously in early seventeenth-century Spain clash again in Lacan's writing. Both traditions are valued by him for the difficulty they promote and for their seeming hostility to the intellectual vice of "good sense." Lacan hands the burden of difficulty back and forth between syntax and sound, between tropes and schemes, between conceited thinking and opulently allusive verbal textures. He is by temperament a Senecan in his handling of syntax, but will turn his hand to a Ciceronian sentence when the injunction "dire toujours Autre-chose" (837) requires it [...] His writing is not always good [...] a time-travelling Quintilian, coming upon declamatory lists of his own rhetorical figures in *Écrits*, might wish to caution Lacan with a list of those vices into which devices may dwindle: Lacan's *accismus, metonymy, catachresis, antiphrasis, hypallage* and *litotes* (466) might be countered, after an inspection of his writing, by *anoiconometon, cacosyntheton, cululatio, nugatio, periergia* and *scurra*.[17]

Yet all the same, the Baroque nature and pattern of Lacan's psychoanalytic discourse, as well as of Luhmann's writings, in their rhetorical figurations, is worthy of note, for both corpuses of work seem to need a kind of Baroque reconstruction as complex pieces of what I call chapters of the philosophical

---

[17] Bowie 150.

Baroque. Both are part and parcel of a larger unavowed cultural legacy of today's late Baroque modernity.

One already adduced key text in an analysis of Lacan's rhetoric would be the French scholar and historian Michel de Certeau's essay entitled, "Lacan: An Ethics of Speech" from his *Heterologies: Discourse on the Other* (1986). One of de Certeau's contentions is that "'Lacan' designates a rhetoric of withdrawal,"[18] which allows him to operate with more autonomy (Luhmann would call it "autopoiesis") as he moves from one institution to the next in his teaching and writing career. Lacan's rhetorical skill in capturing a large seminar audience constitutes another interest here; suffice it to say that Lacan's audience was very much theatrically drawn into the centre of Lacan's discourse. Lacan's seminars in this context offer for our study a wealth of concrete material, since Lacan concentrated his energy in precisely this direction.

As for the pro and the contra of Lacan's rhetoric, some may consider him in his *Seminar* a kind of French state actor performing an allegory of his own psychoanalytic edifice as a Baroque play-text for late twentieth-century Paris. Another perspective would show that he enacts a kind of mimetic desire, which René Girard has formulated in a series of intriguing works, and so communicates a desire for the desire of others in his *commedia dell'arte*, as Michel de Certeau has put it. The desire flowing to Lacan helps to explain the large audiences that his seminars drew. The mimetic space that constituted his seminars is what the critics have not noticed to a sufficient extent. A whole social history remains to be written about the powerful impact of these seminars on a whole generation of analysts and important intellectuals. Ladislav Rieger observes not irrelevantly here that

> Philosophical texts are the result of a continuous tension between the situation of philosophizing and the system of language that is directly or indirectly (paradox, antinomy) reflected in the text. *But a special analysis of philosophizing itself is a major task* that, even in outline, exceeds both our present goal and the bounds of this article.[19]

[18] Michel de Certeau, "Lacan: An Ethics of Speech," *Heterologies: Discourse on the Other*, trans. Brian Massumi (Minneapolis: University of Minnesota Press, 1986) 47.

[19] Rieger 88. My emphasis.

In this light, Lacan's form of philosophizing constitutes too the content of his teachings.

For some the whole rhetorical performance of Lacan is a kind of spoof. Others claim that we come with Lacan to inhabit a verbal world. In Luhmann we come to inhabit ever expanding concentric circles of concepts. In both cases, rhetoric is a good road into the universes of Lacan and of Luhmann, discursive edifices not irrelevant to the construction and to the apprehension of the world society of our future. That both were non-dogmatic syncretists to a large degree in the wide range of cultural reference they used reminds one of what Josef Vachek writes of

> the maxim Mathesius often instilled in the minds of his students, viz. that language should be treated as a fortress which must be besieged with all possible weapons attacking it from all sides. Clearly, also Mathesius's non-dogmatic approach may set a valuable example even to present-day linguistic research pursued both in Mathesius's own country and abroad.[20]

Mathesius may also offer a sterling example of what comparative cultural research can be motivated by into the future of intellectual work. The relation of Mathesius's work to that of Lacan or of Luhmann evades direct transposition, since neither of them refers to him directly, and yet their general sensibility has some concordance with it in terms of a parallel dynamic.

Certainly Lacan's explorative, syncretistic, and non-dogmatic rhetoric exploits the dramatic possibilities of language to an unusual effect. Lacan dramatizes the unconscious itself in his pedagogic method and verbal style that enlists silence and uncommon uses of the throat to communicate certain emotive states and blocs of sensation. De Certeau comments on this aspect:

> a starring role is assumed by the speaking body, and especially by this body's throat. Coughing, slightly grumbling, clearing the throat – like tattoos on the process of phonation – punctuate the chain of words and indicate all their secret of being "for the other" and

---

[20] Josef Vachek, "The Czech Editor's Postscript," *Praguiana* 285.

of producing for the listeners the effects of meaning, of the signified
[...] These corporal indicators bring speech to what they do not
know.[21]

Lacan's wild idea of a seminar also allowed him to turn his sense of
reference to an astonishing array of disciplines and figures that he rolls
in for illustrative and comparative purposes. Further than this, de Certeau
argues of the Lacan *Seminar*: "This exercise resembles a prayer to which
and for which nothing would answer."[22] This sounds rather like an
enactment of non-violence and of forces of separation of "un-power"
(Maurice Blanchot) and also of power which links phenomena and
relates to the injunction Lacan once gave: "I am asking you to refuse
what I am giving to you because that's not it."[23] This rather paradoxical
statement refers to something that evades the easy habits of
schematization and of taxonomization. Moreover, it can be said to avoid
simple representationalism which leads to imprecise and unreliable
conclusions.

Other scholars such as the renowned linguist Noam Chomsky
execrate Lacan's discourse and argue that Lacan is a charlatan, or what
one might prefer to call a magnificent windbag. But this surely does not
tell the whole story. For Lacan's theatre of rhetoric taps into the play of
the unconscious, which itself eludes direct representation by lexical
choices alone (linguisticalization), whence the enormous suggestiveness
of Lacan's language, in print and on stage, and pedagogic persona. The force
of Lacan comes from his ability to teach above all even more than to
write. And indeed for some scholars his true work was his seminars, and
not so much his writings. In this way, Lacan broaches interesting
questions about the role of language in our modernity controlled by the
dominating power of scientific discourse and capitalism. At times one
can even hear the violence of Lacan and of modernity both in his
rhetoric.[24]

---

[21]   de Certeau 50.
[22]   de Certeau 50.
[23]   de Certeau 51.
[24]   See a video of an impassioned Lacan on the unconscious: http://youtu.be/
       URsYj-TVFjc, accessed on 24 September 2012.

Now it has to be said that at times the greyish jargon of Lacan and of Luhmann as well betrays their standing as academics; yet that both display a rare capacity of rhetorical giftedness cannot be doubted. For both are stylists and rhetoricians of the very first rank in prose. On the surface, it may be argued that at times Lacan is purely decorative, whereas Luhmann is rather more sturdy conceptually and lacks the burnish and lustre of Lacan's rhetorical firepower. Yet actually both possess similar verbal powers as far as their lexical equipment goes. What cannot be doubted is that both contain an ability to question their whole enterprises, and so are capable of an admirable kind of self-problematization that opens out onto a possible intellectual self-completion. Perhaps the whole effect of their work in language is an effect of the violence of rhetorical representation and awaits a more mature adjudication with the passage of time.

To put some of the foregoing otherwise, if Lacan then expresses his insights in dramatic form, Luhmann does so in a rather more mechanical and systematic way and yet his rhetoric is populated with considerable conceptual armaments and verbal prowess of comparable stature to Lacan's as far as lexical choices go. For how else are we to judge the rhetorical sub-structure of their theories?

As far as humour goes, Lacan has the critical edge over Luhmann who in spite of having a keen sense of play and irony lacks the humour that so often thrives in Lacan. As I have already noted, both tap into the generative role of interdisciplinarity to equally excellent effect and in so doing they add to the good kind of violence of complexity of their investigations and limit the bad kind of violence of reductiveness. Both offer big theories about reality not least with regard to this complex of a highly sophisticated conceptual and intellectual strategy. To some, however, the abstraction of their theories seems preposterous, and that is the negative side of the wide-ranging ambitious scope of their sense of reference. Both of their rhetorics celebrate a special love of theory that goes against the grain of an age not so amenable to such abstract intellectual work; for these rhetorics do not fit the temporality of the digital and entertainment period of time in which we are. As such I find the idea attractive that both are among our most valid contemporaries, for they do not fit well into our commodified times.

Be that as it may, in the theatrical Baroque texts of Lacan we witness a special quality of chattishness that could be of the idle sort were it not for the aesthetic fact that the rhetorical flights are intense and truly dramatic, and diagnostic of the functioning and of the rhetorical possibilities of the unconscious. Here then the aesthetic and rhetorical quality run together.

To liberate the rhetoric and aesthetics of Lacan, who constructed a body of work which Alain Badiou, Jean-Luc Nancy, et al., engage as well, requires the kind of interdisciplinary approach that he himself espoused in his pedagogic work and in his writing. Rieger aids us here when he asserts that

> philosophical texts are usually polysemous, that is, they allow multiple interpretations. These interpretations, however, are not arbitrary; they always relate to a particular situation. If we are concerned with the original situation – the one in which the text was created by the author – then the most important thing ultimately is our ability to move our thought into a relevant framework, that is, the ability to seize an analogous situation [...] new concepts of the world are most often generated by original creations which, consequently, place the thought of the philosopher against the collective or official view of the period.[25]

This fits Lacan well because his discourse, which so often challenges orthodox or rather more standardized accounts of issues in the psychoanalytic tradition, invites plural interpretive perspectives. To understand Luhmann's writings requires even more than merely this, since his rhetorical chitchat is even more demanding in terms of the reader's powers of concentration, for he lacks the rhetorical effervescence that so marks Lacan's language in his seminars. To demonstrate this, Nico Stehr and Gotthard Bechmann write that

> Luhmann's strict, austere artificial language is not due to any affectation but rather to the stringency of his theoretical program [...] In this respect one should take seriously the penultimate

---

[25] Rieger 98.

sentence of the *Society of Societies*, according to which an adequate modern theory of society requires the sacrifice of mere pleasure of recognition and the judging of theory construction on its own merits.[26]

And yet both Lacan and Luhmann are now enjoying a major afterlife some twenty-one and fourteen years respectively after their deaths. As such their stylish rhetorics live on.

A considerable amount of critical and institutional energy is now paid to Lacan, more today than ever with so many of his former students now as senior psychoanalysts who have found the time to write on their mentor, not to mention the academic chairs, academic leaders, philosophers and cultural theorists who now find him worthy of their critical attention; the popular Slavoj Žižek builds preeminently on Lacan and Hegel in his cultural work. Luhmann studies meanwhile, as I have already suggested above, continue to grow in the English-speaking world with his works steadily but surely being more and more addressed; Luhmann's demanding writing becomes more and more difficult to ignore and the rhetorics of both reverberate more and more as descriptions of our contemporaneity.

If Lacan's operatively closed and autopoietic seminars are a far-reaching allegory of the unconscious, then the allegorical intellectualism of Luhmann's linguistic outputs has a similar function within the global system. As such they both delineate systems that are at once uncontrollable and evade easy fixings, yet are the very picture of modernity. Both raise disturbing questions about the violence of representation, while shaking off received academic thinking. For instance, both take a long view of economic, social and cultural developments in their works that pursue problems originating in the sixteenth century. And both see the subject itself as an effect of representation, a necessary violence for us perhaps, but a fiction all the same that needs a new semantics to articulate a possible new relationship between representation and violence for another politics of representation and another economy of violence/non-violence.

[26] Nico Stehr and Gotthard Bechmann, "Introduction," Niklas Luhmann, *Risk: A Sociological Theory*, trans. Rhodes Barrett (Piscataway, NJ: Aldine Transaction, 2002) xx-xxi.

The memorable drama that is the cultural activity of reading both Lacan and Luhmann might be outfitted by the idea that the unconscious gives autopoiesis a new flavour for more open and less homogeneous communities. Autopoiesis as a world soft force or un-power is still to come. Social and cultural autopoiesis awaits its inhabitants. The ungroundedness of the unconscious and of dissemination meanwhile nicely articulates the Baroque linguistic virtuosity of Lacan. Nothing in the Lacanian vision is more important than his pedagogic rhetoric. Nothing in Luhmann's intellectual intentions is more crucial than his ability to create conceptual and rhetorical models for our own linguistic and intellectual growth. And in this regard his key mentor by far is none other than Edmund Husserl; or, as Hans-Georg Moeller makes clear, Luhmann

> suggests nothing less than that Husserl had already employed a theory of second-order cybernetics, operationally-closed autopoietic systems and radical constructivism [...B]y attempting to continue the old project of epistemological idealism, Husserl missed the opportunity to understand the broader functionalist relevance of his own theory. He was too much of an epistemologist, in the traditional sense, to realize that he had already detected some of the most general mechanisms of autopoiesis.[27]

The contents of a tradition "of second-order cybernetics" for Luhmann are thus born with Husserl's intellectual output.

Similar to Luhmann's corpus of texts, Lacan's *Seminar* functions recursively (self-referentially). Thereby both works illustrate Luhmann's point that "the accumulation of internal complexity is possible only through operative closure."[28] This is what allows rhetoric too to function in more horizontal and direct access societies as against hierarchical and mediated access societies. In this way the *communitas* dimension of society may have new chances for being, for what militates against community is the reductively false form of the violence of representation.

[27] Moeller 181-82.
[28] Niklas Luhmann, *Law As a Social System*, eds. Fatima Kastner, Richard Nobles, David Schiff and Rosamund Ziegert, trans. Klaus A. Ziegert (Oxford: Oxford University Press, 2004) 80.

By mobilizing the recursivity of the unconscious, Lacan's rhetoric allows the construction of another discourse of modernity. This is not unlike the way Luhmann's work enables us to think even more conceptually of the international discourse of that modernity. If the ancient trivium that divided disciplines into grammar, dialectic and rhetoric still allows for the rhetoric of words if not of titles to capture one true substance of things, then a freer concept articulating the mediated relation between representation and violence is what is needed in the late capitalist Baroque period to minimize these relationships of authority, power and control towards less monochrome and more contrapuntal, free, polyphonic and autopoietic societies.

The current millennial upheaval with regard to the late capitalist Baroque age might look to these vast frescos or tapestries constructed by the two writers not merely as a servant of two masters, but as a master of two servants. For we can read Lacan and Luhmann jointly and in so doing resist the hierarchical preemptive power of the hydraulic and psychodynamic rhetoric of psychoanalysis and the fantasticated rhetoric of systems theory, as we have here just attempted to do even while pointing out the understated role of the Prague School in the epistemic formulation of our target textual projects.

On top of this, if "[t]he structure of truth, for the Baroque, is theatrical"[29] and if what is distinguishing about the unconscious for Freud and for Lacan is that it has a structure, and if for Luhmann structure and autopoiesis must replace reason, will and feeling and if "as Brazilian theorist Irlemar Chiampi puts it, "the Baroque is the aesthetic of Counter-Reformation, the Neo-Baroque is the aesthetic of counter-modernity,"[30] then it can be claimed that Lacan's diatribes against modernity and its pulverizing impact on the subject are not radicalized by Luhmann who gets rid of the subject altogether when he opts instead for communication as the basic cell of society. This conceptual investment in the functionalistic aspect and importance of communication for the system of language, epistemically speaking for thought later in the twentieth century, is without a doubt influenced by the Prague School,

[29] Egginton 51.
[30] Egginton 70.

since its founding document propounds as much. For example, we read of "The Conception of Language as a Functional System"[31] in which "[w]hether we analyze language as expression or communication, the speaker's intention is the most evident and most natural explanation."[32]

Both the rhetoric of Lacan and that of Luhmann end not on a note of self-indulgent optimism but of a hardheaded realism; as William Rasch puts it of Luhmann, "It is not a utopic vista that Luhmann paints, but simply an improbable and, he seems to think, highly fragile condition. And it is this condition – not project – of modernity that he invests with an ethical imperative."[33] As for Lacan, Jonathan Scott Lee remarks that "[b]y the end of his life Lacan seems to situate the very power and success of psychoanalytic theory in its ultimately necessary failure. This is the true significance of the human subject's encounter with the real: failure is success, and success is failure."[34] Hence, both of our conceptual systems articulate something for the benefit and clarification of the cultural Baroque modernity, our four centuries of experience of modern society.

Luhmann's idea of "the autopoiesis of society as communication system"[35] should remind us that linking the two thinkers was also a desire to activate the happy risk of communication for our theoretical offerings. If communication as such creates, and thus even processes, society one wonders whether the violence of representation can be minimized by this sharing, circulation and experimentation, in which a good level of rhetorical charm remains and awaits some kind of factual-practical if not ideological marriage. If a shift of tone is underway, then this is perhaps because Lacan's and Luhmann's rhetoric unconsciously articulate but do not precisely define what might be something like a new form of togetherness and sacred, or a new freedom; and yet maybe this constitutes the overall unconscious strategy of their work for its ultimate unconscious net effect. Luhmann himself after all once said that "[a]utopoiesis presupposes a recurring need for renewal,"[36]

---

31   "Theses Presented to the First Congress of Slavic Philologists in Prague, 1929" 5.
32   "Theses Presented to the First Congress of Slavic Philologists in Prague, 1929" 5.
33   William Rasch, *Niklas Luhmann's Modernity: The Paradoxes of Differentiation* (Stanford, CA: Stanford University Press, 2000) 149-50.
34   Jonathan Scott Lee, *Jacques Lacan* (Boston: Twayne Publishers, 1990) 199.
35   Luhmann, *Risk: A Sociological Theory* 115.
36   Niklas Luhmann, *Essays on Self-Reference* (New York: Columbia University Press, 1990) 8.

even as "what is proper to time itself is only its irreversibility";[37] therefore there is a demand that the meaning of the dialectically petrifying and liberating powers of time, of violence and of representation should be reformulated, so that we can contribute to a better solution of these ancient problems. Time, violence and representation develop structures of their own to continue autopoietically to exist in various social systems; the question therefore is, how can the distinctions between structure and autopoiesis be put in the better service of the globalized Baroque modernity?

What is remarkable about the violence of our globalized spectacle society is how much it misses; so what of the autopoietic unconscious and of communicative structures working instead in communicative tandem? When Luhmann writes that "interpretation is the creation of more text,"[38] it captures one essence of our contribution for rethinking violence and representation, or figuratively speaking, putting old libations in new bottles.

As a feat of achievement, the Prague Linguistic Circle was foundationally significant for the creative periods and outputs that were the teaching and writing careers of Lacan and of Luhmann. To separate the mediate from the immediate, the Circle shifted the terms and concepts of the debate and of the critical ground upon which our chosen thinkers stood in a twentieth-century European world. The spirit circulating between these cultural parties, Lacan – Luhmann, continues today in a concert of inflows and outflows for their powerful tours de force. Although their formidable scholarly works cannot yet postulate a complete circulation, their individual projects remain in the kaleidoscope of an antifoundationalist Baroque modernity in wait, even as the insights of the Prague School and related thinkers (e.g., Husserl) do too. Consequently, the Prague code is invariant, and the aforesaid constitutes a point of departure for keeping the Aspidistra of a post-Husserlian autopoiesis flying; such would invest the Circle with life.

---

37 Luhmann, *Essays on Self-Reference* 43.
38 Luhmann, *Law as A Social System* 306.

JAN GROSSMAN, PRAGUE STRUCTURALISM, AND THE GROTESQUE

Ondřej Pilný

> The difference between being a man and being a coffee-mill is art.
> — Tristan Tzara in Tom Stoppard's *Travesties*

Widely regarded as one of the most influential Czech theatre directors of the twentieth century, an esteemed writer on the theatre and literary critic, Jan Grossman (1925-1993) ranks also among prominent inheritors of the Prague Structuralist school. From 1945, he was a student of comparative literature and aesthetics at Charles University, taking courses by the eminent literary critic Václav Černý and the leading Structuralist theoretician Jan Mukařovský. After the arrival of the communist rule in 1948, Grossman was expelled from university, and for the subsequent four decades had to struggle with persistent harassment by the Czechoslovak communist authorities. The 1960s saw a moderate thaw in censorship and Grossman quickly came to the fore with his version of the theatre of the absurd, collaborating closely with the up-and-coming playwright Václav Havel at the Prague theatre Na zábradlí (At the Balustrade); his most powerful productions included Alfred Jarry's *Král Ubu* (King Ubu, 1964), Havel's *Vyrozumění* (The Memorandum, 1965), and an adaptation of *The Trial* by Franz Kafka (*Proces*, 1966). This essay examines the role of Structuralist methodology in Grossman's writing and theatrical practice, with a focus on the politics of the grotesque as an issue that has influenced his particular form of engagement with Structuralism, Grossman's version of Jarry being employed as a remarkable example.

Unlike Martin Esslin, who perceived the theatre of the absurd as being linked with the catastrophe of World War II – the shattering of both religious and secular beliefs – Grossman saw absurdist theatre as a reaction to the debilitating effect of modernity on individual selfhood and on creativity:

> The theatre of the absurd essentially focuses on a single basic phenomenon: the uniformity, banality, forcing into the line, and standardization caused by modern civilization – a phenomenon which is paradoxically associated with a world that is labelled as the world of social restructuring and scientific and technological discovery.[1]

The "core and the source" of the universal mediocrity that is produced by this "civilization" according to Grossman is parochialism (*maloměšťáctví*). While the literal meaning of the Czech term apparently foregrounds its historical linkage with the petit bourgeoisie (it translates as "the quality of being petit bourgeois"), and had originally been used to criticize the attitudes of the urban middle classes under capitalism, Grossman links it rather with an opportunistic, materialist existence that is complicit with the political tide regardless of its nature. Parochialism is thus defined as a "state of mind [...], manipulating the world and exploiting, degrading and depreciating all values." The parochialist basis of absurdity "rests in the tension between a passionate longing for the absolute and a dilettantism which degrades this longing into a parodic deformation of true creativity."[2] Grossman's phrasing is deliberately, even strategically vague; and the direct relevance of his view to the atmosphere in communist Czechoslovakia would have been manifest to any contemporary reader.

One of the principal features of the theatre of the absurd, if we disregard the respective pitch of its definition for the moment, is its

---

[1] Jan Grossman, "Uvedení *Zahradní slavnosti*" (Opening of *The Garden Party*), Václav Havel, *Zahradní slavnost* (Praha: Orbis, 1964), repr. in Jan Grossman, *Texty o divadle – první část* (Texts on the Theatre, Vol. 1), eds. Miloslav Klíma, Jan Dvořák, Zuzana Jindrová (Praha: Pražská scéna, 1999) 138. All translations from Czech in this essay are mine.

[2] Grossman, "Uvedení *Zahradní slavnosti*" 138.

frequent employment of the grotesque. As Wolfgang Kayser has observed, the essential ingredients of the grotesque include a "mixture of heterogeneous elements, confusion, fantastic quality, and [... an] alienation of the world."[3] Moreover, the grotesque "depersonalizes the individual and makes him the agent of something strange and inhuman,"[4] a feature that often results in a depiction of the world in which instruments and mechanisms "unfold a dangerous life of their own" and where "human bodies [are] reduced to puppets, marionettes, and automata."[5] A fundamental awareness of these traits of the grotesque is manifest in Grossman's essays on absurdist plays, grotesque imagery even coming to permeate vital passages, such as the following which merits being quoted at length:

> The parochial mentality is truly embodied [in the theatre of the absurd]: its imaginings, dreams and interpretations seem to be planted in a climatically favourable environment, where they proliferate as tropical vegetation out of all proportion. Characters in these plays are not portrayed with photographic realism any more, nor are they mere Daumieresque caricatures. They are creatures developed by outrageous fantasy akin to that of Hieronymus Bosch: caretakers thus turn into monsters, professors really kill their pupils with their Spanish lessons, inhabitants of entire cities are transformed into rhinoceroses. Objects grow over into an unnatural dimension, as do the people, albeit in a different sense. Made by humans, things slip out of human control, cease serving people, and devour them instead.[6]

Indeed, mechanization was highlighted by Grossman in the plays of both Václav Havel and Alfred Jarry, and formed one of the central motifs in his stagings of both authors, as we shall see in our subsequent discussion of *Král Ubu*.

The affinity of grotesque art in a broad sense with Grossman's theatrical practice is further underlined in an effect he desired for his productions – that of an ambivalent laughter: "I was the happiest when

3   Wolfgang Kayser, *The Grotesque in Art and Literature* (1957), trans. Ulrich Weisstein (New York and Toronto: McGraw-Hill, 1966) 51.
4   Kayser 197 n. 12.
5   Kayser 183.
6   Grossman, "Uvedení *Zahradní slavnosti*" 138.

people said after the show [...] that they laughed while simultaneously feeling a chill in the spine."[7] This kind of laughter has been associated with the grotesque by its theorists and practitioners alike at least since Christoph Martin Wieland's *Unterredungen mit dem Pfarrer von **** (1775), and its utility (or lack thereof) has become one of the most vexed issues pertaining to the study of the grotesque.[8] Grossman's view on its role was unequivocal, however: he regarded the intermingling of merriment with horror as an ideal premise for a true dialogue between the stage and the auditorium, and between fellow human beings.[9] This in turn demonstrates that Grossman's concept of the theatre of the absurd entails a vital ethical component: in his words,

> The theatre of the absurd is analytical and produces, if you wish, a cold diagnosis. As a matter of principle, it does not offer solutions. Nevertheless, I would argue that its adherence to such principles does not stem from a certainty that the solution does not exist, but rather from the conviction that the solution will never be *given* to us in any way by anybody anywhere. If the theatre be a doctor, it does not wish to cure by issuing the customary prescriptions, but instead by confronting the patient in the most drastic manner with his potentially imminent destruction. Not in order to bring this destruction about, but rather to prevent it from happening.[10]

It is by turning towards the individual and the private, and by simultaneously historicizing the present that the theatre "unmasks evil in a broad context," an evil that is more dangerous than that of a Richard III in Grossman's view, because it has turned "quite ordinary."[11] Given this perspective, it is clear why Grossman maintained that the origins of the

---

7   Jan Grossman, "Předmluva" (Foreword), Václav Havel, *Protokoly* (Protocols) (Praha: Mladá fronta, 1966), repr. in Grossman, *Texty o divadle – první část* 149.
8   On Wieland, see Kayser 30-32. Kayser's view of "grotesque laughter" is ultimately inconclusive, as he is ready to admit of it merely as an involuntary, "abysmal" reaction to that "which cannot be handled in any other way," since for him, the grotesque is essentially bleak. Cf. Kayser 186-88.
9   Grossman, "Předmluva" 149.
10   Grossman, "Uvedení *Zahradní slavnosti*" 141.
11   Grossman, "Uvedení *Zahradní slavnosti*" 140-41.

theatre of the absurd were to be seen in Realism rather than in Romanticism, despite the centrality of the grotesque for absurdist playwrights. He asserted that absurdity was created by hyperbole; however, "only that which has been first stated with precision may be hyperbolized."[12] Absurdism was consequently to be perceived as a type of hyper-realism, of which Franz Kafka was the epitome, standing alongside Alfred Jarry as an ur-father of the theatre of the absurd.[13]

To anyone familiar with Jarry's *Ubu* plays or the details of the scandalous first performance of *Ubu roi*, Grossman's production of *Král Ubu* would have come across as surprising, because it was couched in realism. There were no outrageous or amateurish costumes or decorations, the acting was of a high standard, and the vulgarity of the language was subdued and sounded commonplace, as instantiated by the opening scene in which Pa Ubu's notorious "merdre" was muttered as part of the everyday routine of getting up which was enacted in naturalist style.[14] In light of the director's view on the origins of the theatre of the absurd, his dramaturgical choice is only natural. Grossman has moreover left an extraordinary document in the form of an extensive commentary on the production, where he meticulously outlined the reasons for his directorial decisions and concluded with a reiteration of his perspective on the purpose of absurdist theatre.[15] In this manuscript, he explains that his team did not wish to reconstruct the Rabelaisian puppetry and anarchic fireworks of Jarry's original, since that would have resulted only in a retrospective curio production – attractive as that might have been. Instead, they opted for creating what they hoped would be a fully resonant reinterpretation. Grossman asserts that this meant to focus on

[12] Grossman, "Uvedení *Zahradní slavnosti*" 138-39.
[13] Grossman, "Uvedení *Zahradní slavnosti*" 139. "The classical author of absurd realism is Franz Kafka." (ibid.) See also Jan Grossman, "Král Ubu" (King Ubu), *Texty o divadle – první část* 154.
[14] The production was recorded in 1968 by Czech Television, and released in 2006 on DVD by the magazine *Reflex* as part of its theatre series.
[15] The typescript of 95pp dated 1966 was lodged at the Theatre Institute in Prague, and remained unpublished until the late 1990s edition of his collected works, where it appeared under the title "Král Ubu." See Grossman, *Texty o divadle – první část* 153-78. References given in parentheses in the text of the present essay are to this edition.

what he termed the "overall structure" of Jarry's play, and replace those of its elements that were bound up with the historical context of the time of its origin by others that would be able to "impart the same or analogous meanings now." (154) The ultimate objective was to "force the spectator to receive the production not as a dazzling spectacle, but as a challenge and as an enquiry that solicits an answer. In other words, to renew the shock caused by Jarry." (155) The extent to which the original was adapted may be judged most immediately by considering the alterations to Jarry's text: Grossman and his collaborator Miloš Macourek in fact welded together *Ubu roi* with the dramatically less accomplished *Ubu enchaîné*, the play that was of the greatest interest to them as it had not been produced in Czechoslovakia previously and since it "mercilessly unmasked bureaucratized liberty – a liberty which has become a strictly enforced decree." (155-56) The relevance of the theme in a totalitarian state of the Eastern Bloc which ostentatiously promoted its social arrangement as the ultimate achievement of freedom and guarantor of universal joy hardly requires further comment. The text was complemented by passages from *Ubu sur la butte* and from Jarry's novel *Gestes et opinions du docteur Faustroll, pataphysicien*, while individual speeches were added wherever it was deemed necessary.

Grossman proceeds to chronologically detail all the elements of his production in his commentary and conscientiously notes further textual and dramaturgical alterations, together with his stylistic decisions. This is where his exposure to Structuralism comes most prominently to the fore: in the manner of a rigorous Structuralist, Grossman discusses all the layers that are joined in creating the meaning of the performance, beginning with elements of the plot and setting, and proceeding through details of stage design, acting and scenic gesture, costume and props, music and its orchestration. The individual units are presented as combining into a seamless whole, which is conceived of as a "travestied Shakespearean history play." (171) This "history play" traverses several periods: the feudal realm of King Wenceslas which is turned into a centralized monarchy by the usurper Ubu, which is then in turn succeeded by a bourgeois republic of "free people." In a final evolution, the republic is gradually and inconspicuously converted into a state where freedom becomes an obligation and in which the indomitable opportunist Ubu swiftly comprehends that in order to triumph again, he must make himself over into a slave and a prisoner, which he duly does. His new proletarian guise finally brings him back his crown. Significantly, Grossman puts specifications of the individual eras, such as "feudal," "centralized," and "bourgeois" into brackets in his text and appends them with a question mark, arguing against an excess of specificity and preferring a "multiplicity of topical interpretations." (156) Notwithstanding his explicit argument, it must be kept in mind that an overt historical allegory starring Ubu the anti-hero would hardly have escaped the notice of the communist censors and would simply not have been allowed on the stage, not to mention the personal repercussions that would inevitably have ensued for those involved in its creation. This is probably also why the final era – arguably that of Eastern Bloc communism – is outlined most obliquely in Grossman's notes, and more importantly, was the only one whose specific contours were not readily distinguishable from that of the democratic republic in the actual production, at least in contrast to the clear depiction provided of feudal rule and absolutist monarchy respectively.

While certain elements were of necessity recondite, others were not: the meaning of prominent elements of the stage design such as the dust bins, stove pipes, and assorted junk was quite obvious in the performance as these helped to demarcate the acting space as a rubbish dump, where the "sublime" drama of "big history" was depicted as unfolding.[16] The mechanical puppetry of the inhabitants of this junkyard complemented the image of a world "where people do not use mechanisms and where mechanisms use people instead" (177), a picture that was further enhanced by the presence onstage of a pataphysical machine made of destroyed objects of everyday use, such as spoons, toothbrushes, light bulbs, broken pots, a smoothing iron and assorted wiring. The machine "functioned perfectly, moving, humming, and emitting light. It had only the one fault: it was devoid of any use. It became an image of senseless activity, moving in a circle, from nowhere to nowhere and with no purpose." (158) In order to drive the point home, drawings of the pataphysical machine were included in the programme

---

[16] Grossman's intention as regards this theme is sketched out in "Král Ubu" 156.

notes for the performance and were complemented by a pseudo-scientific treatise on its operation.

Any activity on the stage came down to an engagement in a constant struggle for power in which, inevitably, Pa Ubu and his wife were triumphant. This was Grossman's way of intimating that a purposeless world becomes dominated by the sort of parochialism that grows in Pa Ubu from a "banal and lousy" individual quality into an overwhelming essence, whereby parochialism is transformed into "an almighty divinity." (177) The clear political edge of this reinterpretation of Jarry's work provides a vivid illustration of Grossman's perception of the theatre of the absurd: there is no trace of resignation in the face of the absurdity of existence, no despair over the loss of direction that is caused by the disappearance of God or any of his ideological substitutes. Instead, Grossman's production takes Jarry's exuberant, anarchic grotesque and transforms it into a grotesque with a satirical purpose that questions the viability of the political status quo; or, as the director put it, the theatre's technique attempts to "create points of contact between fantastically grotesque action and our contemporary experience." (164)

We have seen that Grossman described his approach to the staging of Jarry as being founded on an adherence to the "overall structure" of the work. Outstanding as his production was, the description of the technique is suspect: what exactly is this "overall structure" of a play supposed to be, particularly in a situation where it is produced from a collage of texts and where a similar approach is used as regards all the other aspects of production, such as acting, stage design, and music? Furthermore, we have also noted that Grossman describes the process of developing the production in the manner of a meticulous Structuralist, which may imply that all the various units of meaning are to combine in a closed and ultimately self-regulating compound. Grossman's use of the term "structure" in fact reflects its definition by Jan Mukařovský, who did not merely conceive of the work of art as an interrelation of the whole and its parts but also stressed its location within a particular artistic tradition on the one hand and within the context of the oeuvre of a specific artist on the other. Moreover, Mukařovský argued that due to the parallel historical development of the arts and the society, individual elements in the structure of the work of art must be seen as constantly rearranging themselves within the hierarchy of their importance.[17] The broad understanding of structure may thus elucidate the use of the term by Grossman; however, this does not mean that the concept itself is unproblematic.

Coincidentally, it was only a year after Grossman completed his commentary on the Ubu production that Jacques Derrida published his seminal essay on the limits of the Structuralist method, arguing that since structure was always already linked with that which remained outside it, the notion of its closed nature collapsed.[18] Derrida deliberately chose to make his point in relation to the very origin of Structuralism in de Saussure's linguistics; his critique consequently becomes all the more potent when applied to the complex development of the method in a general aesthetics theory by Mukařovský. This becomes manifest when Mukařovský needs to inflate the concept of structure so that it refers not only to the work of art itself but also to its context,[19] whereby "structure" becomes all-encompassing, and as a concept rather devoid of utility. Derrida's unravelling of the metaphysical nature of Structuralism, bounded with the notion of a single meaning and a totalizing tendency, is all the more strongly confirmed.

Having said that, it must be admitted that for a linguist engaged in identifying the basic rules of the grammar of a language, the Structuralist method is probably still the best available, Derrida's reservations notwithstanding. Looking at Grossman's argument in contrast, the fact that he uses an essentialist notion of "overall structure" in outlining the guiding principle of his adaptation is frankly of academic significance: Grossman never proceeds to comment on what the essence of Jarry might consist in, and more importantly, the conceptual awkwardness had no detectable impact on the actual production. The concerted weaving together of individual units of structure toward an intended whole in his essay may seem more problematic. Grossman's effort to achieve a harmony of the respective elements of performance

[17] Jan Mukařovský, "O strukturalismu" (On Structuralism, 1946), *Studie z estetiky* (Studies in Aesthetics), ed. Květoslav Chvatík (Praha: Odeon, 1966) 109-110.

[18] See Jacques Derrida, "Structure, Sign and Play in the Discourse of the Humanities" (1967), *Writing and Difference*, trans. Alan Bass (London: Routledge and Kegan Paul, 1978) 278-94.

[19] Mukařovský, "O strukturalismu" 112.

nevertheless involves a remarkable and concurrent conceptualization of individual details as allusions and hints. Momentary changes of acting style, departing from naturalism, are intended as hints towards melodrama, slapstick, or great tragedy; these may still be read within the bounds of Mukařovský's notion of tradition and artistic conventions.[20] However, the historical settings of individual scenes – as outlined above – deliberately lack the specificity that would allow for the attribution of an unambiguous meaning, and combine with the theatrical and other allusions in a web that defies totalization. In Grossman's own words, the consistent use of hints and allusions is intended to "activate the spectator's intelligence and imagination" and invite him/her to a con-versation; the "incomplete and unfinished nature of the hint means something 'in excess' on the stage: it clearly points to a space beyond, whereby it offers the spectator the greatest freedom of interpretation that is possible, provoking at the same time the desire for interpretation and application."[21]

Grossman's adoption of the Structuralist method thus amounts to a significant loosening of its constraints: the individual units of meaning are joined together in a collage that achieves unity and balance in performance, while it simultaneously remains open to multiple interpretations due to its relentless use of allusion in the context of the grotesque. Paradoxical as it may seem, the resulting "structure" is harmonious and open at the same time. In the theatre, it is ultimately the nature of the production that is decisive of course, rather than the theoretical underpinnings of a director's position. In the case of *Král Ubu*, however, the latter received a splendid confirmation by the former: while we have noted that the political relevance of Grossman's version of Jarry to communist Czechoslovakia was evident, the production maintained a significant level of ambiguity which prevented it from being perceived merely as a satirical brand of agit-prop. It is here that

---

[20] Cf. Mukařovský, "O strukturalismu" 109.
[21] Grossman, "Král Ubu" 162. Grossman's emphasis on the importance of the hint and of multiple meaning is further developed in his remarkable essay on Kafka and on his 1966 adaptation of *The Trial* for the stage. See Jan Grossman, "Kafkova divadelnost?" (Kafka's Theatricality?), *Divadlo* 15.9 (1964): 1-17, repr. in Grossman, *Texty o divadle – první část* 181-203.

the affinity of Grossman's theatre with the epic theatre of Bertolt Brecht, one of the playwrights whose work he admired the most, becomes the most pronounced perhaps: both practitioners aimed at creating an engagé theatre whose principal technique was that of montage and where a reality that was accepted as normal was questioned through new perspectives that were opened by the performance. Yet while many of Brecht's plays and productions have been criticized for their promotion of a distinct political ideology, such an objection is difficult to raise with Grossman's work for the stage, as the case of *Král Ubu* shows.

The Prague Structuralism which provided Grossman with his theoretical apparatus does however contain a restrictive tendency, although the characteristics and the potency of this predisposition are relative to the individual scholars. Of particular relevance in the present context are the remarks of Vilém Mathesius on the relation between the stage and the audience in the theatre and, again, the views of Mukařovský. In a brief essay on Shakespearean theatre, Mathesius conceived of the spectators as being representative of the nation from which the playwright's work had stemmed, and ascribed to the audience a "regulatory function."[22] This is perhaps overly expressive of the limitations of the interpretive framework that forms the basis of Mathesius's scholarly work; a number of his other studies in fact repeatedly stress the need for the national culture to remain open to what lay outside it, while his final essays emphasize the crucial importance of free individual creativity, summarized by the term "creative activism."[23] The work of his follower Jan Mukařovský shares Mathesius's anchoring of art and culture (including the theatre) in the nation. In accordance with the fundamental dialectical basis of his approach, Mukařovský proceeds to depict the relation between the stage

---

[22] Vilém Mathesius, "Kdy mluví drama a divadlo k národu" (When Does Drama and Theatre Speak to the Nation?, 1939, rev. 1944), *Jazyk, kultura a slovesnost* (Language, Culture and Literature), ed. Josef Vachek (Praha: Odeon, 1982) 302, 304.

[23] Vilém Mathesius, "My a skutečnost" (Us and Reality, 1943), *Jazyk, kultura a slovesnost* 345; see also "Tvořivý aktivismus" (Creative Activism, 1942), *Jazyk, kultura a slovesnost* 353-56. For the need of inspiration from external sources, see, e.g., "Vůle ke kultuře" (The Will to Culture, 1928), *Jazyk, kultura a slovesnost* 347.

and the audience more specifically as a dialogue: for him, the dialectic of forces that is enacted on the stage is to continue in the spectator's mind after the performance.[24] This, incidentally, is very much in accord with the effect of the theatre intended by Brecht. However, the totalizing tendency of Mukařovský's approach tellingly gains the upper hand in a subsequent development of the notion, in which the "passionate conversation" of a director with his audience is not only equated with a dialogue of the theatre and the nation, but Mukařovský also decries "any shades of subjectivism": these are emphatically to be "done with." As a result, the dialogue is ultimately conceptualized as one of "the society with itself via the artist."[25] Such dialogue turned monologue stands of course in radical contrast to Grossman's desire to "activate the spectator's intelligence and imagination" and to engage him/her in a conversation.

Grossman termed his practice the "theatre of appeal" (*apelativní divadlo*); in Czech, the primary connotation is that with issuing a challenge (as in 'I appeal for the audience to listen') and with that of pursuing a claim (as in 'I appeal to your sense of justice'), with perhaps an echo of another meaning of the Latin *appellāre* – to put a name to things. The translation of the term into English highlights another quality that is foremost in Grossman's work and which we have bypassed so far: an inherent sense of entertainment and joyousness. These are often the result of simply engaging the audience's imagination in a meaningful way; moreover, they are often caused by the impact of various anecdotes and gags utilized in the production. Grossman was a firm believer in the anecdote as the source of a "pure and a completely natural absurdity" and an energetic force that "analyses and unmasks";[26] when staging *Ubu*, all he

---

24 Jan Mukařovský, "Jevištní řeč v avantgardním divadle" (Language on the Stage in Avant-garde Theatre, 1937), *Studie z estetiky* 162. Mukařovský shares Mathesius's view of the audience as representative of the nation despite his ostentatious negation of this perspective in his 1941 essay "K dnešnímu stavu teorie divadla" (On the Current State of the Theatre Theory), since the same essay subsequently comments on the theatre exclusively in a national context and thus contradicts the initial statement. See *Studie z estetiky* 163-71.

25 Jan Mukařovský, "D34 – D48 ve vývoji českého divadla" (The D34 – D48 Theatre in the Development of Czech Theatre), *Studie z estetiky* 327.

26 Grossman, "Kafkova divadelnost?" 198-99.

had to do was utilize some of the best passages of Jarry's original text in order to make his point. His concerted effort to include numerous gags in the production, from those that involved unexpected changes of acting style, to scenes such as that in which a single soldier emulates whole battalions parading for inspection under an elevated platform of assembled dignitaries, testify to a close collaboration with Václav Havel. Only months before the Ubu production, Havel wrote a brilliant essay entitled "The Anatomy of the Gag,"[27] in which he regards the device as a peculiar instance of estrangement as defined by Viktor Shklovsky. Havel claims that the estrangement produced by the gag reveals an absurdity, and at the same time rouses the spectator from the automatism of their reality. The gag may thus be defined as a "deliberate nonsensification" of an absurd reality,[28] which results in laughter. Havel concludes: "A sense of absurdity, the ability to estrange, absurd humour – these are likely the ways in which the contemporary man achieves catharsis. This may possibly be the only method of 'purification' that is adequate to the world in which we live."[29]

The incongruity that is at the root of the gag brings us back to the concept of the grotesque, which forms the cornerstone of the "appeal" of Grossman's theatre in all the senses of the term as outlined above. The grotesque involves the construction of an ambivalent work of art from incommensurable elements, presents the world as a puppet play and highlights its domination by senseless automatism and mechanization. However, the grotesque in Grossman's work defies the view of the most accomplished theorist of the concept, Wolfgang Kayser, who held that the grotesque was essentially hopeless and was expressive of despair. Bearing a fundamental political charge, Grossman's grotesque emerges as an inheritor of the medieval manifestation of the phenomenon as

---

[27] Václav Havel, "Anatomie gagu" (1963). The essay appeared as part of the collection *Protokoly* which was introduced by Grossman (see notes 7 and 9 above) and included, among others, Havel's play *The Garden Party*, for which Grossman had written an earlier introduction (see note 1ff above), documenting the creative and intellectual interaction between the director and the playwright at the time.

[28] Havel, "Anatomie gagu," The Václav Havel Library Online Archive, accessed 7 November 2012.

[29] Havel, "Anatomie gagu" 8.

conceptualized by Mikhail Bakhtin, who saw in it a "power to liberate from dogmatism, completeness, and limitation"[30] and believed in the regenerative power of laughter in the face of the grotesque – difficult as it may be to maintain that theatre can influence the politics of a modern state.

[30] Mikhail Bakhtin, *Rabelais and His World* (1965), trans. Hélène Iswolsky (Bloomington: Indiana University Press, 1984) 44.

ATTESTING / BEFORE THE FACT

Louis Armand*

What I say for the first time, as if as testimony, is already a repetition, at least a repeatability; it is already an iterability, more than once at once, more than an instant in one instant, at the same time; and that being the case, the instant is always divided at its very point, at the point of its writing. It is always on the verge[*en instance*] of becoming divided, whence the problem of idealization. To the extent that it is repeatable, the singular instant becomes an ideal instant. The root of the testimonial problem of *technē* is to be found here. The technical reproducibility is excluded from testimony, which always calls for the presence of the live voice in the first person. But from the moment that a testimony must be repeated, *technē* is admitted; it is introduced where it excluded. For this one need not wait for cameras, videos, typewriters, and computers. As soon as the sentence is repeatable, that is, from its origin, the instant it is pronounced and becomes intelligible, thus idealisable, it is already instrumentalisable and affected by technology. And virtuality. It is thus the very instant of the instant that seems to be exemplary: exemplary in the very place where it seems unique and irreplaceable, under the seal of unicity. And it is perhaps here, with the technological both as ideality and prosthetic iterability, that the possibility of fiction and lie, simulacrum and literature, that of the right to literature insinuates itself, at the very origin of truthful testimony, autobiography in good faith, sincere confession, as their essential composability.

— Jacques Derrida, *Demeure*[1]

* A version of this essay was originally published in Louis Armand, *Incendiary Devices: Discourses of the Other* (Prague: Karolinum, 2006).

[1] Jacques Derrida, *Demeure. Fiction and Testimony*, trans. Elizabeth Rottenberg (Stanford: Stanford University Press, 2000) 41-42.

I

In his discussion of "radical philology,"[2] Geert Lernout, critiquing certain "theoretical" tendencies that had taken hold in the field of textual genetics, cites a passage by Daniel Ferrer in which the latter in turn cites Jacques Derrida on the "possibility of disengagement and citational graft which belongs to the structure of every mark, spoken or written, and which constitutes every mark in writing before and outside every horizon of semio-linguistic communication" ("Signature, événement, contexte"). Despite the curious irony of this situation, it is worth taking Lernout's objection seriously, that whatever stands "before and outside every horizon of semio-linguistic communication" constitutes – as in Immanuel Kant's *Kritik der praktischen Vernunft* (1788) and Ludwig Wittgenstein's *Tractatus Logico-Philosophicus* (1921) – "that whereof we cannot speak." For Lernout, the anteriority of signification is a matter simply of intuition, and therefore characterises a failure of rigorous methodology.

It is precisely the question of methodology or rather of *method*, however, which may be regarded as being at stake here. For Derrida, the anteriority of signification is indicative of the tautological relation of the instantaneousness of the present (posed in the form of the signifier) to *technē*, and which via the concept of "testimony," devolves in large part upon the impossibility of generalizing the instant, while nevertheless confronting the necessarily generalizing condition of "iterability" as the structural constraint and pre-condition of its signifier as such (i.e., of "the instant" as "une série de contiguïtés matérielle").[3] Derrida argues at length in his 1996 collaboration with Bernard Stiegler, *Échographies*: "que technicité ne soit pas technique, que la pensée de la technique ne soit pas technique, c'est la condition de la pensée."[4] And yet in speaking thus we necessarily generalize this concept, as Derrida warns, both as

---

2   Geert Lernout, "The *Finnegans Wake* Notebooks and Radical Philology," *Probes: Genetic Studies in Joyce*, eds. David Hayman and Sam Slote (Amsterdam: Rodopi, 1995) 19-48.
3   Jacques Derrida et Bernard Stiegler, *Échographies de la télévision: Entretiens filmés* (Paris: Éditions Galilée, 1996) 146.
4   Derrida et Stiegler 149.

an exemplum and as an ideality (viz. the supplementarity of *method*). The point for Lernout, nevertheless, is that whatever stands as an object of anteriority, and hence of intuitive knowledge, is unverifiable; it is not an object of knowledge at all and is therefore irrelevant to the science of philology.

What the science of philology properly is may be debatable, and may assume a variety of forms, from classical hermeneutics or empirical method, to the "radical philology" of textual genetics; likewise operating in any number of contexts, from linguistic historicity to the technics of "language" acquisition, and including all forms of discourse, literary, philosophical or otherwise. In any case the term needs to be qualified, if only for the very practical reason that philology begins with a necessary if apparently contradictory assumption of *incompletion*, and that at every point it must take this into account, above all in its definition of "verifiability." It is in part for this reason, in the excess of method, that Lacan poses the paradoxical formulation "tout langage est métalangage."[5]

Between a conception of semio-linguistic anteriority and of quasi-scientific verifiability, there arises the problem of "prediction." If anteriority is purely a matter of intuition, as Lernout argues, then verifiability itself succumbs to the indeterminacy inherent to all forms of predictive modelling. What is significant is not that this indeterminacy arises as a consequence of the "incompletion" of philology – or from any other limitation of empirical knowledge – but that it is structural and structurally inherent; which is indeed the point of Derrida's statement regarding "possibility" ("the possibility of disengagement and citational graft which belongs to the structure of every mark").

Lernout is obliged to concede that, viewed in this context, "radical philology" can never be more than an approximative method or, rather, an approximative system of knowledge, whose tenets must therefore at some point violate the principle of verifiability. Approximation is in this sense not merely a practical necessity with regard to a certain limit implicit to the *technē* of knowledge, but as a condition bound up with the materiality of "knowledge" – that is, semio-linguistic or *signifying*

---

5   Jacques Lacan, "Metaphore et métonymie," *Le Séminaire de Jacques Lacan, Livre III: Les Psychoses (1955-6)* (Paris: Seuil, 1981) 243-62.

materiality. The logical consequences of viewing "knowledge" as an approximative system which will never be verifiable are thus crucial to an understanding of why the argument about the intuitive character of semio-linguistic anteriority does not hold – and this is the problem which must firstly be addressed, but not, however, as a binary expression of either *praxis* or *poiēsis*, but rather, in the first instance, of their nexus in a common materiality.

With "radical philology," a fictive definitive system of knowledge is established as the basis of epistemological enquiry, with the result that the schematized character of this basis is soon forgotten, and the fictive construction is identified with the actual system. It is with regard to the limits of this construct that semio-linguistic anteriority assumes its "intuitive" character, for Lernout, as that which exceeds "verifiability." The relativism of this system not only contradicts its basic premise of generalizability (something must be generally verifiable, not merely a special instance of verifiability), but it also exposes the system to further logical violations with regard to what we might call "locality" (*vis-à-vis* Derrida's "disengagement and citational graft") and the system's over-dependence upon "context." In short, the predictive limits of textual genetics require that all recourse to context be provisional, and at the same time that the probabilistic feature of this "recourse" NOT be regarded as provisional. Indeed, probability invests the philo-genetic project at every level, consequent upon precisely the "possibility of disengagement and citational graft," as Derrida says, "which belongs to the structure of every mark, spoken or written, and which constitutes every mark in writing before and outside every horizon of semio-linguistic communication."

II

In discussing the claims of logical empiricism with regard to the philosophy of language, Hans Reichenbach has pointed out: "It is one of the elementary laws of approximative procedure that the consequences drawn from a schematized conception do not hold outside the limits of approximation; that in particular no consequences may be drawn from features belonging to the nature of the schematization only and not to the co-ordinate object."[6] The question that obtains here is how approximation avails itself in any way of a consequent realization of its "co-ordinate object," as Reichenbach says. It may well be worth going back over several of the assumptions aired here about language and signification in general, before proposing anything like a response to the above question. According to the tenets of logical empiricism, "symbols" are physical bodies or processes like any other, irrespective of their "function." It makes no difference if we consider a symbol as obtaining meaning through its correspondence to "facts" or to other "symbols." A symbol is itself a fact. In structural terms it is irrelevant what "class" of fact a symbol "corresponds to," or why it is taken as corresponding to it. Its significance, and that of language as a whole, resides in the *possibility* of treating a physical body as a symbol; and symbolization as a function of a possible (meaningful) correspondence between facts.

By treating symbols as facts in this manner contradicts, on the level of semio-linguistic materiality at least, the principle of verifiability. That is, the principle of "truth value," which, as Reichenbach demonstrates, is consequent upon a schematized conception. Moreover, the principle of verifiability is required, in the first instance, to account for the *possibility* of "correspondence," and subsequently to account for the ultimately *approximative* nature of correspondence as such. In this way verifiability cedes to probability and is consequent therefore upon prediction rather than upon a determinate "state of affairs."

The question – and it is a very interesting one – is how, then, we can assume an initial state of signification – the point at which the perception, or indeed contemplation of an object, cedes to the act of "reading." Between the "zero method" of a base materialism, and the resemblance of a semio-linguistic system, what "takes place" that could allow us to account, in more than merely a superficial way, for the phenomenon of reading, or of the "transmission-effect" of sense? What makes such a "reading" possible? What, to complicate things, is its "co-ordinate object," as Reichenbach says? Or, to adopt a terminology closer to Derrida's, what form does this "purely" material signature-effect take, as an "anteriority"

6 Hans Reichenbach, *Experience and Prediction: An Analysis of the Foundation and the Structure of Knowledge* (Chicago: University of Chicago Press, 1961) vi.

of signification? And how do we escape the tautology of addressing this "anteriority" in significatory terms – i.e., as a "co-ordinate object"?

Such questions are evidently not idle, as a vast amount of philological activity has indeed been devoted to enumerating sets of "facts" that correspond, in some way, with *language* – whether on a micro- or macro-scale; whether in symbolic, rhetorical or poetical terms. Each of these assume a certain placement; that *language* is in fact a type of object to be deciphered, dissected, anatomized, classified, and so on – in accordance with something like a hermeneutic fiction. And indeed this too is a fact; is a kind of fact, one among others, that corresponds in some way to an idea of *language* or of *the text*. And in and of themselves, each of these facts is "verifiable," to a certain degree, and yet no idea of *language* is verifiable. It is because the idea is already a schematization – the outcome of a set of predictions centred upon a causal arrangement of symbolic "correspondences" – whose supposed "co-ordinate object" remains barred, because (we may assume) it renders the very notion of verifiability nonsensical.

How does it do this? We might say it does this by exposing all such presuppositions about language to the broadest implications of semio-linguistic materiality and to the radically probabilistic organization of language as a whole.

What would it mean to verify the materiality of a "symbol"? Or, conversely, to "falsify" a symbol? It is by way of certain assumptions with regard to the "falsifiability" of philological research, after all, which has lent it to a logistic conception of text which has always presupposed a connection between signified meaning and verifiability, beyond any system of symbolic representation. One problem is that to *verify* already entails symbolization – here, with regard to a measure of "truth value." Or, as Samuel Beckett puts it in the addenda to his 1953 "roman" *Watt* (affecting a détournement on a well-known motto of sovereign *vérité*): *Honni soit qui symbole y voit.*[7] Another problem is that to assign "truth value" to materiality is tautological. In philosophy the formula S=P provides a simple expression of this effect of semiological "complementarity." It is evident enough that S is not P, and yet the structure of equivalence or

---

[7]   Samuel Beckett, *Watt* (Paris: Éditions de minuit, 1953) 268.

correspondence described here is one which underwrites the entirety of signification: whether it is in the conventional model of the sign (signifier-signified); in the organization of rhetorical tropes or figures (metaphor, metonymy, allegory, analogy, parataxis, and so on); or in the overarching notion of narrative and schema. We might say, therefore, that language proceeds on the basis of what we could term an "inequality" theorem, and that inequality itself provides the measure of verifiability. It may be that language *occurs* as such in the "suspension" of verifiability. Or, we might equally characterize language as proceeding from a structural dependence upon a principle of the "arbitrary" ($S=P$, where S and P can be *any* terms whatsoever) which is nevertheless tied to the arbitration-effect of "correspondence" ($S \neq P$, where S and P are nevertheless mutually determined and interdependent).

III

A note on "signifying materiality": there is a common thread running through the work of Lacan and Derrida, in the relationship between Lacan and "deconstruction" and between Derrida and "psychoanalysis" (in a recent collaboration with Elisabeth Roudinesco, for example, we find Derrida dwelling at length upon the fact of his own intimate relationship with the work of Nicolas Abrahams, and the work of his wife, Marguerite Derrida, psychoanalyst and translator of Melanie Klein),[8] intersecting with various aspects of the thinking of Martin Heidegger, Alexandre Kojève, Maurice Merleau-Ponty, Jean-Luc Nancy and others, which is that of *anteriority* in the elaboration of a theory of language or, perhaps more appropriately, of the *technē* of writing.

To the extent that this takes the form of a theoretical engagement with "psychoanalysis," it does not thereby assert what Derrida terms "les dogmes et les rigidités de la pensée psychanalytique dominante," or the orthodoxies of Jacques-Alain Miller and the remnants of the École freudienne de Paris (EFP 1964-1980), but specifically responds to the question of a certain "nominalism" addressed through the Lacanian

---

8   Jacques Derrida et Elisabeth Roudinesco, *De quoi demain...* (Paris: Éditions Galilée, 2001).

revisioning of Freud. As a foreshadowing of this encounter, and in the absence of a direct address to the spectre of Freud supervising or supervening upon the text of Derrida, it is worth citing Derrida's comments on his relationship with Freud and Lacan in *De quoi demain...* in which Derrida attests, as it were, to a fundamental inadequacy of reading: "J'avais lu Freud de façon très fragmentaire, insuffisante, conventionelle, et Lacan de façon plus lacunaire, à peine preliminaire..."[9] In view of this disclaimer, Derrida specifically addresses the legacy of Freud upon a "materialist" conception of signification in terms of a "suspension" of verifiability, of responsibility *per se* and of a certain "credit accorded to a fiction":

> Parmi les gestes qui m'ont convaincu, séduit en vérité, il y a cette indispensible audace de la pensée, ce que je n'hésite pas à appeler son courage: cela consiste ici à écrire, inscrire, signer, au nom d'un savoir sans alibi (et donc le plus «positif»), des «fictions» théoriques. On reconnaît ainsi deux choses à la fois: *d'une part*, l'irréductible nécessité du stratagème, de la transaction, de la négociation dans le savoir, dans le théorème, dans la *position* de la vérité, dans sa démonstration, dans son «faire savoir» ou dans son «donner à entendre,» et, *d'autre part*, la dette de toute *position* théorique (mais aussi bien juridique, éthique, politique), envers un pouvoir performatif structuré par la *fiction*, par une interventio figurale. Car la convention qui garantit tout performatif inscrit en elle-même le crédit accordé à une fiction.[10]

Where this leads is to the insistence that such (hypothetical) distinctions as between base materiality and semiosis, or between anteriority and a "semio-linguistic system," are themselves "une fiction théorique," situated between a wish for verifiability and the mirage of vérité. The lineaments of this theoretical fiction are seen to converge upon a question of responsibility, stripped of its tranquil assurances, addressed to the relationship between ontico-linguistic subjectivity and the facticity of the Real, or of the Other, in the receipt of language (in advance of itself, as it were, and as a type of credit to which signification accrues in the form of

---

9   Derrida et Roudinesco 275.
10 Derrida et Roudinesco 281-82.

a "symbolic debt"). As Derrida himself has acknowledged, there remains a like debt in elaborating here of what in effect constitutes a "theory" of signifying materiality, to the Freudian unconscious as the "object" of attestation and "site" or "figure" of linguistic anteriority *par excellence*: le *coup d'envoi* freudien ("de voir ce que peuvent vouloir dire des termes comme «répondre devant», «répondre à», «répondre de», «répondre de soi», dès lors qu'on les regarde du point de vue de ce qu'on appelle encore l'«inconscient»).[11]

[11]   Derrida et Roudinesco 286.

CONTRIBUTORS

Louis Armand directs the Centre for Critical and Cultural Theory within the Department of Anglophone Literatures and Cultures at Charles University, Prague. He has published four novels, *Breakfast at Midnight* (2012), *Clair Obscur* (2011), *Menudo* (2005) and *The Garden* (2001). In addition, he is the author of seven collections of poetry – most recently, *Letters from Auslund* (2011) – and of a number of volumes of criticism, including *Literate Technologies: Language, Cognition, Technicity* (2006), *Event States: Discourse, Time, Mediality* (2007) and *Solicitations: Essays on Criticism & Culture* (2008). He is an editor of *VLAK* magazine and is the founder of the Prague Micro-Festival.

Zdeněk Beran is Senior Lecturer at the Department of Anglophone Literatures and Cultures at Charles University, Prague. He specializes in later Victorian literature and publishes articles on specific cultural issues (Pre-Raphaelite art, late-Victorian sexuality, Walter Pater's fiction, etc.) and on the history of the reception of British writers in the Czech lands (Conrad, Wilde, Dickens). Among his translations into Czech are works of popular English writers (M.R. James, a selection of short stories, 1997; Robert Harris, *Pompeii*, 2005; etc.) as well as modern American novelists (Kurt Vonnegut, *God Bless You, Mr Rosewater*, 2009; etc.).

Bohuslav Mánek is Professor of English and American Literary History at the Department of English Language and Literature, University of Hradec Králové. He is the author of *První české překlady Byronovy poezie* (First Czech Translations of Byron's Poetry, 1991) and book chapters and articles in scholarly journals and conference proceedings on Czech (and in some cases also Slovak) reception of Shakespeare, Romantic poetry, G.M. Hopkins, James Joyce, H.G. Wells and others, and on Czech translations and translators from English, e.g., E.B. Kaizl, Primus Sobotka, V.A. Jung and others. He contributed over 200 entries to *Slovník spisovatelů: Anglie...* (An Encyclopaedia of Writers: England..., 1996, 2003). His other publications include over 200 translated poems from contemporary

British and American poets published in literary magazines and anthologies. He is the editor-in-chief of the academic journal *Hradec Králové Journal of Anglophone Studies* and was a Visiting Professor at the University of Worcester, England (1998).

Ondřej Pilný is Associate Professor and Director of the Centre for Irish Studies at Charles University, Prague. He is the author of *Irony and Identity in Modern Irish Drama* (2006) and editor of *J.M. Synge, Hrdina západu: Dramata a próza* (an annotated edition of Synge's work in Czech translation, 2006), *Global Ireland: Irish Literatures in the New Millennium* (with Clare Wallace, 2006), *Time Refigured: Myths, Foundation Texts and Imagined Communities* (with Martin Procházka, 2005), Petr Škrabánek, *A Night Joyce of a Thousand Tiers* (with Louis Armand, 2002), and of two thematic journal issues, *Samuel Beckett: Textual Genesis and Reception* (with Louis Armand, 2007) and *From Brooke to Black Pastoral: Six Studies in Irish Literature and Culture* (2001). His work on Irish drama and fiction has appeared in a number of essay collections and refereed journals across Europe. He has translated plays by J.M. Synge, Brian Friel, Martin McDonagh and Enda Walsh, and Flann O'Brien's novel *The Third Policeman*. He is currently working on a critical study of the grotesque in contemporary drama.

Martin Procházka is Professor of English, American and Comparative Literature and Head of the Department of Anglophone Literatures and Cultures at Charles University, Prague. He is the author of *Romantismus a osobnost* (Romanticism and Personality, 1996), a critical study of English Romantic aesthetics, Coleridge and Byron, *Transversals* (2007), essays on Post-structuralist readings of English and American Romantics, *Ruins in the New World* (2012), a study of apocalypticism and uses of ruins in American culture, and a co-author (with Zdeněk Hrbata) of *Romantismus a romantismy* (Romanticism and Romanticisms, 2005), a comparative study on the chief discourses in the West European, American and Czech Romanticism. With Zdeněk Stříbrný he edited *Slovník spisovatelů: Anglie...* (An Encyclopaedia of Writers: England... 1996, 2003). His other publications include book chapters and articles on Shakespeare, Romanticism and Post-structuralism, a translation of Byron's *Manfred*

(1991) and M.H. Abrams's *The Mirror and the Lamp* into Czech (2001). He is the founding editor of the international academic journal *Litteraria Pragensia* and a Visiting Professor at the universities of Glasgow, Kent and Porto.

Erik S. Roraback received a D.Phil. in English Language and Literature from Oxford University. He teaches U.S. literature, interdisciplinary studies, psychoanalysis, and critical theory at the Department of Anglophone Literatures and Cultures of Charles University, Prague, and international cinema in Prague's film academy, FAMU. In 2005 he was Visiting Professor at the Université de Provence (Aix-Marseille I), France. His book, *The Dialectics of Late Capital and Power: James, Balzac and Critical Theory*, was published in 2007.

Pavla Veselá is Senior Lecturer at the Department in Anglophone Literatures and Cultures at Charles University, Prague. She holds a PhD in Comparative Literature from Duke University. The focus of her work has been modern American and Russian literature (especially utopias and science-fiction), as well as feminist and literary theory. Her most recent articles discuss American poetry after 9/11 (*Poetics Today*) and the critical utopias of Sutton E. Griggs and Samuel S. Schuyler (*Science Fiction Studies*). Her other works has appeared in the journals *Litteraria Pragensia*, *NWSA Journal* and *Espinosa: Revista de filosofía*, as well as in the essay collections *Moderní svět v zrcadle literatury a filosofie* (ed. Miroslav Petříček, 2011) and *Realism's Others* (ed. Geoffrey Baker and Eva Aldea, 2010). She also contributed entries to several encyclopedias, including *Encyclopedia of the Cold War* (Routledge, 2008).

David Vichnar is Research Assistant at the Centre for Critical and Cultural Theory at the Department of Anglophone Literatures and Cultures at Charles University, Prague. He is currently completing his cotutelle PhD thesis (with Université de la Sorbonne Nouvelle, Paris) on James Joyce and the post-war Anglo-American and French literary avant-gardes. He works as an editor, publisher and translator. His publications include *Joyce Against Theory* (2010), *Hypermedia Joyce* (co-edited, 2010), *Thresholds: Essays on the International Prague Poetry Scene* (edited, 2011) and, most recently, *Praharfeast: James Joyce in Prague* (co-edited, 2012). He co-edits the *VLAK* magazine, co-organises the annual Prague Poetry Microfestival, and manages Litteraria Pragensia Books and Equus Press. His articles on contemporary experimental writers (Christine Brooke-Rose, Iain Sinclair, Steve McCaffery, the Oulipo group, et al.) as well as translations of contemporary poetry – Czech, German, French and Anglophone – have appeared in numerous journals and magazines.

Robert J.C. Young is Julius Silver Professor of English and Comparative Literature at New York University. His work in the field of Post-colonial Studies includes *White Mythologies: Writing History and the West* (1990), *Colonial Desire: Hybridity in Culture, Theory and Race* (Routledge, 1995), *Postcolonialism: An Historical Introduction* (Blackwell, 2001), and *Postcolonialism: A Very Short Introduction* (Oxford, 2003). He has also published *Torn Halves: Political Conflict in Literary and Cultural Theory* (Manchester University Press, 1996) and *The Idea of English Ethnicity* (Blackwell, 2008). He is currently writing a book on the theory and philosophy of translation. Prior to moving to New York, Robert Young was Professor of English and Critical Theory and a fellow of Wadham College, Oxford University. He is Editor of the quarterly *Interventions: International Journal of Postcolonial Studies*. His work has been translated into over twenty languages.

Helena Znojemská is Senior Lecturer at the Department of Anglophone Literatures and Cultures at Charles University, Prague. She teaches English mediaeval and Renaissance literature, British studies and literary theory. Her PhD thesis, *Quod Christus cum Hinieldo: readings in the manuscript context of the* Exeter Book, analysed the intertextual links within the codex and their functioning. She has published articles on Old English poetry and religious literature in *Litteraria Pragensia* and *Prague Studies in English*. Her research focus is on Old English religious poetry and on historical narrative from Old to early Middle English period. She also translates Old English poetry and prose and participates in the activities of the Group for English Mediaeval Studies at the Modern Language Association of Prague.

INDEX

A

Aarsleff, Hans, 125, 150
Abrahams, Nicolas, 204
Abrams, M.H., 47, 49
Adams, John, 26
Ælfric, 55
Agamben, Giorgio, 168
Albrecht, Jaroslav, 109, 110
Alexander III of Russia, 124
Alfred of Wessex, 55
Allard, Joe, 75, 76
Alpatov, Vladimir M., 148, 149
Althusser, Louis, 15, 122, 140
Anderson, Benedict, 16, 30
Antiphon the Sophist, 25
Aptekar, Valerian Borisovich, 125
Aristotle, 9, 25, 26, 27, 29, 30, 33, 34
Armand, Louis, 19, 198

B

Badiou, Alain, 178
Baggioni, Daniel, 150
Bakhtin, Mikhail M., 12, 16, 19, 42, 86, 133, 134, 143, 146, 148, 151, 153, 197
Ball, John, 74
Bally, Charles, 25, 38
Barrett, Rhodes, 179
Barthes, Roland, 15, 123
Baskin, Wade, 26
Bass, Alan, 15, 37, 146, 192
Bauer, Otto, 133
Bechmann, Gotthard, 178, 179
Beckett, Samuel, 203

Bede, 75
Beneš, Eduard, 133
Benjamin, Walter, 143, 168
Beran, Zdeněk, 14, 103, 108, 117
Berg, Leo S., 146, 147
Bhabha, Homi K., 146, 153
Blanchot, Maurice, 176
Boas, Franz, 125, 126, 152
Booth, Wayne C., 171
Borovička, Lukáš, 155
Bosch, Hieronymus, 186
Bourdieu, Pierre, 122
Bowie, Malcolm, 171, 172, 173
Bowlt, John E., 147
Brandist, Craig, 133, 146, 148, 149, 153
Breazeale, Daniel, 39
Brecht, Bertolt, 194, 195
Broch, Olaf, 44
Brontë, Emily, 100
Bruche-Schulz, Gisela, 148, 149
Brugmann, Karl, 35
Burbank, John, 20, 170
Burke, Edmund, 26
Byron, George Gordon, Lord, 66, 67

C

Caedmon, 67, 75
Cantineau, J., 127
Cejp, Ladislav, 77
Čelakovský, František Ladislav, 66
Čelakovský, Ladislav, 66, 74
Čermák, Jan, 43, 64, 76
Černý, Václav, 19, 92, 184
Certeau, Michel de, 174, 175, 176

Červenka, Miroslav, 49
Chateaubriand, François-René de, 117
Chaucer, Geoffrey, 13, 61, 65, 67, 71, 72, 73, 82
Cherchi, Marcello, 148
Chiampi, Irlemar, 181
Child, Clarence G., 88
Child, Francis James, 73, 74
Chodakowska, Elżbieta, 126
Chomsky, Noam, 147, 176
Chown, Katya, 148, 149, 153
Chvatík, Květoslav, 156, 157, 192
Chyzhevsky, Dmytro, 57
Cicero, 33
Cohen, Joshua, 26
Conley, C.H., 92
Constantine the Great, 34
Courtenay, Baudoin de, 150
Cram, David, 135
Croce, Benedetto, 12, 41
Croll, Morris W., 87, 88, 89, 91
Crystal, David, 75, 76
Culler, Jonathan, 156, 157

D

Darwin, Charles, 98, 146
Daumier, Honoré, 186
de Man, Paul, 10, 37
Defoe, Daniel, 65
Deleuze, Gilles, 17, 167
Demetz, Peter, 92, 93
Derrida, Jacques, 15, 17, 37, 122, 146, 192, 198, 199, 200, 201, 202, 204, 206
Derrida, Marguerite, 15, 17, 37, 122, 146, 192, 198, 199, 200, 201, 202, 204, 206

Dickens, Charles, 14, 103, 107, 108, 109, 110, 111, 112, 113, 114, 115, 117
Dobrovský, Josef, 34
Dos Passos, John, 100
Dreiser, Theodore, 93
Dugin, Aleksandr, 130
Durantaye, Leland de la, 168, 169
Durdík, Josef, 86
Dušková, Libuše, 33, 43, 64
Dvořák, Jan, 185

E

Eagleton, Terry, 85, 89, 90, 94, 101
Egginton, William, 168, 169, 181
Einstein, Albert, 42
Elizabeth I of England, 108
Elster, John, 26
Emerson, Caryl, 42, 134
Erlich, Victor, 101
Esslin, Martin, 185

F

Fabian, Jeanette, 155, 156
Fanon, Frantz, 122
Faulkner, William, 93
Fearon, James, 26
Fehr, Johannes, 29
Ferrer, Daniel, 199
Feuillerat, Albert, 88
Field, Rachel, 98
Fielding, Henry, 65, 108, 110, 112, 113
Fishkin, James, 26
Flint, F.S., 133
Foucault, Michel, 11, 15
Franklin, Benjamin, 26
Freeman, E.A., 60
Freud, Sigmund, 172, 181, 205

Fülöp-Miller, René, 133

G

Gadet, Françoise, 122, 128, 132, 144
Galan, F.W., 97
Galsworthy, John, 65
Garvin, Paul, 156, 162, 167
Gasparov, Boris, 126, 127, 129, 131, 134, 146, 147, 151
Genghis Khan, 127, 130
Ginsburg, Lidiia Ia., 131
Ginzburg, Carlo, 10, 33, 34
Girard, René, 174
Glorovskii, Georgii, 130
Goethe, Johann Wolfgang von, 70
Goldsmith, Oliver, 66
Góngora y Argote, Luis de, 173
Gooch, George Peabody, 78, 82
Gower, John, 67
Gracián, Baltasar, 173
Gray, Thomas, 66
Green, Alice, 60
Green, J.R., 60
Greenberg, Joseph H., 144
Greenblatt, Stephen, 40
Greene, Robert, 116
Grimm, Jacob, 35
Grossman, Jan, 19, 184, 185, 186, 187, 188, 189, 190, 191, 192, 193, 194, 195, 196
Grundfest Schoepf, Brooke, 141

H

Habermas, Jürgen, 26, 168
Haller, Jiří, 161, 163
Hamilton, Alexander, 26
Hankin, Robert M., 148
Hasty, Olga, 170

Havel, Václav, 19, 184, 185, 186, 187, 196
Havránek, Bohuslav, 18, 48, 156, 157, 159, 161, 162, 163, 165
Hawthorne, Nathaniel, 93
Hayman, David, 199
Hegel, Georg Wilhelm Friedrich, 85, 179
Heidegger, Martin, 168, 204
Hemingway, Ernest, 93, 100, 101
Henry II of England, 60
Herbart, Johann Friedrich, 86
Hladký, Josef, 64
Hodek, Břetislav, 99
Hogarth, Georgina, 117
Holling, Fred, 148
Hollmann, Josef, 66
Holquist, Michael, 134
Honeycutt, Lee, 34
Hornát, Jaroslav, 9, 14, 103, 106, 107, 108, 109, 110, 111, 112, 113, 114, 115, 116, 117, 118
Hostinský, Otakar, 86
Hron, Zdeněk, 73
Husserl, Edmund, 18, 166, 169, 170, 171, 180, 183

I

Ingarden, Roman, 105
Iswolsky, Hélène, 197
Ivasheva, V.V., 117

J

Jacobson, Claire, 141
Jacobson, Manfred, 171
Jahn, Jiljí Vratislav, 67
Jakobson, Roman, 11, 12, 15, 16, 17, 18, 20, 41, 46, 85, 86, 102, 122, 125, 126, 128, 129, 131, 132,

133, 139, 140, 141, 143, 144,
146, 147, 148, 151, 152, 153,
154, 155, 156, 157
James, Henry, 93
James, James Alton, 78, 81
Jameson, Fredric, 94
Jankovič, Milan, 49, 106
Jarry, Alfred, 19, 184, 186, 188, 191,
192, 193, 196
Jay, John, 26
Jefferson, Thomas, 26
Jeřábek, František Věnceslav, 67
Jindrová, Zuzana, 185
Jones, William, 34
Joravsky, David, 147
Joseph, John E., 135
Joyce, James, 19, 199
Jungmann, Josef, 117

K

Kafka, Franz, 19, 184, 188, 193
Kagan, Donald, 25
Kaizl, Edmund Břetislav, 67
Kalivoda, Robert, 106, 107
Kang, Younghill, 98
Kant, Immanuel, 199
Karcevsky, Sergei, 128, 156
Kastner, Fatima, 180
Kayser, Wolfgang, 186, 187, 196
Kelly, Louis G., 125
Kennedy, Michael D., 125
Kettle, Arnold, 117
Khatibi, Abdelkadir, 122
Khlebnikov, Victor, 84
Klein, Melanie, 204
Klíma, Miloslav, 185
Kochis, Bruce, 171
Kocourek, Rostislav, 125
Kojève, Alexandre, 204

Kristeller, Paul Oskar, 33
Kristeva, Julia, 123
Kroeber, Alfred Louis, 125
Kruchenykh, Aleksei Eliseevich, 94
Kubíček, Tomáš, 105, 113
Kumar, Krishan, 60

L

Lacan, Jacques, 9, 10, 15, 17, 18,
146, 166, 167, 168, 169, 171,
172, 173, 174, 175, 176, 177,
178, 179, 180, 181, 182, 183,
200, 204, 205
Lähteenmäki, Mika, 153
Lalande, André, 169
Landman, Friedrich, 88
Langer, František, 117
Langland, William, 76, 77
Laruelle, Marlène, 130
Lawrence, D.H., 95
Lee, Jonathan Scott, 182
Lenin, Vladimir Ilyich, 124, 126,
139
Lernout, Geert, 19, 199, 200, 201
Levington Comfort, Will, 98
Lévi-Strauss, Claude, 15, 17, 122,
141, 142, 156
Lévy-Bruhl, Lucien, 142
Liberman, Anatoly, 127
Liddell, M.H., 49
Lincoln, Abraham, 99
Linda, Josef, 114
Linn, Andrew, 135
Lotman, Iurii M., 131
Luelsdorff, Philip A., 167, 169
Luhmann, Niklas, 9, 10, 18, 166,
167, 168, 169, 170, 171, 173,
174, 175, 177, 178, 179, 180,
181, 182, 183

Lyly, John, 88, 90
Lyotard, Jean-François, 16, 122, 137
Lysenko, Trofim Denisovich, 147, 148

M

Mabillon, Jean, 34
Macek, Emanuel, 66, 78, 82
Macháček, Simeon Karel, 66
Macourek, Miloš, 189
Macpherson, James, 66
Malá, Markéta, 125
Mallet, David, 66
Malory, Thomas, 65
Malý, Jakub, 67
Mánek, Bohuslav, 13, 64, 66
Manning, Paul H., 148
Marek, František, 112
Marr, Nikolay Yakovlevich, 17, 102, 148, 149, 150, 151, 152
Marx, Karl, 149
Masaryk, Tomáš Garrigue, 16, 133
Massumi, Brian, 174
Matejka, L., 86
Mather, Cotton, 89, 91, 101
Mathesius, Vilém, 9, 10, 11, 12, 13, 14, 18, 19, 20, 21, 23, 33, 36, 37, 38, 39, 40, 41, 42, 43, 44, 45, 46, 47, 48, 49, 50, 51, 52, 53, 54, 55, 56, 57, 58, 59, 60, 61, 62, 63, 64, 65, 66, 68, 69, 70, 72, 73, 74, 75, 76, 77, 78, 79, 80, 81, 82, 97, 125, 128, 155, 156, 157, 158, 159, 161, 162, 163, 165, 166, 171, 175, 194, 195
Matich, Olga, 147
Mayakovsky, Vladimir, 84, 126, 140, 154, 155
McCarthy, Joseph, 126

McLean, Hugh, 126
Medvedev, P.N., 86
Melville, Herman, 93, 100
Memmi, Albert, 122
Merleau-Ponty, Maurice, 204
Mill, John Stuart, 26
Miller, Jacques-Alain, 133, 204
Milner, Ian, 107
Milton, John, 66
Moeller, Hans-Georg, 166, 167, 168, 170, 180
Montfaucon, Bernard de, 34
Moore, Thomas, 66
Morávková, Alena, 85
Morley, John, 88
Mourek, Václav Emanuel, 67
Mudimbe, Valentin Y., 122, 123
Mukařovský, Jan, 13, 14, 15, 18, 19, 20, 21, 40, 45, 48, 49, 50, 51, 56, 57, 58, 63, 86, 97, 103, 104, 106, 107, 113, 116, 122, 156, 157, 159, 161, 163, 164, 165, 184, 191, 192, 193, 194, 195
Müller, Friedrich Max, 149
Murra, John V., 148

N

Nakhimovsky, Alexander D., 131
Nancy, Jean-Luc, 178, 204
Nejedlý, Vojtěch, 66
Neruda, Jan, 102, 109
Nezval, Vítězslav, 18, 84, 155, 157, 161, 164
Ngũgĩ Wa Thiong'o, 143
Niederche, Hans-Joseph, 125
Nietzsche, Friedrich, 33, 39
Nisbet, Ada B., 107
Nobles, Richard, 180
Norden, Eduard, 88

North, Richard, 75, 76
Nowak, Elke, 135

O

Osborne, Peter, 135
Osthoff, Hermann, 35

P

Pasternak, Boris, 155
Peklo, Jaroslav, 44
Percy, Thomas, 66, 74
Pešat, Zdeněk, 106
Peter the Great, 131
Petkevič, Vladimír, 45
Petrů, Václav, 67, 75
Pichl, Josef Bojislav, 66
Pilný, Ondřej, 19, 184
Poe, Edgar Allan, 93
Polivanov, Yevgeny, 147
Pomorska, Krystyna, 126
Pope, Alexander, 67
Potebnya, Alexadner, 86
Potter, Lois, 21
Procházka, Martin, 9, 11, 21, 25, 83, 125
Putin, Vladimir, 130

Q

Quintilian, 9, 33, 34, 173
Quis, Ladislav, 66

R

Rabelais, François, 188
Raleigh, Walter, 66
Randé, Karel, 79, 81
Rasch, William, 182
Rawls, John, 26
Reichenbach, Hans, 201, 202

Rhys Roberts, W., 26
Riasanovsky, Nicholas V., 134
Richard III of England, 187
Riedlinger, Albert, 25, 29, 30, 31, 32, 38
Rieger, F.L., 67
Rieger, Ladislav, 18, 166, 172, 174, 178
Roraback, Erik S., 18, 166
Ross, Carne, 26
Ross, W.D., 26
Rostovtsow, J.N., 146
Rottenberg, Elizabeth, 198
Roudinesco, Elisabeth, 204, 206

S

Said, Edward W., 16, 137
Šaldová, Pavlína, 125
Sandburg, Carl, 99
Sandford, Stella, 135
Sapir, Edward, 128
Sartre, Jean-Paul, 122
Saudek, Erik Adolf, 70, 82
Saussure, Ferdinand de, 10, 11, 25, 27, 28, 29, 30, 31, 32, 33, 36, 37, 39, 41, 127, 128, 135, 145, 153, 156, 158, 163, 192
Saussure, Léopold de, 25, 27, 28, 29, 30, 31, 33, 38, 41, 127, 128, 135, 145, 153, 156, 192
Savitskii, Petr Nikolaevich, 130, 136
Schaller, Helmut W., 144
Schiff, David, 30, 180
Schlegel, August Wilhelm von, 35
Schlegel, Karl Wilhelm Friedrich von, 11, 35, 36, 37
Schleicher, August, 36, 143, 149
Schmidt, Johannes, 143
Schuchardt, Hugo, 143, 150

Scott, Walter, 66, 114, 116, 182
Sechehaye, Albert, 25
Sedláček, František, 63
Selby Watson, John, 34
Seneca, 173
Sériot, Patrick, 122, 132, 144, 146, 147, 148, 149
Seton-Watson, Hugh, 124
Shakespeare, William, 21, 45, 47, 50, 63, 65, 66, 67, 70, 82, 91, 102
Shaw, George Bernard, 65, 93, 98
Shelley, Percy Bysshe, 63, 66
Shepherd, David, 133, 146
Sheridan, Alan, 146
Shklovsky, Viktor, 84, 154, 196
Shlapentokh, Dmitry, 130, 131
Škvorecký, Josef, 109, 110, 113
Sládek, Josef Václav, 66, 70
Slote, Sam, 199
Šmidt, Vilém, 109
Smith, Michael G., 124
Smrž, Vladimír, 109
Solovyov, Vladimir, 134
Spencer, Herbert, 90
Spenser, Edmund, 63
Stalin, Joseph, 83, 148
Stehr, Nico, 178, 179
Steiner, Peter, 20, 84, 86, 102, 170
Steiner, Wendy, 171
Stempel, W.-E., 84
Stevens, Wallace, 93
Stevenson, Robert Louis, 108
Stiegler, Bernard, 199
Stone Nakhimovsky, Alice, 131
Stoppard, Tom, 184
Stříbrný, Zdeněk, 20, 21, 88, 92
Striedter, Jurij, 84
Stubbs, William, 60
Summerson, Esther, 117
Suny, Ronald Grigor, 125

Surrey, Henry Howard, Earl of, 66
Suvchinskii, Petr, 130

T

Tablic, Bohuslav, 66
Taine, Hippolyte A., 45, 47, 50, 51, 53, 57, 63
Tait, D.F., 133
Tarde, Gabriel, 146
Tasso, Torquato, 70
Taylor, Ben, 146
Thomas, Lawrence L., 148, 150
Tihanov, Galin, 133, 146
Tilsch, Emanuel, 111, 114
Tilschová, Emanuela, 111, 114
Titunik, I.R., 86, 96
Tocqueville, Alexis de, 26
Todorov, Tzvetan, 123
Toman, Jindřich, 45, 47, 48, 57, 125, 126, 128, 129, 131, 132, 133, 137, 140, 142, 144, 147, 155, 161, 164
Tomashevsky, Boris Viktorovich, 86
Toyen (Marie Čermínová), 84
Trnka, Bohumil, 21, 51, 125, 156, 171
Trubetzkoy, Nikolai Sergeyevich, 11, 15, 16, 17, 18, 20, 125, 126, 127, 128, 129, 130, 131, 132, 133, 134, 136, 137, 138, 141, 142, 143, 144, 145, 148, 149, 151, 152, 153
Twain, Mark, 93, 108
Tynyanov, Yury, 85, 86
Tzara, Tristan, 184

U

Uspenskii, Boris A., 131

V

Vachek, Josef, 33, 36, 40, 45, 47, 51, 64, 156, 167, 171, 175, 194
Valla, Lorenzo, 11, 33, 34
Vančura, Zdeněk, 9, 11, 14, 21, 83, 84, 87, 88, 89, 90, 91, 92, 93, 94, 95, 96, 97, 98, 99, 100, 101, 102, 116, 157
Veeser, Harold Aram, 40
Veselá, Pavla, 14, 83, 116
Veselovsky, Alexander, 86, 90
Vichnar, David, 18, 154
Vine, Brent, 126
Vinkovetsky, Ilya, 130
Vladislav, Jan, 70
Vočadlo, Otakar, 97, 98, 99
Vočadlová, Ludmila, 98
Vodička, Felix, 14, 40, 102, 104, 105, 106, 107, 112, 113, 114, 115, 116, 117, 118
Voloshinov, Valentin Nikolaevich, 86
Voltaire (François-Marie Arouet), 117
Vossler, Karl, 150
Vrba, František, 72, 73
Vrchlický, Jaroslav, 70

W

Ward, Nathaniel, 87, 89

Weingart, Miloš, 162
Weisstein, Ulrich, 186
Wellek, René, 13, 48, 51, 85, 86, 89, 90, 92, 93, 94, 154, 161
Wells, H.G., 13, 65, 78, 79, 80, 81, 97, 98, 101, 138
Whitman, Walt, 93, 95, 96, 100
Whitney, William Dwight, 153
Wieland, Christoph Martin, 187
Wilde, Oscar, 101
Williams, William Carlos, 93, 100
Wittgenstein, Ludwig, 199
Wolker, Jiří, 41
Wycliffe, John, 65, 67

Y

Young, Robert J.C., 15, 16, 17, 18, 121, 122, 135, 139, 145

Z

Zelený, Václav, 67
Zeyer, Julius, 58, 67, 70
Zich, Otakar, 86
Ziegert, Klaus A., 180
Ziegert, Rosamund, 180
Zinoviev, Grigory, 139
Žižek, Slavoj, 179
Znojemská, Helena, 13, 43